2-90

A TRAVELER'S GUIDE TO
VACATION RENTALS IN EUROPE

A TRAVELER'S GUIDE TO

VACATION RENTALS IN EUROPE

APARTMENTS, VILLAS, COTTAGES, CHALETS, FARMHOUSES, AND CONDOS

Michael and Laura Murphy

E. P. DUTTON   New York

Published in the United States by E. P. Dutton,
a division of Penguin Books USA Inc.,
2 Park Avenue, New York, N.Y. 10016.

Published simultaneously in Canada by Fitzhenry and Whiteside, Limited, Toronto.

Library of Congress Cataloging-in-Publication Data

Murphy, Michael, 1927–
  A traveler's guide to vacation rentals in Europe: apartments,
villas, cottages, chalets, farmhouses, and condos / Michael and
Laura Murphy.—1st ed.
        p.   cm.
    ISBN 0-525-48527-9
    1. Vacation homes—Europe—Guide-books.   2. Rental housing—
Europe—Guide-books.   I. Murphy, Laura.   II. Title.
TX907.5.E85M87   1990
647.944—dc20   89-23411
                                                                      CIP

Designed by Stanley S. Drate/Folio Graphics Co. Inc.

Edited by Sandra W. Soule

10 9 8 7 6 5 4 3 2 1

First Edition

ACKNOWLEDGMENTS

◆

We wish to thank the many rental company owners and agents, in both North America and Europe, who provided information and assisted us in making the contacts and inquiries necessary to bring this book to the traveling public. We want especially to thank British Airways, although it is not directly involved with the affairs of vacation rentals, for information on its programs in Britain and for its interest and cooperation. We also appreciate the efforts of Auto Europe and Renault of America in making available very good transportation for our travels throughout Europe.

CONTENTS

◆

PREFACE

◆

The length of this guidebook and the amount of information it contains may suggest that the business of renting a vacation villa, chalet, or apartment in Europe is a complicated affair. To some extent it is, but no more so than planning any kind of successful foreign vacation itinerary. There are, of course, tours on which little or no effort on your part is needed: everything is taken care of for you, from where you stay to where you eat to what you see. Renting is more for travelers and independent vacationers who don't mind putting some effort into assuring that all will go well—and who, in fact, find working with maps and catalogs and brochures and guidebooks a pleasurable precursor to the journey itself.

As for difficulty, a word about the authors and the research for this book will help put things into perspective.

We have always enjoyed travel, and have made pleasure trips to Europe, to Mexico, around the United States and Canada, traveling on a modest budget, avoiding the heavily traveled tourist paths. In 1984 we moved to Europe for almost a year on a book assignment. It was all very new, learning to live independently in foreign countries, but we not only learned how to conduct business there, we gained experience in renting places for ourselves for extended periods as the home bases we were able to return to.

After another book, this time on North America, we began work on this project; the idea emerged largely from the good experiences we had with this style of travel but was reinforced by the escalating costs of travel in Europe and the declining dollar. Working four to six months in advance, we set about making appointments with European rental company owners and other authorities to see their operations and to visit a sampling of their properties. There were dozens of companies, and their offices were in places such as Lilliesleaf, Scotland; Bludenz, Austria; Strove, Italy, and other places we had never heard of. But by following the directions we received and using good maps and a calendar, we laid out our itinerary and time schedule. We never missed an appointment during our three months of travel. We never had a car problem and only rarely became lost in over nine thousand miles of driving. Finding stores in which to buy groceries and the other few things we needed for our many cottages, apartments, and villas was never a problem. Neither was language ever a barrier to our buying what we needed, even though Spanish is our only language besides English.

On the few occasions when we had to spend several nights in a row in different hotels, we were reminded of the pressures of unpacking, packing, and constantly moving on. As we had planned, alternating between longer stays in different regions and our more hurried trips between the regions, enabled us to make a fair comparison between the two styles of travel. Vacation rentals have our unqualified vote, for ourselves and for anyone else who is not compelled, for one reason or another, to travel over great distances in several countries in a very few weeks.

As for the effort needed to select the place you dream of, and then to book it and find it and get your groceries for it, we hope this guidebook will help.

MICHAEL AND LAURA MURPHY

Ashland, Oregon

A TRAVELER'S
GUIDE TO
VACATION
RENTALS
IN EUROPE

1

Rentals and Renting

♦ INTRODUCTION

Vacation rentals throughout Europe are much the same as they are in North America, the Caribbean, Hawaii, and elsewhere in the northern half of the Western Hemisphere, except that there are many more of them and they are more diverse in their standards and character. Although rare in the United States, thatched-roof stone cottages, stuccoed villas, renovated farmhouses, and mountain chalets for rent are common throughout Europe and the United Kingdom—as, of course, are city apartments and beachfront condominiums. Referred to by most English-speaking Europeans as "self-catering" or "holiday" rentals, accommodation is available by the week or the month and comes with a fully equipped kitchen, usually linens and bedding, and maid service on a weekly or daily basis, depending on the terms and price of the rental agreement.

Thousands of equipped vacation rentals are available, and it is not difficult for Europeans to locate and book a villa or flat or cottage in some favorite foreign or domestic spot away from home—they know the ropes and they know how and where to look, whereas most of us do not. We can book a condo in a resort area of Mexico or Hawaii or one of the Caribbean islands through a U.S. or Canadian travel agency with relative ease, but it is far more difficult to do the same thing if the spot we're looking for is an apartment on the Rhine, a small villa in Tuscany, or a flat in central London. Furthermore, most North Americans planning a trip to Europe are accustomed to staying in hotels and eating meals out. But there are alternatives.

One way of finding out about European vacation rentals is by writing the national tourist office of the country in which you are interested and requesting a listing of rental properties registered with it. (Not all the countries have such lists, and none will make booking arrangements for you.) The lists vary in their length and nature, some showing only rental agents, others with brief descriptions of individual properties. It is then up to you to make contact with the owner or agent. Ideally, the owner will be English-speaking, but many on the Continent are not. There is also the problem of paying the deposit and the rent, usually required as a bank draft in the currency of the country in which the property is located. (This means that if the property does not live up to your expectations, it may be difficult to do anything about it once the rent has been paid.)

If you prefer to have the rental arrangements made before your departure, it is important to contact a reputable agent, preferably one who will be readily accessible during both the booking procedure and after you have returned, in case there have been any problems. One of the main purposes of this guide is to provide information on stable and reputable rental companies and agencies, enabling you to make sound decisions about your visit to Europe.

The Agencies

One of the European agents we met asked, "Can you think of any other holiday enterprise in which customers are required to put up all the money in advance to rent a place they have never seen from someone they've never met?" The answer to this very good question is no, which makes it clear why the selection of a sound and reliable agent is well worth the effort.

Most of the agencies listed in this guide are American or Canadian; very few of them directly represent property owners in Europe. Rather, they represent European companies, formally or informally, which in turn represent the property owners. Also included in the guide is a selection of European rental companies, mostly British. Although they are not formally affiliated with North American agencies, we found them to be particularly easy to work with and eager to serve travelers from this side of the Atlantic. They also have good reputations for offering a well-screened selection of short-term rentals at fair prices. By "fair prices" we do not necessarily mean inexpensive; good value is the measure, whether the selection is a simple cottage at $150 per week or a villa estate at $15,000 per week.

Because the choice of a rental agency is so important to the success of your vacation, a substantial part of this guide is devoted to an overview of the agencies (Chapter 3). This chapter describes the rental companies and agencies, and their histories, policies, and operational procedures. It explains how to get the latest informational materials, how and when to book, and in which countries and regions of Europe each agency offers properties. Also noted is whether an agency specializes in deluxe properties or tends toward the more modest ones. You'll learn how the agencies make sure you can find the place you've rented, and find information about the best means of transportation. In short, this guidebook opens up the world of in-depth travel abroad that is made possible by renting a home base from which to explore.

◆ THE COST ADVANTAGE

Currency Rates and Inflation

During times of shifting currency-exchange rates, especially when they become unfavorable to American and Canadian travelers, the plans of Europe-bound North Americans take on a new and important dimension. Combined with high inflation in some European countries, shifting exchange rates mean that plans for long, multicountry journeys may have to be modified. Very modest hotel rooms in European cities, which cost the equivalent of $50 (U.S.) per night in 1985, may now run to $120 and more. A standard room in a typical four-star hotel in London, Paris, Rome, Zurich, and even Madrid costs $150 per night; five-star hotels begin at $225. Multiplied by twenty or thirty nights, the total jumps out of reach even for those who could have afforded such a vacation just a few years ago. Similar increases in the price of restaurant meals, taxis, tips, and the other expenses of keeping on the move can be staggering.

A vacation rental can significantly minimize the effects of unfavorable exchange rates and inflation; find an apartment, cottage, farmhouse or villa in the locale (or locales) of your choice—in the heart of London, in a valley in the Alps, in a village on the Rhine, on the coast of Portugal. Not only are the prices for such accommodations less than those for rooms in hotels of similar standards but the cost of meals can be reduced substantially, even if only breakfasts and a few lunches or dinners are prepared at your home base.

Prices and Locales

The types, sizes, and prices of the rentals are affected by many factors, creating a complex spectrum from which to choose. Prices are governed by the economy of the country in which the rental units are located, combined with factors such as size, luxury, and specific locale. Rentals in the major cities and those closest to prime European vacation spots, such as the Côte d'Azur or the hills of Tuscany, are among the most high priced. Luxury villas in Portugal's Algarve can be expensive, despite the fact that overall prices in Portugal are among the lowest in Europe. Before reaching a decision and putting down a deposit, make sure that the description of any rental property is specific on five counts: standard, size, services included, general locale, and exact location. If you are not sure, inquire further. Generally, we found that bargain prices (except for off-season rates) rarely exist—they are usually low for a reason.

Rates: Hotels Versus Rentals

Because such complex factors affect rates, it is difficult to be precise when comparing hotel prices with those of vacation rentals. Just as a modest room in a fashionable area of London or Zurich will cost more than a deluxe room in a less convenient or less fashionable part of town, so a simple beachfront cottage will cost more than a larger villa inland. However, most of the European rental companies carefully counsel property owners about rents and exert influence over rents to make sure that they are kept well below rates at the hotels, all other factors being equal. Several Europeans told us that they like to keep rents at about 65 percent of the equivalent hotel room rate, standard for standard (this does not mean of similar size; even studio-size apartments tend to be much larger than standard hotel rooms—plus, of course, they have a kitchen and dining area).

Having stayed in countless hotels on a nightly basis and having also lived in many rental properties in Europe, our sense is that overall the cost of rentals is roughly 60 percent that of nightly hotels and eating all meals out. This is not to say that vacation rentals are for budget travelers only—luxury rentals range from spacious jewels in the centers of cities to expansive villas on cliffs overlooking the sea, and they offer a totally different way of visiting abroad. Most properties in this category include daily maid service in the price, and often boast a private swimming pool, a tennis court, a choice location—and even a gardener, cook, and driver if desired. Also in the deluxe category are spacious individual villas or town houses that are part of a resort settlement. Rents for deluxe properties range from $1,500 to $20,000 per week, but these homes are usually large enough to be shared by four to six persons, and sometimes even up to a dozen or more. Some manor houses and estates are often rented for a week or two for large family gatherings or by a group of friends on a shared-cost basis.

◆ FACTORS OTHER THAN PRICE

In addition to cost considerations, there are numerous persuasive reasons to stay in a vacation rental. Although European hotels offer daily maid service, fresh towels and soap, a bar and lobby, and a Continental breakfast of rolls and coffee or tea, rentals offer more space, the convenience of a kitchen, and, we discovered, a sense of independence, privacy, and comfort not found in hotels. Maybe it's the psychology of making your own morning coffee, or raiding the refrigerator in the evening; maybe it's being able to shop at the local market for a sampling of the foods and wines of the area and the opportunity to try them out in your own kitchen. It depends not only on what you can afford but on what is important to you.

The Virtues of In-depth Exploration

Vacation rentals are for travelers who enjoy independence and a self-paced style, exploring a city or two and spending time in villages or regions of interest, as opposed to making a rapid, demanding tour where only the highlights of half a dozen cities can be touched.

Anyone who has traveled on an extensive itinerary fitted into a limited stretch of time knows about the energy and time expended in constantly packing and unpacking, finding hotels and railway stations in unfamiliar cities, looking for a place to eat after a late arrival, and deciding what to see in what always seems like far too short a time. Renting gives you a home base to return to, whether you have been on a day trip or away for several days. It provides a place in which to unpack, unwind, relax, and make plans for the next adventure.

In order to derive the most pleasure from a short-term rental, the right location is vital. It's important to consider what sights or activities lie within reasonable access by highway or rail of your rental unit. In the United Kingdom, for example, every place seems to be fairly accessible, but if two weeks exploring the London area is your aim, then it would be better to look for an apartment in the city or its environs. If a few days in London will be enough, then maybe a cottage base from which to explore Wales or Scotland as well would be best—still within easy traveling distance of London, but situated with a different apportionment of your time in mind.

Through descriptions of regions and cities in the chapters for each country, this guide will help you plan how to be within the best striking distance of the things you want to see and do.

◆ EUROPEAN VARIETY AND STANDARDS

There is no "typical" rental property. Unlike short-term rentals in Hawaii, the Rockies, or the resorts in Mexico and the Caribbean, rental properties in Europe come in an amazingly wide variety, with virtually anything from a castle to a primitive alpine hut available. Large or small, modern or rustic, urban or rural, modest or luxury, all the rental units of the companies and agencies included in this guide are designed and equipped to meet the needs of the travelers who rent them. All have completely equipped kitchens and linen and bedding (sometimes at extra cost) for as many guests as the unit is advertised to accommodate.

Some rentals are furnished exquisitely and some simply; many are conversions from what they once were—a winery, an oasthouse for drying hops, a gate house to a manor, or the manor itself. Some, of course, are in new resort developments, and others are in the older, sophisticated developments such as the Riviera towns of Cannes, Antibes, and Villefranche-sur-Mer.

Bedding and towels are always available, but are not always included in the base price. Look for exceptions in the catalogs for France and rural Britain, where special arrangements for North Americans often must be made. You might actually have to rent your sheets and towels. It seems that many Europeans, especially the British, are accustomed to taking along their own linens and towels when they go on holiday. Fortunately, some rental companies seem to be learning that it's too much to ask that North Americans fly their clean towels to Europe and their damp ones back. To play it safe, if you are renting in rural Britain or in France tell the agent that you will need towels and linens.

Some arrangements include weekly or semiweekly laundry service, some have washers (but seldom dryers), and others leave instructions on how to get to the nearest "launderette." Almost all rentals come with a booklet or other collection of information and instructions about the accommodation and its vicinity.

In the meantime, check the chapters for the countries you plan to visit to see if there are any odd things to watch for. Most important, carefully study the material and descriptions you receive from the agencies. What Europeans take for granted may well catch you by surprise.

◆ RENTAL PERIODS

There are minor differences from country to country in the policies and customs of the rental business, but throughout Europe operations are surprisingly similar. Relevant idiosyncrasies are noted in the appropriate country chapters.

More important are common practices that affect renters throughout Europe. One that will affect your planning and timing is that *virtually all weekly rentals run from Saturday to Saturday.* Typically, you will be advised not to arrive at the property until after 4:00 P.M. on the Saturday your booking begins, and that checkout time is before 10:00 A.M. the following Saturday (or two or three Saturdays later).

Beginning with the airline reservations, schedule your arrival in order to make it to where you are going within the appropriate time period (unless you are traveling with one of the very few rental programs in which you depart at specific times and someone meets you to accompany you to the property). If you have rented or leased a car, you will need to figure in driving time, and if you are going by rail you will need to work with the train schedule. Is it difficult? Not really, and planning is part of the fun. Several thousand North Americans, and several million Europeans, do it every year.

If your rental is not in the immediate area of the city where you are going, an alternative approach is to come into the country or area a day early. Make advance reservations in a hotel somewhere in the area of your rental for a night or two before your scheduled Saturday occupancy begins, then spend a leisurely day or so getting to your destination. For example, if you have rented a cottage in Scotland, plan to arrive in London on a weekday, stay a day or so, then drive or take the train to your destination so you arrive by Saturday afternoon.

If you are planning your trip for the shoulder season or off-season, there are two things besides lower prices and thinner crowds working for you: midweek bookings are possible (ask the agent), and you probably won't have to book a hotel in advance. On arrival, simply find a hotel, or a B&B, within an easy day's travel of your destination. Perhaps it will be reassuring for you to know that we booked ahead only three or four times over a period of a year and a half of European travel, partly because we avoid traveling in the high season, and partly because we almost always drive a car.

♦ MAKING CHOICES

From the wide variety of vacation rental properties available, how do you decide which one to choose? It's usually a process of elimination, beginning with the two most basic determining factors: location and budget. Only you know where you want to visit and how much you are prepared to spend.

The first step is to decide which country, or perhaps two countries, you most want to visit, then turn to the country chapter or chapters of this guide that correspond to your interest. Scanning the appropriate chapter will give you an idea of where rentals are available and will enable you to zero in on special locales that appeal to you. The names of the agencies that own or offer short-term rentals (and the locales in which they operate) are listed at the beginning of each country chapter.

A very helpful part of this process is to work with *two* good maps. Unless you plan to spend all of your time in the United Kingdom, you will need a map of the whole of Europe, plus one of the country and region you are considering for your home base. Although the government tourist offices will send you a free map, we feel the best maps are the ones published by Michelin, Halwag, and, for Britain, those of the British Automobile Association and Royal Automobile Club. If your plans include only Britain, a map of the United Kingdom (and one of London if you are considering a rental there) will suffice. The American Automobile Association also has a selection of reasonably good maps of Europe, but they are less detailed than the other two and often fail to show the small towns needed for proper locating.

Once you settle on one or more locales you'd like to investigate further, refer to Chapter 3, "The Rental Agencies," where there is an alphabetical listing of all North American–based agencies and companies whose properties are covered in the guide. This listing includes the necessary contact information, plus a brief history of each agency, a summary of its policies, and anything else that might be useful in planning to rent abroad. Use this list to locate the agencies shown in the country chapter, then write or telephone for information and brochures on their properties in the cities or regions of your interest.

Booking Two Locations

If you like the idea of staying in two or more different locations on your visit to Europe, consider renting more than one place. This usually means that you will need to plan on a total stay of more than two weeks—one week in each location, this being the normal minimum.

There are, however, some agencies that offer combination options, such as two weeks in a London flat and one week in a cottage in Scotland. Options are noted in the guide in Chapter 3 in the agency descriptions but even if they are not specifically noted, don't hesitate to inquire when you contact the agency. A variety of arrangements is often available, especially during the shoulder seasons of April through May and late September through October—as well as in the winter months in most areas except the ski resorts.

◆ RENTAL AGENTS: HOW TO FIND AND WORK WITH THEM

Although there are many travel agencies in North America that offer vacation rentals, usually as part of a complete tour or travel package, there are relatively few companies that deal principally with rental properties. To be precise, these companies are usually not travel agencies but rental property agents. Indeed, travel agencies often arrange their rentals through these property agents.

Most U.S. property agents concentrate on villas and condominiums in popular vacation spots in the continental United States and Canada, the Caribbean islands, Bermuda, the Virgin Islands, the Bahamas, Hawaii, and Mexico, but more and more are expanding their interests into Europe. Of those that do offer European rentals, virtually all operate as agents for European companies, which sometimes own, but usually represent the owners of, the rental properties.

Although there are dozens of rental agencies throughout Europe, their clientele is mostly European, not North American, and it can be difficult to deal with them from the States. Language differences can complicate communication, both mail and telephone; there is also a time problem involved in corresponding back and forth across the Atlantic. And there can be a problem with making payment if the company takes neither credit cards nor dollar checks. Nevertheless, contact and payment procedures are being streamlined; multilingual staffs handle booking and information operations, and overall access is becoming much easier, even in dealing with the smaller companies in Europe.

Perhaps the most serious problems are those that arise if, for any reason, the property you rent is not satisfactory. These problems are not necessarily due to a lack of responsibility on the part of the European company, but arise because of the difficulty in postvacation communication with a distant agent, particularly if you are seeking reimbursement or other compensation for whatever you felt was not right.

If you have these concerns, and if you want the security of having everything settled before departing for Europe, we suggest booking through an American or Canadian agency. There will usually, but not always, be an added fee or commission to cover the cost of international calls, fax, currency transfers, postage, and problem handling.

On the other hand, if you are willing to begin your planning early and feel that you can handle any risks and complications of dealing directly, or if you are willing to wing it and look for a place after you arrive, we were favorably impressed with the foreign rental companies whose addresses can be found in Appendix B.

Soon after you have contacted a domestic rental agency, a package of brochures and other informational material will arrive, describing everything from the location of the agency's properties to what the rental units are like and giving the prices. When you receive these brochures, take care in figuring the costs. Some prices are shown on a per-unit, and some on a per-person basis; some are shown per week and some for a set minimum time. Be prepared to do a bit of calculation to determine the actual total costs, especially if you are comparing the rates of two companies with rentals in some single town or area in which you are interested. A range of rental rates for each group of properties is shown in the country chapters of this guide, but because inflation and currency exchange rates affect rental prices, be sure to study the latest agency figures before sending a check or credit card number or signing a rental agreement.

Some companies offer services such as having a representative meet you at your destination airport to hand you your key, help arrange transportation to your rental unit, and give you an orientation to the area. Some companies provide transportation to the rental unit, whereas others provide only an information packet (mailed to you before your departure and containing the name, address, and telephone number of their European representative) and leave it to you to make the contact. Others give you detailed instructions on how to get to the property and how to contact the resident manager. In all cases, you can rest assured that everything can be handled very easily; you should never have to leave for Europe without all the information you need to find and settle in to your "self-catering" unit. (Some companies even provide enough groceries to help you get situated and carry you through until you have had the chance to go to the market.)

Be sure to follow these three rules:

1. Be thoughtful and careful in deciding where you want to stay.

2. Don't sign a rental agreement or make a deposit unless the information you receive on any rental unit is complete and you are sure you will be getting what you want.

3. Don't send your final rental check or credit card authorization until you are comfortable with all the arrangements, including how you are going to find your unit and how you are going to get there.

A more thorough discussion of the pros and cons of booking through a North American agency versus direct booking, the services to be expected from each, and additional fees and commissions can be found in Chapter 3.

◆ RENTING WITHOUT RESERVATIONS

Another choice for many vacationers is the season in which to travel. During the off-season in Europe (normally winter, except in the ski resorts), most rentals either stand empty awaiting an occasional booking or are not offered for rent. (For more details on seasons, see the country chapters.) During these times, it's easy to go to an area of interest and look around for a short-term rental. These are usually less difficult to find in the smaller towns and resort areas than in major cities, mainly because of the complexity of cities. Some villages, most towns, and all cities have a tourist assistance office, and virtually all of these offices have listings of places for rent. It's also possible simply to wander the streets looking for a place to rent, a task made easier if you have rented or leased a car (see Chapter 4).

We took this independent approach several years ago when we went to Europe to do research for our first travel guide. We leased a car in Paris, knowing that we wanted to set up a home base in the vicinity of Barcelona. We drove into Spain in February, traveled down the north Mediterranean coast, and spotted numerous signs—ALQUILAR ("To Rent")—along the way. We found a place we liked in the pleasant little coastal town of Sitges, some twenty miles south of Barcelona. It was a small apartment with a view, just across the street from the beach, with a modestly equipped kitchen and dishes, sheets, blankets, and so forth, but no towels. The off-season rent was about $290 per month, including utilities. We found it by scouting the beachside street, and lived there for four months, taking extended drives and boat trips to places as far away as Yugoslavia, Greece, and Tunisia, but always returning "home."

We repeated this procedure when we moved to England later that year, but found that our June arrival put us very close to the high season, when everything is fully booked. We worked things out, but barely in time.

In retrospect, had we arrived in Spain between mid-May and mid-September, or during the three weeks surrounding Easter, we would likely have been out of luck. And even had we, by some good fortune, found an apartment or villa for rent, the cost would have been double the off-season rate.

The lesson is that if you want to rent as you go, plan your visit during the low season of winter, during the spring shoulder months of April and May (but avoiding the three Easter weeks), or in the autumn shoulder months from mid-September to November. Otherwise, reserve well ahead. And again, remember that the period from two weeks before Easter through the week after is a time of peak travel in Europe, especially in the Mediterranean countries. As for December at the fashionable ski resorts, be prepared for peak prices and dense crowds.

There are millions of Europeans who are creatures of habit when it comes to their holidays, and they book their rental places, especially for July and August, many months in advance. Americans who must visit Europe in the peak seasons must learn to do the same.

2

Using This Guide

♦

♦ ORGANIZATION OF THE COUNTRY CHAPTERS

Anyone thinking about renting a vacation place in Europe will find more than just a list of properties and agencies in this guide. It also serves as a travel planner, organized by country, covering major cities and regions. The general locations of rental properties in each country are divided into regions and are arranged geographically. Principal cities within the regions are also listed. The absence of a city or region from a country chapter does not necessarily mean that no rentals are available there, only that they are so scattered or few in number that they are hard to identify and book through a U.S. agency. These scattered properties sometimes appear on a page or two in the catalog of a European company.

The first step in working with this guide is to decide which regions or cities you want to visit. You may already know where you want to go, but if you're unsure, the location descriptions in the country chapters provide a helpful overview of where the rental properties are.

The second step is to tie the region or city of your interest to the agencies that represent properties there—easily done because agencies and the regions they cover are listed at the beginning of each country chapter.

Third, refer to Chapter 3, "The Rental Agencies," to find and learn a little about the agencies that offer rentals in the regions or cities you are considering, then select several to contact for brochures and other information.

The fourth and final step is to choose the right agency. From the information you receive, the descriptions in Chapter 3, and your personal preferences as to location, standards, style, approach, and price level, an informed decision can be reached.

◆ ORGANIZATION OF THE INFORMATION

The List of Agencies

Each country chapter begins with a listing of the names of U.S. and Canadian agencies that offer properties in that country, noting the regions and cities where they operate. The names of these agencies can then be cross-referenced to the alphabetical list in Chapter 3, where their addresses and telephone numbers can be found, along with comments on their policies and procedures regarding deposits, terms, refunds, transportation, guarantees, package arrangements, multilocation programs, and whatever else may be relevant. Included may be recommendations, as well as comments, on any unusual characteristics of the agencies and any warnings that the writers feel may bear upon the success of your rental experience. Don't limit your inquiry to one agency; pick three or four that seem to approach their prospective customers in different ways.

The Country

Following the list of agencies is a brief overview of the country from the perspective of finding a good location in which to rent for a week or two or more. These overviews do not substitute for a good country guidebook; rather, they provide general observations on rentals in the country and describe any unusual rental procedures that could affect your stay. Suggestions on the best times of year to visit may be covered in this section if the country is small or has a fairly consistent climate and consistent tourist season patterns; otherwise, this advice is included in the section dealing with the regions.

The Regions

This section may include descriptive geographical names (such as "South Coast" in the chapter on Spain), or a proper national name (Scotland, in the chapter on the United Kingdom), or the name of a region or province (Brittany, in the chapter on France; Tirol in the one on Austria). The locations of these places are always made evident, but it may also be helpful to check the map near the beginning of each country chapter.

Pertinent information is presented in an order designed to make planning and decision making easy, generally following the same format in each chapter, and includes the following:

ENVIRONS AND ACCOMMODATIONS. These paragraphs describe the region in the vicinity of the rental units. If they are in a city, the type of neighborhood is discussed. The terrain, scenery, and the nature of the village are given for rural units. The typical rental accommodations in the region are described: mountain chalets, flats, apartments in private homes, estates, condominiums, converted farmhouses, or beach apartments. Suggestions on the best time of year to visit may be included here.

LOCATION AND TRANSPORTATION. This section tells about important cities or sites in the region that can be visited by means of a day trip or an overnighter from the rental properties, locates the region in relation to the country and other countries, and notes more distant destinations that can be reached on round-trips of two days or so. For example, from the Lake Country of northern Italy it is not difficult to visit Interlaken and the Bernese Oberland of Switzerland to the northwest, the Tirol and Innsbruck of Austria to the northeast, and Lake Garda and Venice to the south. It is very helpful to work with a detailed map of Europe as you make decisions on where to locate your home base. Also noted here is the accessibility to transportation (railway lines, main and secondary highways, ferry routes). Appropriate suggestions are made regarding the best means of traveling throughout the area. (All the rental agencies should provide detailed information and instructions once a particular property has been decided upon, and, as has been noted, some even provide transportation or someone to accompany you from the airport or railway station to the property.)

PRICES. Nearly all the rental agencies list their prices for the *complete unit*, so the cost per person in your family or party is easily figured. Be careful when making comparisons with hotel rates, because many hotels in Europe show their prices per person, rather than per room, which is the general custom in the United States and Canada.

Some larger properties may seem expensive, but upon examination you may learn that they can accommodate six, eight, or more persons. These units are ideal for families, or for sharing with congenial travel companions.

Note: Because of changing currency exchange rates, inflation, and the addition and deletion of properties from year to year, be sure to check the current rental rates published by the appropriate agencies before reaching a final decision.

ADVANCE BOOKING TIME. This section will tell you how many weeks or months in advance of your planned arrival you must book so that you can be reasonably sure of being able to confirm your booking; the differences depend on the locales of the rental properties and the time of year. Also, some countries observe holidays that are rarely considered by citizens of other countries. For example, foreigners planning to come to the United States usually don't know that hotels and motels and cottages and campsites are booked solid over the Fourth of July and Labor Day weekends. We, on the other hand, have little idea when Britain's midterm holidays are, nor do we know that everything is booked well in advance during those periods. So book early in any case.

◆ THE APPENDICES

Appendix A

The names, addresses, and telephone numbers of North American–based agencies are repeated for convenience.

Appendix B

This is a list of European rental company addresses for travelers who may be in Europe without a pre-arranged booking or who may want to book directly with a European company. The pros and cons of direct booking versus booking through an agency in the United States or Canada are dealt with in Chapter 3. The inclusion of these companies in the guide means only that the authors have had personal contact with the company owners or representatives or have other reason to believe that they will work well with a North American clientele. There may be comments along with some of the company addresses.

Appendix C

This is a listing of the addresses of European national tourist offices in the United States. Upon request, many of these offices can provide a list of rental properties that have been registered with them, but the tourist offices cannot make rental arrangements for you. They are usually also a good source of country, regional, and city maps.

3

The Rental Agencies

◆

The Europeans

Very few of the rental agencies in the United States and Canada actually represent European property owners directly, but rather, they are the agents for European companies that do. The business of seeking out and accumulating long listings of rental properties throughout a region or a country began in Europe long ago and retains a character unlike that of the American companies that manage and rent condominiums in Hawaii or villas in a resort in Mexico or on a Caribbean island.

These European companies advertise and compete with each other in their continuing quest for owners who will rent on a short-term basis to vacationers, while their staffs comb the countryside looking for new properties and making sure that the owners of current properties are keeping up their part of the bargain by maintaining standards. These companies encourage the restoration of ancient buildings and crumbling stone cottages and their conversion into apartments, comfortable villas, and cozy bungalows, and they often help the owners with the process. These European companies also photograph the properties they represent, usually hundreds of them, sometimes thousands, write descriptions, and design the catalogs for distribution to potential customers.

Some companies are two- or three-person operations; others have dozens of staffers, including some who work with sophisticated computer systems, linguists who deal with the international clientele, and overseers of the quality and maintenance of the properties the companies represent. Some of the companies are highly personalized, working closely with both owners and renters and limiting their operating area

17

to locations that are within a half day's drive or less. Others are large, offering properties throughout an entire country, and in a few cases throughout Europe; they rely on their regionally based staff to deal with owners, properties, and renters.

LARGE OR SMALL? As we met and talked with owners and company personnel, we became aware of opposing views on whether smaller or larger meant better. Some people believe that a small company offering properties in a limited region can be more selective about the places it has to offer and can more closely supervise them; others are convinced that the big companies offer better incentives to owners and that their regional personnel can do a good job of finding new properties and maintaining standards. Our conclusion is that there is no predictable relationship between company size and the quality of the properties represented—the important factors are the policies and standards set by the company, whether it's a two-person or a fifty-person organization.

It's a very competitive business, becoming more so, and most of the companies we dealt with in Europe are indeed doing a remarkable job, offering well-described, well-maintained properties at fair prices. Companies that offer shoddy, misrepresented, or grossly overpriced properties will likely fall by the wayside. The knack is to avoid dealing with them during their predictably short lives. One way of doing this is to work through a reputable agency in the United States or Canada; it then becomes the North American agency's task to sort out the good from the bad and the exceptional from the ordinary. There are many reputable agencies on this side of the Atlantic, but the important thing is to find the one that appeals to you, that offers properties in the country and area you want to visit, that best suits your needs, and that you consider to be fair in its pricing policies.

Booking a Vacation Rental

USING A U.S. AGENT VERSUS BOOKING DIRECT. With very few exceptions, it will cost more to book through a North American agency than directly with a European one. For the American or Canadian agency there are the costs of international phone calls, fax or telex charges, costs for accepting credit cards and for the transfer of funds in foreign currency drafts to the European company, mailing of brochures and letters, domestic calls to clients, time and costs of solving problems and settling disputes, costs of printing of informational materials, and costs of travel to Europe to inspect properties or to assure themselves that the European companies do. And there are the costs of maintaining an office on this side of the Atlantic, and, of course, making a profit. The question is: Is it worth the difference?

The answer is: It depends on *how much* the fee or commission is and what services you are getting for your money. Interestingly, it seems that very few vacationers who contact U.S. agencies ask about the fee or commission, perhaps because it is assumed that whatever the amount is it's probably worth it, or perhaps because in the excitement of planning a visit to Europe one doesn't think about there being much of a difference (there can be). Another possibility is the belief that there is no alternative.

The decision is a personal one, based on two main factors: deciding which route offers the best chance of assuring that the place you rent will be what you want and your ability and willingness to deal with a foreign rental company in order to save the additional commission or fees. Bear in mind that you will likely be committing yourselves in either case to a rental period of at least one, and usually two or more, weeks. With some North American agents you will be asked to pay a deposit to begin the process, followed by about one-half of the total rent in order to guarantee the booking, and finally, the remainder of the total amount several weeks before departure. To place this in perspective, it is not unlike renting a house, condominium, or apartment in the United States or Canada for a long term; usually a deposit and the first and last months' rent are required in advance of occupancy. The difference is that if the property is in Europe you are doing it sight unseen.

Dealing with Foreign Rental Companies and Properties

Because of electronic processing of credit card payments, the ease and lower cost of international telephone calls, and the increased use of the English language by persons in the booking offices of foreign companies, many of the obstacles to direct bookings are slowly disappearing. Nevertheless, there is considerable variation among the companies, even in Britain, on the method of payment that will be accepted. Many still do not accept credit cards from overseas and will take bank drafts only in the currency of the country of the home office. Although you can obtain drafts in foreign currencies at most U.S. banks, there is a fee, or at least the cost of the difference between the buy and sell rates of the currencies.

The costs of bank drafts, international phone calls, and postage are not, however, the principal considerations in deciding whether to deal directly or through a U.S. or Canadian agent. Time can be a problem. Mail strikes and other interruptions in service are not uncommon in Europe, and although arrangements can be discussed by long-distance telephone, nothing is firm until written agreements and money have actually changed hands. On the other hand, dealings between a North American agent and a European company can be handled by fax, telex, or telephone. The agent you select should be set up to serve as your guarantor to the European company that the funds have been, or will be, collected from you, the client.

Another thing you should consider before dealing directly is the issue of getting a refund or other settlement if you find upon arrival that the property is not as advertised, or if through no fault of yours the property becomes unavailable after you have paid the rent or put up a deposit. Usually, the company will find another property of equal value and cost acceptable to you, or perhaps one that is even more expensive. If this should occur (and it rarely does), remember that you are legally in the driver's seat. You should never pay more for a replacement, regardless of its listed rental price, unless *you* initiate the substitution. This applies whether you are dealing with a foreign company or a domestic agency. Matters of adjustment, exchange, or any other type of settlement can be more complicated when dealing internationally. Nevertheless, the same warnings hold true. Read the fine print in the rental agreement or terms for booking regardless of where they come from.

DIFFERENCES. Finally, expect differences. Companies in different countries function in various ways, and there are differences in European perspectives relating to accommodation standards. There are differences in amenities, kitchen appliances, sizes of beds, wattage of light bulbs, and even in shopping for groceries. Most of these differences arise from the complex and fascinating differences in history and culture from one European country to another and between Europe and North America. These cultural variations, of course, work both ways; to the majority of French travelers, for example, the absence of bidets in the bathrooms of Britain, the United States, Canada, and elsewhere appears uncivilized. If you are not ready for variety, plan to book only a deluxe villa in a modern development, an apartment in a luxury apartment building, or perhaps turn your sights toward a vacation in Hawaii, the U.S. Virgin islands, or another Western Hemisphere resort area where the accommodations have been influenced or developed by Americans or Canadians.

Sadly, in meetings with owners and representatives of European rental companies from Cornwall to Tuscany, we often heard the assertion, usually delicately couched, that Americans tend to be complainers. One substantial company we visited in England had long been uninterested in the American market—too many petty complaints, too many problems. It was thought that we Americans have a tendency to want a cottage with the comfort, size, style, and amenities of a typical American vacation resort. Someone observed that Americans are used to having a box of paper tissues in the bathroom, and complain if there isn't one. We think that's carrying the criticism too far, although we know it's not baseless. The point is, if you want to get away to a stone farmhouse in

Scotland, a sixteenth-century farmhouse in Italy's Chianti region, or an apartment in an eighteenth-century building off the Champs Elysées, the odds are that there will be little to which you are accustomed. Much of the enjoyment and fascination of foreign travel is that it isn't just like being "at home." This doesn't mean that you should accept shoddiness, discomfort, uncleanliness, or serious variance with what has been described in a brochure—rather that oddities (to American eyes) arising from the age of buildings, curious locations, or different cultural perspectives should be taken in stride.

Often, idiosyncrasies that are known about in advance can be dealt with easily, improving one's comfort and overall enjoyment. Many things that North Americans take for granted are often absent in European vacation rentals, so in direct dealings with a foreign rental agency (or even a North American one for that matter), the burden is on you to understand fully what is being supplied. Again, sheets and towels are not always included and must be inquired about at the time of booking. If not, you could find yourself in your remote castle with no linens and none to be found. (If they are not included, they can be provided, but you *must inquire in advance*. This is usually spelled out in the catalogs or property profiles you will receive.)

Most North American travelers can deal with a variety of situations, but at the same time it is nice to know what to expect, especially when there may not be someone on the spot to take care of the trivia, as in a hotel. Small unexpected things can complicate your stay, but if anticipated, they can be dealt with. Where appropriate, the country chapters advise on potentially troublesome peculiarities and how best to deal with them. Don't worry about asking questions before you book; we were told that the unhappy clients are those who arrive uninformed and unprepared.

European Company/North American Agency Relationships

A majority of the European rental companies have one or more agents in the United States, associated in a variety of ways ranging from formal and exclusive to very loose. If you contact a foreign company and the reply to your inquiry comes from a company in the United States or Canada (often with a different name), you will know that your inquiry has been referred and that a formal relationship exists and is being respected. If this occurs, but you wish to work directly with a European firm, you will need to try another foreign company, one with no formal agency relationship here. However, if the first company has the properties in which you are interested, it will be necessary to work with the

American or Canadian agent. If you receive information and a booking form directly from Europe, it tells you nothing; the company may have no U.S. or Canadian representation, or it may have informal arrangements with no obligation to refer inquiries to its "agents." If this occurs, feel free to work with that company if its properties are of interest and its terms seem satisfactory.

Despite the tendency of European companies to establish some sort of agency relationships in order to reach the North American market, we found a number of good companies that prefer to work directly with American and Canadian customers without an agent, and a few that will work either way. Most of these are British, and they feel they can offer their rental properties without the added fees and commissions of a U.S. agent and still provide good service, ease of booking, business dealings in a similar language, and excellent reputations. Still others, although they are not inclined to meddle in the financial affairs of their agents, do put caps on what the agents can charge overall. They are concerned that the layers of administrative levels between the property owners and the renters could increase rental prices unreasonably, raising them into hotel price ranges. Because of this danger, it is important for you to determine if the fee or commission is consistent with the services being provided. A few key points on the issue, and some questions to ask yourselves and the agencies, are discussed in "Commissions and Fees," later in this chapter.

Our view is that by and large the services provided by the North American agencies are worthwhile, in terms of making it easier and more expedient to obtain information and to book. It's easier to pay by credit card or dollar check than by a foreign currency bank draft. It's also good to know that an agency is at hand to deal with problems that may arise. Just be sure that the agency you are about to work with does indeed offer this kind of service in addition to having the property you want.

Although we found some foreign companies not equipped to accept credit cards or dollar checks or bank drafts, we found none that we felt to be dishonest or disreputable. The main problem, and it is not a great one, is that some companies had different property standards than Americans do; that is, a rental they may consider to be above average in size, furnishings, and amenities might be rather average to most Americans. This is usually a matter of differences in culture and economy, not of intent.

For persons willing to make the extra effort, and to accept the few risks noted above, or who feel independent enough to go to Europe during one of the off-seasons without prebooked accommodations, the names and addresses of a few selected rental agencies in Britain and on the Continent are listed in Appendix B.

North American Rental Agencies

During the past two years, as the dollar has declined against most foreign currencies and as inflation in Europe has played havoc with everything from clothes to cars and restaurant meals to hotel room prices, the business of renting vacation properties has grown, especially in the United States, where the number of agencies specializing in short-term European rentals has almost tripled. When we began work on this guide there were some twenty companies; now, over sixty are included.

Unfortunately, it is not too difficult to get into the business. All that is needed are the names and addresses of some rental companies in Europe, letterhead, and a telephone. Many European companies will accept a booking from, and offer a commission to, any second party on behalf of a third party. It usually takes just a letter or phone call to the owner or manager of the foreign company, ideally along with one or two potential bookings. Many successful and legitimate companies began this way, but the point is that it's important to know with whom you are dealing. And because it is more difficult to determine the integrity of the European company, the trustworthiness of the North American agency needs to be considered. At a *minimum*, the owner or some key staff member of the domestic agency should be personally familiar with the foreign territory; he or she should have inspected at least a sampling of the properties, met the management of the foreign companies or the property owners, and have a good idea of what the area is like. Although some agencies represent literally thousands of properties throughout the world, someone should be able to provide an accurate description of at least the general area where your rental property is before you commit to it. Sometimes this is very well handled in a brochure or catalog, sometimes not. If you are unsure, either persist until you are satisfied or try another agency. There is nothing more ruinous to a vacation than being unpleasantly surprised by your accommodations.

It is not the purpose of this guide to compare and contrast these agencies; ownerships and managements change, as do policies on commissions and fees and the European companies that each agency represents. Thus, what is true today may not be tomorrow.

What this guide provides, among other information and insights, is a rather complete list, with brief descriptions, of North American agencies—and a scattering of selected European companies in Appendix B—enabling you to make contacts, gather the specific information you need, and ask the appropriate questions, all so that you can make informed decisions and better find the vacation rental that suits your needs and your dreams.

THREE BASIC STEPS. From the list of agencies in each country chapter, select those companies with properties in the region or city you want to visit. Then look up the agency names in the alphabetical list provided in this chapter. This list gives a summary of information about each agency. The next two steps are those of information exchange: your initial contact with the agency and its response to you.

Although asking questions is important, your first and most important job is to *define exactly what you are looking for.* Once you have selected the country(ies) and region(s) or city(ies) in which you are interested, prepare a list of the important specifics: location, size, style, type, standard, number in your party, dates, budget, and special needs. Remember that flexibility is important throughout the selection process.

LOCATION: Where do you want to be? On the beach, within a mile of the beach, in the center of a village, in a remote rural area, anywhere in central London or in a specific area such as Bloomsbury or Kensington, near a golf course, on the Rhine, near a ski lift, close to salmon streams, anywhere in central Paris or specifically in Montmartre, in Florence or in the Tuscan hills nearby? Keep in mind your budget, and prioritize your list. You might even draw a line between those locale features that are essential (you won't settle for less) and those that are desirable but not essential; perhaps they will be unaffordable or unavailable. Use a good area map and guidebook to determine possible daytrips and area activities.

SIZE: How large a place do you want? A studio, one bedroom, two bedrooms, total square footage, and so on. In most European catalogs the area is given in square meters, or m^2; multiply this figure by 10.5 to find the approximate square feet. Some European catalogs do not include the kitchen in the room count; that is, a two-room apartment may have a bedroom, a sitting/dining room, and a kitchen. As in the United States and Canada, the bathroom is not included in the room count.

STYLE: What architectural style do you fancy? A contemporary or historic dwelling, stone cottage, castle, farmhouse, stately home, mountain chalet, or whatever.

TYPE: What type of rental do you prefer? An apartment, detached house, town house, single or multilevel dwelling, etc. Considerable differences exist between the American English and British or Continental English names of particular types or styles of buildings; these are "translated" in the appropriate country chapters.

STANDARDS: Define the quality you prefer. Most vacation rentals are not the principal homes of the owners (although some are), and may not be furnished or equipped like your own home. The exceptions are usually in the luxury category. Common terms are "simple," "standard," "deluxe," "luxury," and, increasingly, rentals are given a number of "stars," as hotels are. Bear in mind that even five-star accommodations may have been built well before the age of indoor plumbing in the cities as well as the country, so don't be surprised to find exposed pipes and bathrooms in odd places. Garbage disposals are rare, and dishwashers are uncommon (but becoming less so); you will sometimes find automatic clothes washers but seldom dryers.

NUMBER IN YOUR PARTY: How many adults? How many children?

DATES: When are you going? Allow some flexibility if possible, and aim for shoulder or off-season travel; check the price lists or catalogs for peak, high, middle, and low seasons, and the corresponding price differences. Check the country chapters for more information.

BUDGET: How much can you spend? The amount per week you are comfortable with, and the maximum amount per week you are willing to pay. You may discover that you will have to lower your sights, or you may be pleasantly surprised that you can spend less, or have a nicer place than you anticipated. (If you are traveling with friends, be sure you are all involved in working out these financial details.)

SPECIAL NEEDS: Are there any features required by a disabled person in your party? Do you need wheelchair access? Will you have a vehicle, or must you be within walking distance of public transportation and grocery stores? Need a garage?

There are two reasons for working out this information. First, many agencies *do not* send catalogs to prospective customers, but rather ask for a complete description of what you are looking for. After receiving the information by mail or telephone, the agency matches your description with properties it has and compiles a collection of property profiles fitting the general requirements of your description. The packet is sent for your consideration and selection. (If the packet does not include prices, ask for them or look for another agency.) Second, if the agency does use a pictorial and descriptive catalog, videotape, or slides to display its offerings, rather than matching your description to its properties, you can use the information you have worked out to screen the properties. With the catalog/visual approach, the selection procedure becomes your responsibility. It's an enjoyable one—perusing illustrations and descriptions of the exotic sounding places. As above, if prices are not included, either ask for the list or look for another agency.

FINDING THE RIGHT AGENCY. You must first identify the agencies that offer properties in the locale(s) in which you are interested and find out more about them. It is the competence and integrity of the agency that are of primary concern; after all, what good is a glowing property description if it is not accurate? Ask the agency for details of its firsthand knowledge of any rental you are considering.

Although the short descriptions in this chapter will help you choose the kind of agency that suits you, it's best to find out for yourselves the most current information pertinent to your particular needs and interests.

Specific and detailed information on the properties offered should be contained in the agency's catalog, property profile sheets, or, in a very few cases, on videotape.

Details should include the number of bedrooms, approximate size of the unit, and location (distances from beach, ski lift, lakefront, railway, bus or subway station, and any other appropriate markers). They should describe the style and type of property, and at least try to capture the atmosphere.

Specific terms, ranging from "standard" or "simple" to "luxury" or "elegant," should describe each rental but *look beyond these words* to the descriptions of the properties themselves; try to get a sense of the trustworthiness of the agencies you are dealing with.

Determine the nature of the property; any agency should be able to tell you if the unit is isolated and private, in a bustling area, or tranquil and sedate.

Amenities such as a private swimming pool or access to a community pool, fireplace, laundry facilities, unusual appliances (for European rentals) such as microwave and dishwasher, tennis courts, or stables should be specified.

Supplies, especially linens and towels, should be noted, and if not supplied as part of the rent, then information on arranging for them and the cost must be made clear. How often are linens and towels changed? There should be information on whether or not electricity and other utilities are included, and if not, how they are handled. The same is true for heat or air-conditioning.

Is there a damage or cleaning or utility deposit, and if so, to whom is it paid? (For example, one large company requires that you hand the owner a deposit in local currency upon arrival; it can be the equivalent of several hundred dollars, so it is vital that you go to the bank before arriving at the property so that you will have the cash on hand. The deposit is refunded, also in cash, upon your departure if all is well.

Services should be described: Is maid service included in the rent? If so, how often? If not, is it available, and what is the cost? Who is responsible for the final cleaning, and is there an extra charge for it?

If all of the above information is not covered or described to your satisfaction somehwere in the catalog, profile sheets, tapes, or other informational literature you receive from an agency, either try to get more information or find another agency.

OTHER QUESTIONS TO ASK. By far the majority of the agencies and foreign companies we dealt with, and the owners in whose homes, apartments, cottages, and villas we stayed in or visited while gathering information for this guide, are of such nature that there would never be intentional misrepresentation or intent to delude or defraud the traveling public. This is not to say that no undesirable and opportunistic agencies exist, but that there are very few. Neither is it to say that there are never problems, but only that most arise from misunderstandings—failures of communication between agency and client—rather than bad intent or lack of integrity. Some problems may be due to poor description of properties by the agency or to a poor interpretation of what the client is looking for, and some due to the client's failure to read the booking or fee terms accurately or to interpret property descriptions well. And there are always the less sophisticated travelers who expect American standards in a Welsh cottage. It is imperative to deal with all the property and services details and to feel comfortable about the agency you are dealing with. Even among the most established and reputable agencies there is a wide variation in pricing and fee practices. Don't be afraid to ask questions.

Although answers to the following questions are usually contained in the brochures, rental terms, and other materials you receive, sometimes they are not. In any case, this is a good checklist of questions to be answered.

CONTACTS: In case of problems with the property, is there anyone on or near the property who can be contacted? Is there a person in Europe affiliated with the agency? Who, if anyone, will show us to the property, or how do we obtain the key?

REFUNDS: What are the agency's policies regarding refund of the deposit or rent paid in the event of cancellation before departure? What if the agency or the owner cancels the agreement before we depart or take occupancy? Is the deposit kept in a bank in North America, or is it transferred to a European bank? How long, in either case, does it take to receive a refund? Is cancellation insurance available?

INSPECTION AND PERSONAL KNOWLEDGE: Does someone in the agency inspect the properties the agency offers? How often? If not, is the agency associated with a reputable European company that does? Is that company listed by the government tourist authority for that country? Is someone in the agency in regular personal contact with the agency's European associate? How many properties does the firm represent? (Some large agencies represent thousands of rental properties throughout the world, usually through a network of separate companies. In these cases it is rare for the agency's personnel to have personally inspected the properties. Instead they rely on the company in each country. Personal knowledge of properties is thus replaced by the reputation of the American company, which, in turn, depends on the quality and honesty of the foreign companies. These large agencies tend to be quite reliable and should be able to answer your questions.)

PROFESSIONAL AND BUSINESS PRACTICES: How long has the company been in business? How do we pay—by credit card, personal check? Is the agency a member of the American Society of Travel Agents (ASTA)? (ASTA membership carries no guarantees for clients, but indicates a company's interest in and support of the travel industry.) Is fax, telephone, or mail used in communicating with the agency's European associates in confirming bookings? (The first two are faster and more reliable than the last, and suggest a certain professionalism.)

COMMISSIONS AND FEES: These practices are important not only to you, the renter, but affect the entire international business of renting vacation properties. For example, suppose you pay $900 a week for a villa on the sea somewhere and later learn that you could have rented the same place for $600 a week had you booked directly with the foreign company. That equates to a 33 percent commission. You are rightfully angry, you pass the word, and the legitimate and fair agencies are hurt.

What, then, is fair? Again, it depends partly on what services you receive for your money and partly on what services you feel you need. Some agencies are ideal for the independent traveler, offering a descriptive photographic catalog, sometimes for a small charge ($5 to $15 is not unreasonable, depending on catalog size), from which to choose a property. The selection is up to you, and the agency doesn't have to make an effort to search for the properties that match your description. To this is usually added a flat booking fee ($50 to $100 is reasonable) at the time you actually reserve. The agency will provide you with the details you need to find your place and settle in. It's that simple if you don't mind taking the initiative and being pretty much on your own. At this level of service you should find that the U.S. price list is nearly the same as the one for booking in Europe.

Some agencies receive an adequate, or almost adequate, commission from the European company with which they are working, and in addition are sharp enough to operate on a small margin. In these cases the prices to North American clients are the same, or almost the same, as they are to Europeans. With these agencies, ideally it will be a *matching* process: you tell them where you want to go and the other details, and they will return a selection of comprehensive profiles from which you can select. Another approach is similar, but instead of detailed profiles you receive pages from catalogs selected to meet your criteria. You should not have to pay a fee to start this procedure.

Other agencies receive little or no commission from the European companies (or perhaps they feel that they need to have a larger profit margin), so they add a percentage to the prices published by the European company. In these cases the price list you receive will be typed in the United States or Canada, usually in dollars, but sometimes in the foreign currency with an exchange rate multiplier. The prices will be higher than those found in the original foreign price list. The difference, in our view, should never exceed about 25 percent unless the agency is providing a complete turnkey service; that is, you should be virtually free from any effort in making arrangements.

Finally, some agencies charge a considerable fee for matching your description with their properties, although those that do often apply the fee toward the rent. This assumes, of course, that you will rent from them rather than relinquish the fee. We consider the *matching* approach to be a good one, and it eliminates the difficulty of selecting the property you want from hundreds or thousands of others, but we think that it should be part of the cost of doing business. Before paying a "membership" fee or registration charge, find out if there is also a commission involved. Again, it doesn't seem reasonable to have to pay a large fee, plus a commission, simply to give the agency the opportunity to try to find a vacation rental for you.

From the foregoing basic outline of commission and fee structures, work out what is most comfortable for you, then carefully study the materials you receive from the agencies you have contacted, especially the terms and conditions. The materials may not include a catalog or any other property-related information, but will always tell you how this can be obtained. If it requires a modest fee and the information already received is of interest to you, then it would probably be worthwhile to pay the fee. Remember that the agency wants you as a client and should not be charging you a substantial sum to become one. Most don't, but catalogs and mass mailings are costly, and we find a charge of a *few* dollars to be not unreasonable. But when there is a fee involved, find out what services and materials you will receive for your money. Remember, this fee is usually just to research their property files and see if there is one that matches your requirements—there are no guarantees. We found most of the agencies very open and forthcoming, but from a few we received little or no response to our queries. Those responses are reflected in the amount of information in the following agency listings.

◆ AGENCY INFORMATION AND OVERVIEWS

We have found that almost all of the following agencies have faces and personalities and interested and interesting people, informative, cooperative, and eager to have their part of the world of travel better known and understood in America and Canada, as it has been for so long in Europe.

In the profile listing that follows, the number of rental units shown after most agency addresses is approximate, varying from year to year, and is shown only to indicate the comparative sizes of the agencies.

In a few instances, you will note that the agency descriptions seem very similar. This is because several divisions of one company may have been incorporated separately in the United States and function accordingly, or because different U.S. agencies represent the same European company. In the latter case, compare the offerings to see if one company is better suited to your needs than the other.

After each agency address is a listing of the principal European countries, regions, and main cities in which the agency offers vacation properties for rent.

The term *"Approach"* used in most of the profiles means the procedure that the agency uses in its response to inquiries and its procedure for arranging bookings. For example: "Sends a catalog to select from" or "Matches your requirements to properties in its inventory and sends you selected property profiles." The fee, if any, is noted.

In general, when making an information-gathering contact with a North American agency, either call or send a note stating the countries and regions you are interested in. If you are considering booking directly with a European company, it's best to telephone your request. This will reduce mail time delay and indicate that you are serious about booking. In either case, a telephone call before final booking will assure that all the details are taken care of.

Two alternative properties should be selected from the catalog or from the property profile sheets in case your first selection is unavailable.

   A NOTE FOR FAMILIES TRAVELING WITH CHILDREN. Compared to the confinement of hotel rooms, vacation rentals are ideal for families with children. Most owners and agents welcome children in their properties and promote the advantages of space, kitchens, and a more relaxed atmosphere. A few may have some restrictions because of the nature and quality of the furnishings. Some luxury rentals are furnished with fine period pieces, elegant carpeting, and antiques. When traveling with children under the age of twelve, ask the agent about any age restrictions. Ask also about proximity to suitable play areas for younger children.

Because agents and rental companies handle many properties of different standards, it is impossible to apply any single rule regarding children.

A NOTE ON PROBLEMS AND COMPLAINTS. Problems do sometimes arise, and are typically handled by the agencies in two ways. For on-site problems—a faulty appliance, a leaky pipe, a missing utensil you cannot do without—contact the caretaker, manager, or owner who is on or near the property. If no one is around, contact the company representative whose name and phone number have been provided before your departure. (If you do not receive all this information soon after you book, contact the agency. It is risky to depart for Europe without it.) Complaints of a larger nature, such as finding that the property is not as it was advertised, or not where it was advertised, are dealt with on your return by the U.S. or Canadian agency. However, you should also notify the European company that the North American agent represents.

When agencies depart from this standard procedure, the differences are noted in the following descriptions.

If you booked directly with a European company, you should attempt to resolve any major complaint before leaving Europe. Despite the best intentions of the Europeans, it can be difficult to resolve problems across the Atlantic and across language barriers.

NOTES ON THE COUNTRIES, REGIONS, AND TOWNS. The regions or provinces in which the agency has rental properties follow the name of each country; if the agency offers rentals in the region's internationally known towns, they are shown next. For example, "Riviera—Cannes, Cap Ferrat, Cap d'Antibes," means that properties are available in these three towns in the Riviera area. Large destination cities that we have treated as distinct regions are also noted. If there are specific districts in the cities where the properties of the agency are located, they follow the city name; for example, "London—Kensington, Mayfair, Chelsea."

Where there is little information about an agency, it means that we have received little or no response to our inquiries.

Alphabetical Listing of Agencies

AARP TRAVEL SERVICE
5855 Green Valley Circle
Culver City, California 90230
Tel: 800-227-7737
        212-417-2277

Austria: Vienna.
France: Cannes, Paris.
Portugal: The Algarve—Alvor, near Portimâo.
Spain: Costa del Sol—Torremolinos; Canary Islands—Tenerife; Puerto de
la Cruz)
England: London—Westminster, Mayfair.

AARP Travel Service is the contracted agent of the American Association
of Retired Persons. Unlike those of the other agencies included in this
guide, the apartments rented under the AARP travel program are available only as part of a tour package. The tours include air and surface
transportation, set time periods, and, often, paired destinations such as
Paris/London, Costa del Sol/Madrid, Algarve/Cascais/Madeira, Costa del
Sol/Tenerife. In some cases the accommodations include a hotel in one
of the destinations.

ABACUS AGENCY
P.O. Box 15295
Ann Arbor, Michigan 48106
Tel: 313-572-0700

England: London—Chelsea, South Kensington, Knightsbridge, Mayfair.

This is a subsidiary of Abacus Agency, 20 Park Hill, Ealing, London W5
2JN, which owns short- and long-term rental apartments at this address
and off Sloane Square in Chelsea. The properties are on the luxury end
and are fairly priced, although most Chelsea apartments tend toward the
high side due to location and vogue. Abacus also serves as agent for
other properties, in the moderate to luxury class and price range.

Approach: Phone or write for brochures and other information.
Deposit at Time of Booking: 35 to 50 percent of rental.
Minimum Stay: Three days to one week, depending on time of year
        and the property.

Maid Service (and postrental cleaning): Included in the price of
London apartment rentals. Linens and towels are always provided, and are changed at different frequencies, depending on the
property.

Getting There: Apartment address is provided at the time of booking.

Because the U.S. company is a subsidiary, there is no additional commission to pay for booking in the United States.

AT HOME ABROAD
405 East 56th Street
New York, New York 10022
Tel: 212-421-9165

Approx. No. of Rentals: 2,600, including Mexico and Caribbean.
France: Côte d'Azur—Cannes, Cap Ferrat, Grasse; Avignon area; Brittany
and Normandy; the Dordogne.
Ireland: Stately homes, scattered.
Italy: Amalfi Coast; Tuscany; Veneto.
Portugal: The Algarve—Carvoeiro to Lagos, Salema.
Spain: Costa Brava, Costa del Sol.
England: Sussex and West Country. London.

This relatively large company is not a formal agent for any European
companies.

Approach: Matching, no catalog; in response to inquiries a brochure
and registration form will be sent. The form (not a booking form)
asks appropriate questions relating to country, region, type, size,
and price range you are seeking; upon receiving the form (with a
registration fee, currently $50), the company will send descriptive
profiles and color photos of properties that match your requirements. The fee covers one year and includes a newsletter. Inspections of properties are carried out by New York office staff. Offers a
wide range of types and styles, principally high standard to
deluxe.

Deposit at Time of Booking: 35 to 50 percent of rental; no credit
cards.

Minimum Stay: Two to four weeks, depending on time of year and
the property. One week in the United Kingdom.

Maid Service: Daily service and postrental cleaning service optional, usually available at extra cost. Linens and towels are normally exchanged weekly unless other arrangements are made.

Getting There: Instructions, address and directions to property, and information on the owner's or agent's contact in Europe are provided upon booking.

Children are welcome in almost all properties. The company has been in business since 1960 and enjoys a good reputation in the trade and with clientele; personal inspections and property selections by company staff assure consistently high standards, but of course add to the overhead. The $50 registration fee is, we believe, a negative factor. The agency offers a wide range of types and styles, principally high standard to deluxe.

B. & D. DE VOGÜE TRAVEL SERVICES
1830 South Mooney Boulevard
Suite 113
Visalia, California 93277
Tel: 800-727-4748
      209-733-7119

Approx. No. of Rentals: 510.

France: Atlantic Coast; the Auvergne; Brittany; the Dordogne; Loire Valley; Normandy; valleys of the Garonne and Lot. East Provence, Alps, and Côte d'Azur; West Provence and Rhône Valley. Paris.

Italy: Tuscany (a few).

Portugal: Costa da Prato (north of Lisbon)—Caldas da Rainha, Foz do Arelho, Óbidos.

Specializing in France, the de Vogüe agency represents two excellent European companies, the highly regarded PSR in Paris, and Bowhill's, one of the more respected British companies dealing with properties in rural and village France and Portugal. De Vogüe is a very good combination of American, French, and English companies. It offers a good variety of properties in almost all categories from simple to luxurious, which we believe to be carefully selected.

This is also the U.S. agent for Château Accueil, an association of castle and manor house owners throughout France who offer a look into "La Vie de Château," château life as it is lived today. The resident owners, such as Vicomte and Vicomtesse de Bonneval of Château de Thaumiers, and Comte and Comtesse A. de Vogüe of Château de la Verrerie, open their estates to guests. Some offer apartments in the château or other estate buildings, others provide guest rooms with meals. Prices are on the high end, but the experience is unique and the châteaus are elegant.

Approach: For France (except Paris) and Portugal, de Vogüe will, upon request, send an illustrated, descriptive catalog from which you make your choices; the agency determines availability and provides advice. For Paris, it is a one-way matching process. A reservation form is included with a brochure about de Vogüe/PSR apartments; after you mail back the completed form with your requirements and price limits, the agency will make the closest match and notify you.

For Château Accueil, you select a locale and château of interest from an illustrated booklet, then discuss prices, dates, and arrangements by phone. There is no fee.

Deposit at Time of Booking: 25 percent of full rental for rural, 50 percent for Paris.

Minimum Stay: Usually one week; two weeks during peak season. Seasons vary with location. In the châteaus, minimums vary with the site.

Maid Service (and postrental cleanup): Optional in rural properties, usually available at extra cost; in Paris, weekly maid service and postrental cleanup are included in the price. Daily maid service optional at extra cost. For Château Accueil, everything is included.

Getting There: De Vogüe can arrange air travel if desired; also, Peugeot lease (purchase/buyback) or Hertz car rental arranged at discount. All information and directions supplied at time of booking. Rural: agent or owner will be on-site with key and assistance. Paris: collect key and final instructions at PSR office on Champs Elysées. Château hosts always there.

Good reputation, fairly priced properties; we also like all three of the associated European companies. Children are welcome in most properties, but be sure to check about this if you are interested in one of the châteaus.

BEDS ABROAD, LTD.
188 Highwood Avenue
Tenafly, New Jersey 07670
Tel: 201-569-5245

England: London—Belgravia, Knightsbridge, Pimlico.

The owner of this small company represents several apartment blocks in London, but claimed at the time of our interview to have all the business he needs. Perhaps this means that the agency is doing something right.

Approach: Write or telephone the company for brochures, then select a first choice and an alternate. Upon confirmation of availability from London, you will be notified and invoiced for your deposit. Payment of deposit by check or money order; payment in London in sterling or major credit card except at 30 Beaufort Gardens. No fee.

Deposit at Time of Booking: 50 percent of full rental. After arrival in London pay the full rental (that is, you have now paid 150 percent) upon your departure, your 50 percent deposit will be refunded in London by the apartment management.

Minimum Stay: Usually one week.

Maid Service: Six days per week, included in rent.

Getting There: Directions are provided upon final payment of rent. There is a manager at each of the properties, so it is simply a matter of going to the address and getting the key.

The brochures are informative and straightforward; some of the apartments are simple, as the brochure notes. Prices compared to others are fair. All apartments are heavily booked during high season (April 1–November 1), so reserve several months in advance for this period. The Chester House apartments at 28 Sloane Gardens are very well located, but we would be reluctant to pay $475 a week for a standard small studio in high season; a one-bedroom runs $715. At the 30 Beaufort Gardens apartments (also well located in Knightsbridge), a one-bedroom is about $850 in high season, $775 in low. We did not visit these apartments.

The agency's response to our inquiry was slow. Prefers to work with clientele east of Chicago.

BLAKE'S VACATIONS
4939 Dempster Street
Skokie, Illinois 60077
Tel: 800-628-8118
     312-982-0561

Approx. No. of Rentals: 2,200.

France: Normandy; Brittany; Loire Valley; Garonne and Lot river valleys; the Dordogne; Landes; the Basque Provinces; Gironde; Provence; Alsace; Languedoc.

Ireland: Scattered in Counties Clare, Cork, Kerry, Limerick.

United Kingdom: England—Cornwall; Devon; Kent; Lake Country; Norfolk; Suffolk; Sussex; West Country; Yorkshire. Throughout Wales and Scotland. Some on island of Guernsey.

This is the U.S. agent for Blake's Country Cottages—one of England's largest vacation rental companies—based in Wroxham, Norfolk. More than seventy-five years ago, Blake's rented "Yachts, Boats & Wherries" for sailing the vast East Anglian network of rivers, sloughs, marshes, and lakes known generally as the Norfolk Broads. The company still does this, in a big way. Everything from sailboats and houseboats to small and large motor cruisers can be rented by the day or week by anyone old enough to drive a car. Many of the vacation rentals are near the hundreds of miles of shoreline of these inland waterways; a combined cottage rental and discounted dayboat rental makes for a unique holiday.

The majority of properties are modest, renting in high season in the $300-to-$400-per-week range, but many are at the low end in the $200 category. A few go for more than $1,000, and are mostly large rather than deluxe accommodations. All must meet set company standards.

> *Approach:* Catalog selection. An inquiry will bring you a nearly 200-page color photo catalog, geographically divided, with short descriptions that seemed accurate in our sampling. There is no fee. A booking form and terms details are part of the catalog, along with a well laid-out price list. Prices from the U.S. agency are the same as in the United Kingdom. Property inspections are carried out at least annually by main office and regional company staff.
>
> *Deposit at Time of Booking:* 25 to 35 percent, enclosed with your booking form. If one of the properties you choose is not available when you want it, the deposit is refunded. MasterCard and Visa are accepted. Booking can be made by telephone.
>
> *Minimum Stay:* One week; three days in low season.
>
> *Maid Service:* Rarely included, but can be arranged in some properties.
>
> *Getting There:* Complete directions and information upon payment of rent. There is usually a local contact. Be sure to have a good, high-detail map before trying to find any specific property in the United Kingdom.

Blake's seems to specialize in comfortable, family properties at reasonable prices; nothing spectacular, but many types and locations.

BRITISH TRAVEL ASSOCIATION
P.O. Box 299
Elkton, Virginia 22827
Tel: 800-327-6097
 703-289-6512

Approx. No. of Rentals: 3,000.
France: Scattered throughout, via a British company.
Italy: Scattered throughout, via a British company.
United Kingdom: Throughout England, Scotland, and Wales.

This agency is one of several U.S. representatives of probably the largest, and one of the best managed, vacation rental companies in the United Kingdom. It also formally or informally represents other companies (as most agencies do), thus offering a very wide selection of properties in virtually all prices, types, standards, and locations. Of particular interest are rentals in the vicinity west of London (Thames Valley) and in Cornwall. Launched as a travel newsletter publisher, the agency has expanded over the past decade and offers very competitive prices. Many other programs are available (car rentals, air transportation, maid service).

> *Approach:* Usually the British Travel Association matches your description with its inventory, but ask for the basic catalog ($2). If you prefer to pick your own properties, ask for more catalogs, designating the region or regions of your interest. The company employs a contracted agent based in London to assist with bookings. There are no flat fees. Property inspection is left to the British companies, which inspect at least annually or more often. The U.S. staff makes periodic inspections of a sampling of properties.
>
> *Deposit at Time of Booking:* 25 to 50 percent depending on the property and company. Major credit cards are accepted for deposit and payment.
>
> *Minimum Stay:* One week; three-plus-day periods available off-season.
>
> *Maid Service:* Available for some, but far from all, of the properties; postrental cleaning also optional at extra cost in most cases.
>
> *Getting There:* Specific instructions, and directions to the property, are given when deposit is received (most companies wait until the rent is paid in full).

Your best approach with this agency is to define your needs accurately, then to telephone in the information. By understanding your desired standards (from simple to deluxe), the agency can make the best selection of properties. Confirms bookings very quickly.

CASTLES, COTTAGES & FLATS OF IRELAND
　& THE U.K., LTD.
P.O. Box 261
Westwood, Massachusetts 02090
Tel: 617-329-4680

Approx. No. of Rentals: 1,100.
Ireland: Counties Clare, Cork, Donegal, Galway, Kerry, Leitrim, Mayo,
　Roscommon, Tipperary, Waterford, and Wexford.
United Kingdom: England—All areas, but especially good properties in
　Cornwall; the Cotswolds; Devon; Kent; Shakespeare Country of Strat-
　ford and Evesham; Sussex; Thames Valley; Bath. London—Blooms-
　bury and City. Scotland—All areas, especially Borders; Central West
　Coast and islands; Dumphries and Galloway; Far North. Aberdeen,
　Edinburgh. Wales—Most areas.

This is a small agency operated by Michael Wynne-Willson, a vigorous
man of English birth who, after retiring from the Royal Air Force, came to
the United States. During the decades since, he has remained in close
touch with his homeland. In its relatively short life, the agency has
established associations with more than ten British and Irish rental
companies, some as exclusive agent, but most not. In addition to the
more modest Irish cottages, the agency also represents Elegant Ireland,
which offers shorter stays in hosted elegant Irish homes, manors, and
castles.

> *Approach:* By catalog *or*, if you prefer, matching your requirements
> with the properties of the appropriate company. Catalogs cost less
> than five dollars, but commissions are on the high side, offset by
> capable service and reliably good properties at fair prices. Proper-
> ties are inspected by their respective British or Irish rental com-
> panies.
> *Deposit at Time of Booking:* Normally 50 percent; both deposit and
> full rent can be paid by check, Visa, or MasterCard.
> *Minimum Stay:* One week in summer and peak national holiday
> periods; three to four days off-season.
> *Maid Service:* Not included, but usually available with advance
> notice and at extra cost. Same for postrental cleaning.
> *Getting There:* As is usually the case with British and Irish rentals,
> procedural information, and directions on how to find the prop-
> erty and obtain the key, are provided at the time of booking. For
> most rural properties, a car is important. If you will not have one,
> make this clear before you book.

This is a helpful agent, especially for first-time visitors to the United Kingdom or Ireland. It is possible to specify the British companies you want this agency to use. We were especially impressed by Holiday Cottages (Scotland) Ltd., and by Heart of England Cottages, which specializes in the Cotswolds and Stratford areas. Also excellent is the Devon-based company Independent Traveller; this firm, which offers well-selected, fairly priced rentals in southwest England and apartments in London, will go to great lengths to find exactly what you want. For Sussex and Kent, Freedom Holiday Homes seems to be the best bet, and for an elegant apartment in Bath, ask about Fountain House. We found the Cornwall properties of Cornish Traditional Cottage Company to be excellent.

Castles, Cottages & Flats is one of the few agencies dealing with rentals in Ireland. We did not visit the companies or sample the cottages in Ireland, but we rely on the integrity of the U.S. agent and the Irish companies he represents.

CHEZ VOUS
220 Redwood Highway
Suite 129E
Mill Valley, California 94941
Tel: 415-331-2535

Approx. No. of Rentals: 150.
France: Southwest France—the Dordogne and valleys of the Lot and Garonne rivers.

In effect, this small agency represents itself. An English partner lives in the village of La Capelle Biron, near the town of Cahors; from this vantage, the properties in the very desirable region can be selected and watched over carefully. Because of the small area it covers, the company can oversee properties, assure that they are well maintained, and provide personal service.

The majority of rentals are modest in character and price, renting in high season in the $200-to-$400-per-week range, about one-third less in spring and late autumn, and almost half during winter.

> *Approach:* Upon contact the agency will send a descriptive catalog. Because this is a small agency, service is personalized, and it is best to specify what type of rental you are looking for and the general locale you are interested in. No fee to begin the process.
> *Deposit at Time of Booking:* 30 to 50 percent of rental.

Minimum Stay: Usually two weeks in July and August; one week can often be arranged other times of the year. Normal period Saturday to Saturday.

Maid Service: Not usually included. These tend to be tranquil rural and village get-away places with few frills. Make sure towels and linens are supplied or are available.

Getting There: Instructions and directions given at time of booking; although two mainline rail routes run through the area out of Bordeaux, a vehicle is an important asset if you wish to explore.

Personal and personable service, and fair rent prices.

COAST TO COAST RESORTS
860 Solar Building
1000 16th Street N.W.
Washington, DC 20036
Tel: 800-368-5721
         202-293-8000

Approx. No. of Rentals: 2,200.

France: Aquitaine; Atlantic Coast; Brittany; the Dordogne and Lot river valleys; Normandy.

West Germany: Baden-Württemberg and Rhineland.

Switzerland: Canton of Uri—near Lucerne.

United Kingdom: Throughout England; some in Scotland and Wales.

This is the largest of several U.S. agencies representing Hoseasons Holidays, Ltd. of England, which, in turn, is one of Britain's largest vacation rental companies. In addition to cottage rentals throughout England, Scotland, and, to a lesser extent, Wales, Hoseasons also offers boat rentals on the Norfolk Broads, renting anything from day cruisers and sailboats to cruiser-type houseboats by the week for up to eight persons. It is also a good company from which to arrange canal barge rentals in Britain, France, Holland, and Denmark.

As with a few of the larger British companies (see Blake's Vacations, for example), Hoseasons has expanded its vacation rental operation into Continental Europe, principally for its British clientele, but certainly available to all. Its West German properties are mostly in rural "bungalow parks," not in towns. The Swiss rentals are apartments in a chalet in Seelisberg. The company is growing.

Approach: A color-illustrated, descriptive catalog will be sent. There is no fee.

Deposit at Time of Booking: 50 percent of rent; checks and major credit cards accepted.

Minimum Stay: In the United Kingdom, one week June through September; three to four days off-season. Other countries, usually two weeks in July and August, one week rest of year.

Maid Service: Daily service is very rare, weekly exchange of linens and towels is usual.

Getting There: This is a typical British operation principally for British vacationers who know the ropes, both in the United Kingdom and on the Continent, but procedures are not difficult for North Americans. All instructions and directions are given at time of booking.

Many of the rentals in Britain are in *holiday parks* (planned vacation developments), which, it seems to us, defeats for North Americans a primary purpose for visiting the United Kingdom. These rentals are often referred to as "purpose-built." Unless you want a rental in a vacation development, state that you prefer a farm or village cottage. The same applies to the West German properties, except there are fewer alternatives available from the United States.

We are not sure how closely the French and Swiss properties are inspected and overseen, but Hoseasons has a good reputation in England for offering modest accommodations at reasonable prices. One concern is that the strings grow long, stretching from U.S. agency to British agency to owners in other countries.

Coast to Coast, a large and reputable company, also represents Eurocamp, which arranges camping tours throughout Europe.

CONDO VACATIONS
717 West Pender Street, 3rd Floor
Vancouver, British Columbia V6C 1G9
Canada
Tel: 800-663-0368 (toll-free, British Columbia only)
        604-688-2504

Approx. No. of Rentals: 3,500.
United Kingdom: Throughout England, Scotland, and Wales.

This is one of the surprisingly few Canadian agencies that offer vacation rentals in Britain. The firm's name refers principally to rental properties in the United States—especially Hawaii, Palm Springs, and Palm Desert—but does not represent the British cottages, which are on the other end of the spectrum from resort condos. The Lancashire-based company represented by Condo Vacations is one of the largest in Britain and one of the two or three most sophisticated in terms of public relations and customer affairs. With such a large selection to choose from, it is possible to find exactly what you want where you want it. The prices are fair and are published up front, available to all potential customers for all the properties listed.

>*Approach:* Ask for the catalog and agency brochure if you prefer to peruse properties and select you own; there is no charge. If you want more personalized help, write or phone with information on what kind of rental you are looking for, the location you prefer, and your budget; the agency will send several property profiles matching your needs. There is no fee.
>
>*Deposit at Time of Booking:* Normally 50 percent, less for longer-term rental periods.
>
>*Minimum Stay:* One week; three days during low season.
>
>*Maid Service:* Seldom provided, but may be available in select properties. Inquire.
>
>*Getting There:* All directions and instructions are provided at the time of final payment of the rent.

Given its size and the number of listings, the catalog is adequately descriptive. The agency seems well organized and efficient, yet small enough to offer peronsalized service and advice; response time is good. Air transportation and car rental can be arranged because this is also a full-service travel agency.

CUENDET-POSARELLI VACATIONS
180 Kinderkamack Road
Park Ridge, New Jersey 07656
Tel: 201-573-9558

Approx. No. of Rentals: 1,500.
Italy: Elba; Sicily; Tuscany—Arezzo, Chianti, Florence, Lucca, Pisa, Siena; Umbria—Assisi, Orvieto, Perugia.

Posarelli Vacations represents the large Swiss-Italian rental organization Cuendet & Cie., located in Strove, near Siena. Cuendet offers the largest single collection of properties in the Tuscany/Umbria region, perhaps in Italy overall. The principal focus is central Italy, where hundreds of ancient stone country houses that dot the hill country have been converted into villas and apartments for rent (see Chapter 9). There are even castles available.

Cuendet, a highly professional and progressive organization, demands high standards from the owners it represents. An associate with Posarelli Vacations is the son of a member of Cuendet's board of directors, so he knows the company, as well as the country, intimately. (Another, and very good, U.S. agent for Cuendet is Susan T. Pidduck, who is listed below.) In Canada, contact Der Tours (see agency listing in this chapter).

Approach: The key to the Cuendet operation is its catalog, a full-color, 200 + -page compendium of properties and other information about Tuscany and Umbria. The catalog costs $12, but even if you don't book, it is worth the money for its view of the countryside and its introduction to the variety of properties available. From the catalog, pick one property of interest and two alternates; phone or write the agency with your choices. It will notify you of availability within three days. You then send the booking form, the deposit, and the $45 booking fee to the agent within three days.

The written descriptions are brief but accurate. The catalog also contains information about the booking and renting process and, most important, a 30 + -page price list, thus assuring U.S. and Canadian clients that the prices are the same as those paid by booking directly in Europe. The only additional cost for booking through the agent (besides the catalog) is a $45 flat booking fee. This is a good approach, and it guarantees that there are no hidden agent fees.

Deposit at Time of Booking: 25 percent, balance due eight weeks before departure; you'll receive a voucher to give the owner on arrival.

Minimum Stay: Prices are shown per week for a two-week rental; for one week there is a 20 percent surcharge. Period is normally Saturday to Saturday.

Maid Service: Usually not included except for postrental cleanup. May be arranged in some cases.

Getting There: Explicit instructions are provided upon final payment.

There are many rules and instructions to wade through with Cuendet, but the variety of rentals is worth it. The catalog clearly establishes five "comfort" categories (and price ranges). The prices, and the absence of an add-on commission, are very fair. Most of the properties are in the modest-to-moderate range, with a scattering of more elegant and expensive villas.

DE LOOF LIMITED
111 South Fourth Avenue
Ann Arbor, Michigan 48104
Tel: 800-553-2582
313-995-4400

Approx. No. of Rentals: 150.
England: London—Belgravia, Chelsea, Mayfair, Sloane Square, South
Kensington, others.

De Loof's principal London property is a block of ten decidedly pleasant,
almost deluxe, flats on Sloane Square, an excellent location in London.
Others range from modest to well above average in standards. Because
they are both well-situated and relatively spacious, the Sloane Square
studio and one-bedroom flats run from $1,000 to $1,400 per week from
January through April, higher in high season; a two-bedroom typically
runs $2,500. Other apartments are less expensive, but the agency tends
toward the upper range.

> *Approach:* Upon inquiry a brochure briefly describing the properties
> is sent, from which you can get a good idea of what they are like
> and their prices. Then telephone to discuss your requirements.
> There are no registration or booking fees.
> *Deposit at Time of Booking:* 50 percent of rental.
> *Minimum Stay:* Normally one week (Saturday to Saturday) from late
> spring to early winter, but three to four days can sometimes be
> arranged; three to four days rest of the year.
> *Maid Service:* Daily in Sloane Square; optional in others. Linens and
> towels always provided and included.
> *Getting There:* All directions and instructions provided upon book-
> ing and payment.

Founded in 1983; small enough to be personal in working with potential
clients.

DER TOURS
1290 Bay Street
Toronto, Ontario M5R 2C3
Canada
Tel: 416-964-3290

Approx. No. of Rentals: 1,500.
Italy: Elba; Sicily; Tuscany—Arezzo, Chianti, Florence, Lucca, Pisa,
Siena; Umbria—Assisi, Orvieto, Perugia. Rome.

This large full-service travel agency is the Canadian agent for the Swiss-Italian rental organization Cuendet & Cie., located in Strove, near Siena, Italy. Cuendet offers the largest selection of rental properties in Italy. For more information on Cuendet, see either "Cuendet-Posarelli Vacations" or "Susan T. Pidduck, Cuendet Agent" in this chapter. All inquiries and bookings from Canada should be addressed to DER Tours in Toronto; all inquiries and bookings from the U.S. should be made to either Posarelli or Pidduck. The price structure is the same through all the companies.

EASTONE OVERSEAS ACCOMMODATIONS
6682 141st Lane North
Palm Beach Gardens, Florida 33418
Tel: 407-622-0777

Approx. No. of Rentals: 2,000.
Austria, France, Italy, Spain, Switzerland: See Interhome, Inc. USA listing below.
United Kingdom: Throughout England and Scotland, scattered in Wales. Individual property—Sudley Castle in Gloucestershire. London—Chelsea, Kensington, Knightsbridge, Mayfair, and other areas. Edinburgh.

This agency formally represents a good selection of moderately priced apartments in London, and is one of two U.S. agents of an Edinburgh-based company with several hundred reasonably priced and adequate properties in Scotland. It can also offer a broad range of cottages in every price range throughout England and Wales through reputable companies there. Its rentals on the Continent—except for an individual one in southwest France and a few in Paris—are handled through Interhome, a large Swiss company that has a U.S. agent, so we see no purpose in booking these through Eastone.

> *Approach:* Upon contact, the company will mail you a brochure and property information from which to make your prioritized selections. After you return the information, they will verify availability, confirm the rent, and advise you accordingly. There is no fee for this process.
> *Deposit at Time of Booking:* If you accept what they offer, a check or money order in the amount of one week's rent must be sent to confirm. The remainder to be paid within thirty to sixty days prior to departure.
> *Minimum Stay:* One week is typical for rural and village properties

(Saturday to Saturday), but shorter "lets" may be available in low and shoulder seasons; three to four days for London and Paris.

Maid Service: Due to the number and variety of properties offered by Eastone, this service varies widely. For rural properties, weekly service is typical. For city apartments, weekly, semiweekly, or daily service can usually be arranged if it is not included. Work this out individually to meet your requirements.

Getting There: The agency can arrange transatlantic flights. To get from the destination airport to the rural property, follow the directions supplied at the time of booking.

The agency was founded in 1982 and has a good reputation. The English properties are fine, but for rentals in Scotland you may also wish to look at other agencies' offerings.

EUROPA-LET, INC.
P.O. Box 3537
Ashland, Oregon 97520
Tel: 800-462-4486
    503-482-5806

Approx. No. of Rentals: 1,200.

Austria: Tirol—Innsbruck, Kitzbühle, Seefeld, St. Anton; Voralberg—Montafon Villages, Bregenz Woods; Tirol; Salzburg Province—Salzburg; Provinces of Carinthia, Burgenland, Upper and Lower Austria; Vienna.

France: Riviera—Antibes, Cannes, Juan le Pins, Nice, Hill country; Paris; Southwest France.

Italy: Tuscany Hills—Florence, Lucca, Pisa, Siena; Tuscan Coast; Umbrian Hills—Arezzo, Perugia, Lakes; Amalfi Coast; Northern Lakes—Como, Garda, Lugano, Maggiore; Capri and Sardinia; Aeolean Islands; Rome and environs; Venice and environs

Portugal: The Algarve; West Coast—Lisbon area, Estoril, Cascais.

United Kingdom: England—throughout; London—Bayswater, Belgravia, Bloomsbury, Chelsea, Kensington, Mayfair, and environs. Scotland—Highlands and Lowlands; Hebrides; Edinburgh. Wales.

This small company uses a personal approach to match the client's interests to the rental and its specific location, offering good advice on where to be as well as on the nature of the property. It also specializes in providing short-term apartments in key cities for business travelers. Anyone planning a stay of two and a half weeks or more should ask about their car purchase/repurchase (lease) program on the Continent (see Chapter 4 for information on this type of vehicle program). Although not a travel agency, the company can arrange air transportation.

Approach: Matching and catalogs. A descriptive selection of appropriate properties will be sent, along with a booking form. Available catalogs or other brochures will be sent if desired.

Deposit at Time of Booking: One-third of the rent. Full payment 30 to 60 days before departure. Prefers personal or cashiers check, but Visa and MasterCard are accepted.

Minimum Stay: One week in high season (summer, or peak winter months in ski resorts areas), Saturday to Saturday as usual; three days possible in low season in rural areas of Britain, France, and Italy. Three- to four-day lets are available in some London and Paris apartments, especially in low or shoulder seasons.

Maid service: Seldom available in rural properties, but can be arranged for in deluxe villas; usually provided in city apartments.

Getting There: All instructions and directions are sent after final payment is made.

Although the agency is relatively new, the principals have a personal familiarity with Europe and the independent style of travel as well as the business of renting. The European companies they represent are carefully chosen, mostly small, with fair prices and established reputations for dependability. Commissions and fees, and information on the companies Europa-Let represents, are discussed openly. Not large, but offers a good choice.

FAMILIES ABROAD, INC.
194 Riverside Drive
New York, New York 10025
Tel: 212-787-2434
       718-766-6185

Approx. No. of Rentals: 2,500.
France: Brittany; Burgundy; the Dordogne; Hérault; Loire Valley; Maritime Alps; Pyrenees; Riviera and Riviera Hills; Savoy Alps (Haute Savoie); Tarn and Var. Paris.
Ireland: Counties Dublin, Galway, Sligo.
Italy: Tuscany; Umbria; Veneto.
United Kingdom: England—Cornwall; Devon; Hampshire; Sussex. London. Scotland—Edinburgh.

One of the larger agencies in the United States, Families Abroad enjoys a good reputation. It handles two types of rental arrangements—short-term vacations and longer-term (six months or more) sabbaticals. For the former, the commission is built in, for the latter, rent is based on duration as well as location, size, and standards, and the commission is quoted separately. The built-in commission seems fair. The selection of Paris apartments is very good, and prices run the gamut from $700 per month for a small studio on the Île St. Louis (4th arrondissement) to over $1,000 per week. It is one of the few agencies with rentals in Dublin.

> *Approach:* Matching. Describe the kind of rental you need; the country, region, or city; the number in your party; and your price range.
> *Deposit at Time of Booking:* Normally 50 percent for vacation rentals; two months' rent for the long-term types.
> *Minimum Stay:* One to two weeks (depending on season) in all countries; a few rentals in Paris have one-month minimums; six months on the sabbatical types.
> *Maid Service:* Rare in rural properties; optional in many Paris, London, and Edinburgh apartments; and included in some of the more deluxe apartments. The client must specify.
> *Getting There:* All information is provided upon booking.

This is an unusually personal agency for its size, and it has the experience to provide good service.

FOUR SEASONS VILLAS
P.O. Box 848
Marblehead, Massachusetts 01945
Tel: 800-338-0474
    617-639-1055

Approx. No. of Rentals: 500, plus Caribbean.
England: All areas; London—Knightsbridge, South Kensington, Pimlico, Westminster.

Formed in 1984 to handle private properties in the Caribbean, Four Seasons added England later. The rural properties are represented by two British companies known to be reputable. In London, most apartments are in the modest-to-moderate price range.

> *Approach:* Matching. Describe the kind of rental you need, the region of England or area of London, the number in your party, and your price range.

Deposit at Time of Booking: Normally 50 percent on vacation rentals.

Minimum Stay: One week; three days in off-season (there may be a 10 percent surcharge for less than one week in London).

Maid Service: Seldom available in rural England, but special arrangements can sometimes be made.

Getting There: Four Seasons is affiliated with a major travel agency, so all travel arrangements can be made. Specific directions to the rental are provided upon booking.

The modestly priced London apartments ($550 to $650 per week for a studio, $600 to $730 for a one-bedroom) are scattered private apartments represented by a London firm, not Four Seasons directly; the drawback is that the agency has probably not seen the apartment being booked for you. Nevertheless, the prices are fair. If you want something more deluxe or better known tell the agency; it also represents a few rentals in these categories.

FOUR STAR LIVING, INC.
964 Third Avenue, 39th Floor
New York, New York 10022
Tel: 212-758-2236

Approx. No. of Rentals: 15,000 (worldwide).
Austria, France, West Germany, Ireland, Italy, Portugal, Spain, Switzerland, United Kingdom.

This is a large real estate company dealing not only in vacation rentals but also in home sales, exchanges and barters, and even yachts. The material we received in response to our inquiry (as writers) consisted of two form letters to the "trade," copies of various newspaper and magazine articles, and complimentary letters from clients (mostly corporate). A single sheet with basic facts about the agency included a perforated card to fill in with information about your needs.

Approach: Upon receipt of your specifications for a rental, and a *registration fee* of $45 (applied to the rent, but not refundable if no booking is made), the agency will match a selection of its properties to your needs and return color profiles to you. After you make your choices, the agency will confirm availability and negotiate the best price with the owner or associate company on your behalf and inform you of the details. There is no catalog.

Deposit at Time of Booking: 50 percent of the full rental.

Minimum Stay: Two weeks in high seasons in the more deluxe properties, otherwise one week in most rural areas, three to four days in the cities.

Maid Service: Almost all possibilities exist and must be worked out individually.

We have very little information, but the agency seems to assume that out of its vast number of properties it will almost assuredly find one for you. Prices are not revealed until rather late in the process. Properties tend to be upscale in both quality and price.

FRANCE GRANDES VACANCES
P.O. Box 2517
Venice, California 90924
Tel: 213-450-1304

Approx. No. of Rentals: 265.

France: The Atlantic Coast; the Riviera/Côte d'Azur—Antibes, Cagnes-sur-Mer, Eze-sur-Mer, Les Issambres Hills, Saint-Aygulf, Sainte-Maxime, Villefranche-sur-Mer, Villeneuve Loubet.

Switzerland: Jura Alps, near Nyon.

This small company was founded in 1987 by Christian Lucas, a very hardworking man of Dutch birth who has a knack for finding good property companies in France. The inventory is limited, but the variety is wide. Of special interest are the private villas in the Riviera hills; the prices are modest compared to those of similar properties in the better-known towns. There is also a good selection in Cagnes-sur-Mer, a pleasant but not upscale town where prices are comparatively lower. (Avoid booking an apartment on the noisy seafront street, Bord de Mer.) If a moderate-to-luxurious private villa in a planned development is of interest, ask about Villeneuve Loubet (near Antibes). The Atlantic coastal properties are mostly private villas and bungalows; the area north of the Gironde River estuary is of most interest.

In Switzerland the properties are managed condominiums in an area carved out of the woods near St. Cergue (20 minutes from the Geneva airport).

Approach: Upon contact, the company will send descriptive material, and advise that there is a small fee (less than $5) for the catalog to defray production and mailing costs. Although it is a slim book, this fee is reasonable in light of the attentive service you will receive. In effect, Christian Lucas serves as your personal agent in dealing with the European companies.

Deposit at Time of Booking: 30 percent, check or money order; no credit cards.

Minimum Stay: Two weeks to one month in some villas in high season, one to two weeks in apartments in high season. One week stays can be arranged September 14 to June 9.

Maid Service: Varies, depending on the property; linens and towels not always included, but can be provided. Advise the agent of your preferences.

Getting There: The agency does not provide transportation, but instructions on getting the key in France, and directions, are provided at the time of booking. There is a resident owner at the Swiss apartments.

What this new agency lacks in PR and promotion it makes up for in its eagerness to please. The European company we contacted in Cagnes-sur-Mer seems capable and fair, and is in touch with American perspectives.

THE FRENCH EXPERIENCE
171 Madison Avenue
New York, New York 10016
Tel: 212-986-3800

Approx. No. of Rentals: 20,000.

France: Throughout France, especially Alps, Alsace, Brittany, Burgundy, the Dordogne, Normandy, Riviera hill country. Paris—Center, Left and Right banks of the Seine.

This agency specializes in self-drive tours of France as well as straight rentals. Many of the properties are rural *gîtes* that can be very hard to book through the normal French channels (see Chapter 6, "France"). In addition to these rural houses, modest to moderate apartments are available in most regions of France, with the private villas mostly located in Brittany and the Riviera area.

Approach: Matching, no catalog. Write for brochure with application form. If you are interested in a *gîte,* or any other property, return the form that lists your requirements in detail. The agency will respond with a choice of proposed properties. A *$20 fee is charged upon application.*

Deposit at Time of Booking: 50 percent, check or money order; no credit cards.

Minimum Stay: One week, except two weeks during July and August.

Maid Service: Not included; daily service can be arranged in some of the more deluxe rentals, but seldom in *gîtes*.

Getting There: Air transportation is not provided, but complete instructions and directions are given at time of booking. The self-drive tours include the price of a car rental, to be picked up at the main city of the selected region.

The company appears versatile enough to put together the kind of French visit the client wants, from a totally independent stay to car/hotel and car/villa combinations.

FRENCH HOME RENTALS (Meeting Points, Inc.)
5515 Milwaukie Avenue
Portland, Oregon 97502
Tel: 503-233-1224

Approx. No. of Rentals: 250.
France: Southwest France—the Dordogne, the Lot River Valley. Paris.

Representing a company based in the southwest of France, this agency offers rentals throughout the southwest as well as a few carefully selected apartments in Paris. Rural rentals are scattered but well located, chosen for convenience as well as picturesque neighborhoods. The Paris apartments are principally individual units, from studios to two-bedrooms, in buildings dating from the seventeenth century to modern times.

Approach: Catalog (property descriptions) and price list are sent upon request. No fee.

Deposit at Time of Booking: 50 percent of rent.

Minimum Stay: One week, except two weeks for large apartments near Montparnasse area of Paris. Some rural properties are not available during winter, and some may be rented daily in low season.

Maid Service: Available at extra cost in some properties; postrental maid service is included in rent.

Getting There: Complete instructions are provided upon final payment of rent.

Apartments are inspected annually by someone from the U.S. agency, and two to three times annually by the French company. Any complaints that arise while in Paris are handled by a local agent. The apartment selection by the small company is very personal.

GRAND CIRCLE TRAVEL, INC.
347 Congress Street
Boston, Massachusetts 02210
Tel: 800-831-8880
    617-350-7500

Austria: Baden (near Vienna), Seefeld (near Innsbruck).
Spain: Costa del Sol—Torremolinos; Nerja; Balearic Islands; Canary Islands.
Switzerland: Davos, Gstaad, Interlaken, Locarno, Lucerne.
England: London—Pimlico.

Grand Circle Travel is not a rental agency, but is included in this guide because it provides extended "live abroad" vacations in which apartments or houses are part of a package. Typically included are air fare, a welcome at your destination, a company representative (host or hostess) available during your stay, a hospitality desk at your hotel or apartment building, and discounts on travel cards. You have a choice of staying in a hotel (and eating meals out at your expense) or in an "aparthotel," usually in a studio apartment with a kitchenette. (An aparthotel is a building of apartments with hotel amenities: a concierge or manager, maid service. In the United Kingdom these units are referred to as "serviced apartments" or "serviced blocks." The package costs more than an independently arranged rental, but the extra services may be helpful to many travelers. Baltic Sea and river cruises, and conducted tours, are available.

> *Approach:* Send for a descriptive catalog of programs; prices are included.
> *Deposit at Time of Booking:* $150 per person; deposit and full payment may be made by credit card (American Express, Master-Card, or Visa).
> *Minimum Stay:* Two weeks.
> *Maid Service:* Included.
> *Getting There:* Air transportation is included in the price; all arrangements for arrival at the unit are taken care of.

The company has selected good locations, and the rental properties, while not deluxe, are very acceptable. The company caters to mature travelers.

GRANT-REID COMMUNICATION
P.O. Box 810216

Dallas, Texas 75381
Tel: 800-327-1849
      214-243-6748

Approx. No. of Rentals: 1,200 (200 in London).
United Kingdom: England, Scotland, and Wales. London—Bayswater, Kensington, Knightsbridge, Mayfair, Pimlico.

One of the two U.S. representatives of London Apartments, Ltd., this agency offers a good apartment selection in terms of price, standards, and location, and charges fairly. Its rural properties throughout Britain are farmhouses and cottages associated with farms; these tend to be simple but comfortable and modestly priced.

Approach: For London, the agency sends a brochure describing typical apartments in several price categories and elaborating on the nature of the city's various areas. For farm properties, the best approach is to phone or write after you have decided where you prefer to stay and how much you want to pay; the agency will match available properties to your description. If a farm holiday appeals, but you don't know where you want to go, ask for a catalog. For both London and rural properties, prices are converted directly from the British company prices in pounds sterling to U.S. dollars (that is, you pay no extra commission).

Deposit at Time of Booking: Normally 50 percent. No additional fees.

Minimum Stay: One week in high season; three days low season; weekends in some rural properties in low season.

Maid Service: Usually provided from three to six days per week in London; may be optional in some apartments. Rarely available in farm properties.

Getting There: All information is provided at time of booking; for the rural properties a detailed map of the area is usually essential.

We were impressed with the way the London company operates. We stayed at its 51 Kensington Court property, a moderately priced, well-located Edwardian, only one block from busy Kensington High Street and Hyde Park. For modest elegance, the Allen Street apartments in Kensington and Lees Place in Mayfair are good choices. For economy, consider the Pimlico apartments. Compared to hotels of equal standards, figure 20 to 40 percent less for these apartments (the higher the rating—and price—the greater the difference). Children are welcome in most apartments.

HASTINGWOOD ASSOC., LTD.
104 East Main Street
Stockingbridge, Michigan 49285
Tel: 800-992-2925
517-851-8000

Approx. No. of Rentals: 50.
England: London—Belgravia, Knightsbridge. Bath.

This is the U.S. office of a London-based organization that deals with upscale, somewhat exclusive properties at 3 Sloane Gardens in Chelsea and at 41 Beaufort Gardens in Knightsbridge. Both are ideally located in terms of proximity to the central city, transportation, good shops, and restaurants. Apartments in these London properties, are, on occasion, for sale, entitling their owners to membership in the 3 Sloane Gardens Club or the Parkes Club. The company manages the apartments for owner/members, renting them short-term when the owners are not in residence. Rates range from $1,000 to $1,250 per week for a studio (two persons), to $1,500 to $2,100 for a two-bedroom (up to six persons), depending on the season. April through December 1 are the high months (plus mid-December to January 7 at the Parkes). Rich woods, thick carpets, and beveled glass characterize apartment decor.

Hastingwood is also an agent for Fountain House, in the splendid city of Bath.

Approach: Telephone toll-free; the agency will send descriptive brochures on London or Bath properties.

Deposit at Time of Booking: 50 percent of rent; payable by check or money order.

Minimum Stay: Usually a week in high season, but three-day minimum is possible.

Maid Service: Daily, included in the rent. Also photocopying service, secretarial service, in-house theater booking, fresh flowers in the apartments, and other amenities.

The Sloane Square apartments are impeccable in all respects, and the Parkes Hotel apartments in Beaufort Gardens are equally elegant. Both properties are full service, and can easily be equated to a four-star hotel, except that the accommodations are much larger than a hotel room. Very private. The agency can arrange air and ground transportation.

Fountain House is a short walk from the heart of Bath, and is in every way desirable. The one-, two-, and three-bedroom apartments are spacious, tastefully designed and furnished; with daily maid service, laundry and valet services, and Continental breakfast served in the suite, this property meets five-star standards.

HEART OF ENGLAND COTTAGES
P.O. Box 888
Eufaula, Alabama 36027
Tel: 205-687-9800

Approx. No. of Rentals: 200.
England: Cotswolds; Hereford; Shakespeare Country; Thames Valley; Wiltshire.

Heart of England does not imply a geographical area alone; it also refers to the rural pleasures and rustic charms sought by visitors who want the England of "olde" in tandem with access to the new. The properties are in a most desirable area of England and are popular with North American visitors. Special activities (hunting, Shakespeare plays at Stratford, and so forth) can be arranged.

> *Approach:* Write or phone for a catalog; after deciding on one or two properties plus an alternate, contact the agency (by telephone is best). While agents are determining availability, complete and send the booking form with a deposit. Confirmation is returned with an invoice for the balance. Access, MasterCard, and Visa accepted.
> *Deposit at Time of Booking:* One-third of the rent.
> *Minimum Stay:* One week in summer, Saturday to Saturday as usual; three days possible in low season.
> *Maid Service:* Seldom available; postrental cleaning is included in price, but renters must leave place neat.
> *Getting There:* Instructions are sent after final payment is made.

With nearly twenty years' experience, this British company runs a smooth, personalized, and efficient operation. We were very impressed with the properties we visited, obviously carefully selected by the company. The U.S. agency is helpful, and the prices are fair.

HEARTHSTONE HOLIDAYS
P.O. Box 8625, Station L
Edmonton, Alberta T6C 4J4
Canada
Tel: 403-465-2874

Approx. No. of Rentals: 5,000-plus.
United Kingdom: Throughout England, Scotland, and Wales.

Hearthstone, a new agency that became operational in January 1989, is one of the few Canadian firms offering rental properties in Britain. It began operations after selecting a handful of British companies to represent in Canada, a formidable task given the numbers and varieties. We are personally familiar with all but one of the British companies, and believe that Hearthstone has done admirably. There is considerable territorial overlap among the companies, but because demand for rentals in Britain and the rest of Europe is rapidly increasing it is good to have a depth of selections. If you want to ask for a specific company, we are especially impressed with Heart of England (U.K.) for cottages in the Cotswolds and vicinity, Cornish Traditional Cottages for Cornwall, Holiday Cottages (Scotland) Ltd. for rural Scotland and Edinburgh, North Wales Holiday Cottages for rural Wales, and English Country Cottages for properties scattered throughout Britain. For boating on the Norfolk Broads (associated with a rental cottage, if you wish), ask about Blake's.

> *Approach:* Matching; phone or write with information on what your interests are. Specify size, general or specific location, and your budget. A selection of profiles will be sent for your consideration. No fee.
> *Deposit at Time of Booking:* Usually 50 percent.
> *Minimum Stay:* One week in summer, Saturday to Saturday as usual; three days possible in low season.
> *Maid Service:* Seldom available; postrental cleaning included in price, but renters must leave place neat.
> *Getting There:* Instructions are sent after final payment is made.

Because Hearthstone is so new it has no track record to evaluate. However, we know it to be a small organization at present, aimed at providing a personalized service. From interviewing the owner we sense that this is a fair, well-run agency.

HERITAGE OF ENGLAND
P.O. Box 297
Falls Village, Connecticut 06031
Tel: 800-533-5405
    203-824-5155

Approx. No. of Rentals: 2,500.
United Kingdom: Throughout England, Scotland, and Wales.

As the U.S. agency for the formidable English Country Cottages, Heritage of England represents a large number of consistently good cottages throughout England and a fairly broad selection in Scotland and Wales. Several competitors in various parts of Britain spoke highly of the properties and operation of this Norfolk-based company, a good sign that it is one of the best.

English Country Cottages sets very high standards and much attention is paid to detail and atmosphere, both inside the rentals and out, from comfort and cleanliness to location and grounds. Before a property is included in the listings, these standards come into play, and are upheld afterward by employees who live in various parts of the country and monitor company affairs on a regional basis. The main office staff of about thirty is located in the market town of Fakenham, Norfolk, and those staff members we talked with were courteous and helpful. More than 250,000 inquiries are handled each year, so the operation is necessarily computerized and otherwise well organized. The U.S. agency also has a good reputation, and we believe that any slowness in response is due to the suddenly increasing demand in the U.S. for British rentals. While we feel that this will become less of a problem, it suggests the need for travelers to book early. In any case, the wait is never distressingly long. Book six months ahead for July and August, three months for June and September, and a few weeks for other months.

Approach: Send $5 for a thick, very well done descriptive catalog.

Deposit at Time of Booking: 50 percent of the rental price.

Minimum Stay: Normally one week in June, July, August, and some of the holiday seasons; Saturday to Saturday as is customary in the United Kingdom and elsewhere in Europe; three days, the rest of the year.

Maid Service: Rarely provided, but may be arranged in some of the larger properties.

Getting There: The agency provides complete directions at the time of booking; rental cars can be arranged, and information on air and train schedules is available. Again, get a good British road atlas.

Children are welcome in most properties. The prices seem fair, and no additional commission is added for U.S. or Canadian bookings. The catalog is certainly worth the $5. We are favorably impressed with this operation.

Heritage of England also handles rentals in France and Italy under the names of Vacances en Campagne and Vacanze in Italia, respectively (same address, see listing in this chapter and Appendix B).

HIDEAWAYS INTERNATIONAL
P.O. Box 1464
Littleton, Massachusetts 01460
Tel: 800-843-4433
    617-486-8955

Approx. No. of Rentals: 1,500.
France: The Riviera; Paris—all areas.
Ireland: Scattered.
Italy: Amalfi Coast; Sardinia; Tuscany—Florence, Siena; Umbria.
Portugal: The Algarve.
Spain: Balearic Islands—Ibiza; Costa del Sol.
England: London—Buckingham Gate, Kensington.
  (Also Canada, the Caribbean, Hawaii, Mexico, and the continental
  United States.)

Hideaways, established in 1979, is basically a travel club; members
receive a very slick directory detailing all the features of the organization
and the properties it represents throughout the world. In addition, the
company acts as agent for a large Italian firm with a good selection of
properties, from modest to elegant. Hideaways also works through a U.S.
agency, which, in turn, represents a very good organization in Paris that
has a large selection of apartments throughout the city. In London, the
apartments of the company Hideaways represents are upscale, well-
located, and fairly priced by local standards.
   Some of the European rentals, as well as a majority of those in the
Western Hemisphere, are high-quality apartments and villas listed in
the directory by private owners for a fee. Club members then contact the
owners directly and negotiate dates, prices, and other details for the
rental.

  Approach: Membership/catalog. Phone or write for a Hideaways
    Directory (price: $9.95). If you are looking for rentals in Italy, also
    ask for the separate Solemar catalog (free). If you find no property
    of interest, then you have wasted $9.95. Should you find a rental
    you like, regardless of which Hideaways source you have selected
    it from, you must join Hideaways in order to book. The annual
    membership fee, currently $75, gets you two semiannual directo-
    ries and four newsletters. The money spent on the catalog will be
    credited against the membership fee. There is an additional $50
    flat booking fee for European rentals selected from the Solemar
    catalog or other brochure sent by Hideaways, but not listed in the
    directory. Membership also lets you consider car rentals, travel-
    planning services, and other discounts, if you wish.

Deposit at Time of Booking: 50 percent for rentals arranged through European companies; negotiate with owner for private properties in the directory.

Minimum Stay: Varies.

Maid Service: Seldom provided in rural Italian rentals. Often provided in Paris and London apartments, but varies among locations and types.

Getting There: For private property listings in the directory, the owner will provide details; for European company properties, all directions are provided at the time rent is paid. London apartments are managed, so it is just a matter of getting a bus or taxi to the address and getting the key at the office or desk.

This company is a departure from most of the others, and seems well suited to persons wanting to negotiate directly with owners of quality properties. The apartments in both London locations are very good and equitably priced. However, for European rentals not listed in the Hideaways directory, membership seems like an awkward process to go through, and the $75 membership fee before you can book seems high. The flat $50 booking fee is reasonable if, as the company states, the rental prices are those shown by the European company. The best measure of this is a European price list included with the catalog from Italy. As for Paris and London apartments—unless you wish to join a club, there are many properties available through agencies that do not charge membership fees.

HOMETOURS INTERNATIONAL
1170 Broadway
New York, New York 10001
Tel: 800-367-4668
      212-691-2361

Approx. No. of Rentals: 5,000 (including Israel).

France: Atlantic Coast; Brittany; Normandy; Riviera—Nice; Savoy Alps (Haute Savoie). Paris; centers of major cities.

Italy: Amalfi Coast—Positano, Latium—south of Rome; Tuscany; Tuscany Coast—Forte dei Marmi, Tellaro.

Spain: Costa Blanca—Villajoyosa; Costa del Sol—Fuengirola. Madrid.

Switzerland: Throughout—Alpine towns. Interlaken.

England: London.

Established in 1984, this agency offers apartments and villas in areas carefully selected to appeal to business travelers as well as vacationers.

An apartment in London, Madrid, Paris, or Tel Aviv, for example, represents enormous conveniences and savings over hotels in these expensive cities. In addition, this is one of the very few agencies with rentals throughout Israel and along Spain's Costa Blanca. Hometours is not a large agency, and it tends to personalize its service.

> *Approach:* Matching. Telephone for information and to give an overview of your needs. Follow up the call with a letter stating your needs and preferences in location, type, style, dates, and price limit, and enclose a check or money order for $25 to initiate the search and the booking process. Brochures on properties will be sent to help in the selection process. If a suitable rental is not found, $15 will be refunded (a good policy).
>
> *Deposit at Time of Booking:* 50 percent of the rent.
>
> *Minimum Stay:* Varies widely. In London, Paris, and Madrid, it is usually three days, one week in peak season. For rural and coastal Italy, Spain, and Israel, the minimum is normally one week. Periods are Saturday to Saturday.
>
> *Maid Service:* Usually included, from three to seven days per week in the better city apartments; always included in aparthotels. Rare in rural Italy; standard in resort villas of Spain and France.
>
> *Getting There:* All instructions and directions are provided at the time rent is paid.

Hometours is quick to respond, easy to work with, and is up front with its property and price list. It is very sensitive to complaints, and will initiate an investigation on behalf of dissatisfied clients. It reduces the chances of problems by selecting properties carefully and by describing the dwelling and other relevant factors before the final booking decision is made. A caveat on the Ulya residence hotel in Nice: The rates are very modest, but it faces the busy and noisy Promenade des Anglais. Otherwise, the Hometours properties we know of consistently offer good value. If seeking economy apartments in Paris, inquire about Residence Trousseau near the Gare de Lyon; for luxury, ask about the Residence du Roi. The "Duke" in London is a well-located building of moderate-to-luxury apartments.

Packages can be arranged, including air and ground transportation.

IDYLL, LTD.
P.O. Box 405
Media, Pennsylvania 19063
Tel: 215-565-5242

Approx. No. of Rentals: 250.

Austria: Salzburg Province—villages south of Salzburg.

West Germany: Rhine Valley, Lorelei Region between Koblenz and Mainz.

Switzerland: Villages on the Thuner See near Interlaken and in the vicinity of Meiringen, between Lucerne and Interlaken.

United Kingdom: England—London. Scotland; Wales.

Idyll's "Untours," with their unique approach to renting, are a cross between do-it-yourself vacations and package tours. Visitors may stay in one location or, in the United Kingdom, in a pair of locations—for example, two weeks in a London apartment and a week in Scotland or Wales. There is also a choice of two plans; Classic includes air transportation and Custom does not. Both include counseling during the selection process. Except in the United Kingdom, an Idyll staff member will escort you to your apartment from your destination airport. Clients who rent a car will meet with an Idyll staff member at the airport for orientation, instructions, and assistance in renting the vehicle. Idyll's programs are seasonal, April to October.

> *Approach:* Brochures with brief location and property descriptions, explanation of the "Untours," and prices are sent upon request.
>
> *Deposit at Time of Booking:* $100 per adult, $50 per child.
>
> *Minimum Stay:* Normally three weeks; special arrangements for two weeks.
>
> *Maid Service:* Not included; postrental cleaning included.
>
> *Getting There:* In most cases in West Germany, Switzerland, and Austria, an Idyll representative will escort you from the airport to your rental. In the United Kingdom, a representative will give you instructions at the airport.

All else being equal, the Idyll programs cost more than arranging your own rental. However, they are good for those who want more support and assistance, yet do not want to be tied to a conventional bus-and-hotel type of tour. The locations in Switzerland, Austria, and West Germany are all excellent. The London apartments are not elegant, but are above average and comfortable; different rates apply depending upon the London area. If within your budget, we recommend those in central locations at the slightly higher price; mention the Apartment Services, Ltd. apartments (modest but consistently good).

   There are many variables in the programs—length of stay, season, with or without airfare, number in party, and so forth—but a basic two-week London "Untour" runs about $900 per person; for Scotland and

Wales the cost is about $500 per person for two weeks. Continental rentals run about $600 per person for three weeks. A $50 supplement must be paid if you arrange your own air transportation.

IN THE ENGLISH MANNER
P.O. Box 936
Alamo, California 94507
Tel: 415-935-7065 (call collect)

Approx. No. of Rentals: 200.
Ireland: Countryside.
United Kingdom: Scattered throughout England. London and environs—
Chelsea, Kensington, Knightsbridge, Mayfair.

The rentals in the English and Irish countryside are in stately homes and manor houses. Meals are taken with the resident owners, and tickets to special events (theater, cricket matches) can be ordered. A smaller number of similar situations are offered in France. These are *not* vacation rental apartments or cottages. The London apartments are in various prime locations, in standards ranging from moderate to luxury (more toward the latter).

> *Approach:* Upon request a color brochure is sent, followed by additional details (including prices) after you have indicated an interest in one or more of the apartments.
>
> *Deposit at Time of Booking:* 30 percent of invoice plus a *fee* of $50 for first-time clients.
>
> *Minimum Stay:* London—one week except in low season; one to three days in country manors.
>
> *Maid Service:* Varies, but is usually daily in the better London apartments; included in the rent.
>
> *Getting There:* Instructions are given at time of payment of rent; nearly all apartments have on-site managers.

The agency offers a number of personalized itineraries, including car rental, chauffeured tours of London and the countryside, even a night as a manor house guest if a break from a London apartment is desired.

INTERHOME, INC. USA
36 Carlos Drive
Fairfield, New Jersey 07006
Tel: 201-882-6864

Approx. No. of Rentals: 20,000.
Throughout Continental Europe.

This agency represents Interhome of Zurich, Switzerland, the largest rental company in Europe, with properties in virtually every popular destination, vacation spot, and resort on the Continent, plus many in out-of-the-way areas. Although the largest concentration of rentals is in Switzerland, your choices range much farther afield.

> *Approach:* A company this large cannot provide catalogs and descriptions for all its properties, but the New Jersey office can send you a sample catalog principally covering the Alpine resort areas of Switzerland, Austria, eastern France, and northern Italy. The price list, in U.S. dollars, comes with the catalog.
> *Deposit at Time of Booking:* 30 percent.
> *Minimum Stay:* One week.
> *Maid Service:* Varies considerably. Most properties include only weekly service and postrental cleanup. If more is required, advise the agent.
> *Getting There:* Again, this varies greatly, depending on the property, but usually full instructions are issued at the time of final payment. Saturday to Saturday is the rent week, especially in July and August, but this may be negotiated during low and mid seasons.

Not a highly personalized operation, Interhome is large, slick, and efficient; it appeals greatly to Europeans looking for consistently good values rather than deluxe accommodations or advice (they know the ropes). This company is best for seasoned travelers on a moderate budget.

INTERNATIONAL LODGING CORP.
89-27 182nd Street
Hollis, New York 11423
Tel: 718-291-1342

Approx. No of Rentals: 150.
Spain: Balearic Islands—Ibiza; Majorca; Costa Brava; Costa del Sol—Marbella, Nerja. Madrid.

One owner of this company, Maria Santos, is a Spanish woman who spends part of the year near Madrid; she has collected a wide selection of beachfront apartments, individual villas, and *fincas* (restored farm or country houses, often with some land). Standards and prices vary widely.

Approach: Request a catalog, specifying areas you are interested in; what is actually sent is a collection of profile sheets on appropriate properties. The best action, after deciding on one or two possible properties, is to telephone the agency to discuss details. There is a $25 booking fee.

Deposit at Time of Booking: 50 percent of full rental.

Minimum Stay: One week, except two weeks in high season (July to mid-September).

Maid Service: Daily in some of the apartment hotels, weekly in most of the *fincas* and villas (but more frequent service can be arranged if required).

Getting There: Instructions upon payment of rent. All apartments have on-site managers, and directions to rural properties and arrangements for keys are made clear.

This agency is one of the best sources of apartments on the Costa Brava, but read the fine print in the descriptions if you are seeking beachfront rentals. For the Costa del Sol, the El Capistrano resort at Nerja is the best unless you crave the high life and nightlife of the Marbella/Torremolinos area (see Chapter 11, "Spain"). The company can assist with air travel arrangements and car rental in Spain.

INTERNATIONAL SERVICES
Piazza di Spagna 35
00187 Rome, Italy
Tel: (011-39-6) 684-0288
    and
110 East End Avenue
New York, New York 10028
Tel: 212-794-1434

Approx. No. of Rentals: 300.
Italy: All areas; Cortina, Florence, Lucca, Milan, Portofino, Rome, Venice. Islands of Capri, Panarea, Ponza, Sardinia, Sicily.

Directed and partly owned by Jacqueline Stamato, an American living in Rome, this agency has a multinational, multilingual staff. Employees of the main Rome office seek villas and apartments that are best suited to North American standards, yet are representative of Italy and the region in which they are located. Many of the rentals are private homes, either vacation homes or primary residences rented out when the owners are away. The properties range from simple apartments and villas to super-luxury estates, and are personally checked by the director. International

Services is an excellent (and rare) source for rentals on the islands of the Tyrrhenian Sea.

> *Approach:* Contact the U.S. representative shown above to give them an idea of where you would like to locate, the type of property, and the price range. You will receive a selection of photos and profiles, with prices. They are well informed and know the company operations.
>
> *Deposit at Time of Booking:* 20 percent of the full rent.
>
> *Minimum Stay:* Varies; usually two weeks in high season, one week in off-seasons. Some larger properties may require one-month stays.
>
> *Maid Service:* Depends on the property. In general, the smaller rentals have weekly service; for larger, more deluxe rentals any arrangement can be worked out.
>
> *Getting There:* Complete instructions upon booking. Agents ask that you advise them of your airline, flight number, and arrival information. Clients are met at the property by a staff person, owner, or property manager.

It is rare for an American to be the director and part-owner of a European company. Agents provide assistance, but the prices are the same whether rentals are booked directly or through the U.S. agent. For the larger, more luxurious villas and estates, or even the moderate ones, a good idea is to telephone Rome and speak with Jacqueline Stamato, who knows the properties personally. Many other services are available: long-term rentals, sales, travel and sight-seeing, art purchases, translation, receptions, and corporate affairs.

ITALIAN VILLA RENTALS
P.O. Box 1145
Bellevue, Washington 98009
Tel: 206-827-3694

Approx. No. of Rentals: 400.
Italy: Amalfi Coast; Chianti Valley; Tuscany coast—Marina di Pietrasanta.

This agency represents two Italian rental companies. One, Toscanamare Villas at Marina di Pietrasanta, on the coast between Pisa and La Spezia, is owned and operated by the daughter and son-in-law of the U.S. agent. (This provides Italian Villa Rentals with access to and supervision of the properties it rents in North America.) Marina di Pietrasanta is one of a long string of beach resorts that should be avoided in the crowded months of July and August. The other company has properties scattered in several good locations, including apartments in a large, interesting villa just east of Florence.

> *Approach:* A catalog/brochure is sent immediately upon request. After making a selection, notify the agent, who then contacts the Italian office to confirm availability.
>
> *Deposit at Time of Booking:* 30 percent upon confirmation.
>
> *Minimum Stay:* One week, Saturday to Saturday.
>
> *Maid Service:* Daily service in most of the properties. Client is responsible for buying cleaning supplies, although the implements are provided.
>
> *Getting There:* Instructions provided at time of booking. A vehicle is very useful in the Marina di Pietrasanta area.

Access to the beach clubs, which provide umbrellas and changing rooms, is available to villa clients at discounted rates. Tours and car rentals can be arranged at Toscanamare Villas offices. This beach resort area is popular with Europeans, so early booking is important for high-season rentals. In the low season, the beach resorts are pretty well shut down; September is the best month, followed by April to mid-June.

LaCURE VILLAS
11661 San Vicente Boulevard
Suite 1010
Los Angeles, California 90049
Tel: 800-387-2726
    800-387-2515
    800-387-2720

275 Spadina Road
Toronto, Ontario M5R 2V3
Canada
Tel: 800-387-1201
    (Ontario and Quebec)
    416-968-2374

Approx. No. of Rentals: 50 Europe, 400 overall.
France: Riviera—Nice, Saint-Jean–Cap Ferrat, Saint-Tropez.
Portugal: The Algarve.
Spain: Costa del Sol—Marbella.

LaCure operates as an agent for privately owned villas in the Caribbean, Mexico, Hawaii, Florida, and some locations in Europe. The company specializes in elegant homes in spectacular settings with a wide range of prices ($2,800 to $30,000 for two weeks).

> *Approach:* Matching. A general brochure is available. Telephone the agency to give its staff an idea of what you are seeking and where. You will be asked to send the specifics in a letter, along with a fee

of $25 (this is reasonable for the effort they put in). After research-ing the areas of interest for suitable properties, photos and de-scriptions are sent for your consideration. If you book, the fee is applied to the rent; if not, the fee is forfeited.

Deposit at Time of Booking: 30 percent. Full payment is required forty-five days before departure.

Minimum Stay: Two weeks; occasionally one week.

Maid Service: Usually available daily. Negotiable.

Getting There: All information and directions are provided at the time of payment; someone will always meet the client at the property.

This capable and professional organization, a Canadian company estab-lished in 1980, has expanded into the U.S. market and also into property offerings in Europe. Its properties are not for the budget-minded.

LISMORE TRAVEL
106 East 31st Street
New York, New York 10016
Tel: 800-547-6673
212-685-0100

Approx. No. of Rentals: 200.

Ireland: Counties Clare, Cork, Donegal, Galway, Kerry, Leitrim, Limerick, Mayo, Roscommon, Waterford.

Lismore represents Irish Cottage Holiday Homes and Rent-an-Irish-Cot-tage, which primarily handle privately owned clusters of vacation cot-tages, plus some individual properties. Also a tour agency, Lismore offers a selection of hosted and self-drive trips throughout Ireland.

Approach: Catalogs sent upon request. The Cottage Holiday Homes catalog lists addresses for direct contact, as well as prices in Irish pounds. However, these properties can be booked most conve-niently through Lismore, and the prices are the same.

Deposit at Time of Booking: 30 percent.

Minimum Stay: One week, Saturday to Saturday is normal; half-week stays can be arranged in off-seasons (see Chapter 8, "Republic of Ireland").

Maid Service: Usually not available, except as postrental cleaning. Be sure to state that towels and linens are needed.

Getting There: Directions to the properties are given at the time of booking. In all cases someone will meet you at the property. As noted in the chapter on Ireland, few rentals are near railroad stations, so a rental car is important. Lismore can arrange car rentals out of Dublin, Shannon Airport, and many major towns.

This is a reputable company offering well-selected and vetted cottages. Although most of the rentals are in a rustic Irish style, they are comfortable, with modern amenities.

LIVINGSTONE HOLIDAYS
1720 East Garry Avenue
Suite 204
Santa Ana, California 92705
Tel: 714-476-2823

Approx. No. of Rentals: 800.
United Kingdom: England—Cotswolds; Hereford; Wiltshire; Shakespeare Country; Thames Valley; southeast, southwest, and northern England. London, Bath. Scotland—Scattered in Highlands and Lowlands.

Livingston represents several excellent British rental companies. One concentrates in the Heart of England, which refers to a time as well as a place, the rural England of bygone days. Well chosen and impeccably kept, these properties are in a very desirable and popular area of England. Another company offers rentals of unusually elegant stately homes, manor houses, and castles scattered throughout England and Scotland. For an executive apartment in Bath, ask about Fountain House. Often, special activities such as hunting or Shakespeare plays, can be arranged.

Approach: Write or phone for a catalog, specifying which type of rental you are seeking (a country cottage; or a larger, more elegant, country home; or an apartment in London or Bath). After choosing one or two plus an alternate, contact the agency (telephone contact is best). While agents are determining availability, complete and send the booking form with a deposit. Confirmation is returned with an invoice for the balance. Access, MasterCard, and Visa are accepted.

Deposit at Time of Booking: One-third of the rent.

Minimum Stay: One week in summer, Saturday to Saturday as usual; three days possible in low season.

Maid Service: Seldom available in country cottages, but may be arranged. Postrental cleaning included in rent, but renters must leave place neat.

Getting There: Instructions are sent after final payment is made.

Almost twenty years in the business by one of the British companies have resulted in a smooth, personalized, and efficient operation. We were very impressed with the carefully selected properties we visited. Elizabeth Livingstone, owner of the U.S. agency, is helpful and, having been raised in England, knows the country and the properties well. Prices, we feel, are fair.

LONDON APARTMENTS (USA) LTD.
5 Hidden Valley Road
Lafayette, California 94549
Tel: 800-366-8748
       415-283-4280

Approx. No. of Rentals: 500 London, 1,200 others.
United Kingdom: England (principally London)—Bayswater, Bloomsbury, Kensington, Knightsbridge, Mayfair, Pimlico; throughout rural
counties. Also in Scotland and Wales.

This is one of the principal North American agents for the British company of the same name (London Apartments Ltd.), which owns an
Edwardian apartment building, formerly a residence of the Aga Khan. It is
well located at 51 Kensington Court, one block off bustling Kensington
High Street, across from Kensington Gardens. Other apartments represented by the firm are grouped in three categories: Grade C (economy),
Grade B (standard), and Grade A (superior). The ratings are accurate,
allowing clients to determine both the price and standards, as well as
location. This impresses us as a straightforward operation with no
hidden costs or excess fees. No commissions are charged; the rent
prices are the same whether booked directly or through the agency. The
rural cottages—a nice selection of modest-to-moderately-priced properties—are available through an arrangement with another reliable company.

Approach: Matching. A brochure on 51 Kensington Court will be
sent on request, and a overview of other apartments is also
available. For the apartments not owned by the company, it is best
to decide on a location and price range, then discuss the matter
with the agent by telephone.
Deposit at Time of Booking: The equivalent of £200 for London,
payable by personal check; 30 percent of rent for rural properties.
Remainder is payable by check at least thirty days prior to departure.
Minimum Stay: Normally one week; shorter periods in low seasons
are negotiable.

Maid Service: Varies among categories. From five days per week to daily is typical in London. Rarely provided in rural properties.

Getting There: Upon payment, a voucher, maps, and all instructions will be provided. A minicab pickup at Heathrow or Gatwick can be arranged in advance if desired.

We like the wide choice offered by this company, and its division of apartments into three standards/price categories. Due to location, some higher-category apartments rent for less than some units in lower categories.

LYNOTT TOURS
350 Fifth Avenue
Suite 2619
New York, New York 10018
Tel: 800-221-2474
    212-760-0101

Approx. No. of Rentals: 70.
Ireland: Counties Clare, Cork, Donegal, Galway, Limerick, Mayo, and Tipperary.

This is principally a tour company, offering conducted and self-drive tours throughout Britain and Ireland, including prearranged stays at manor houses and B&Bs. Lynott does, however, offer a small selection of traditional, but modern, Irish country cottages in the southwest counties. Also, through the well-respected Rent-an-Irish-Cottage based at Shannon Airport, an additional number of properties in the west coast and central-west countries can be booked. This is a well-established agency, familiar to travelers to Ireland.

Approach: Two catalogs are sent upon request; when you select a rental and an alternate, the agency will determine availability and advise you of how to proceed.

Deposit at Time of Booking: 30 percent, payable by check or major credit card.

Minimum Stay: One week, Saturday to Saturday; shorter periods possible during low seasons (season dates are included in the catalogs).

Maid Service: Other than postrental cleaning, maid service is not included; if desired, it must be paid for separately.

Getting There: Instructions and directions are provided upon booking. Most locations (and car rental) are best handled by arrival at Shannon International Airport. Rent a car in Dublin if arriving from Britain.

This is a very straightforward rental operation run by a reputable organization; the catalogs are explicit and the cottages meet their specifications.

NW BED & BREAKFAST—TRAVEL UNLIMITED
610 S.W. Broadway
Portland, Oregon 97205
Tel: 503-243-7616

Approx. No. of Rentals: 70.
France: Scattered châteaus; canal boats.
England: London—Chelsea, Knightsbridge, Pimlico. Also B&Bs and canal boats in Britain.

This versatile company primarily handles arrangements for Bed & Breakfasts in Britain, Austria, France, West Germany, Italy, Switzerland, and the Benelux countries. It also offers guest accommodations, and a very few apartments, in large French châteaus. Third, it books barges and self-drive canal boats in Britain and France. But a good selection of London apartments is offered, ranging from ones of moderate prices and standards in Pimlico to more elegant ones in Chelsea and Knightsbridge. The company works mostly through travel agents, but will deal directly with the public.

> *Approach:* Contact the company for booklets and brochures. After making a selection, send a check for the $20 booking fee along with your reservation request, arrival and departure dates, number in party, type, and price category preferred. The booking fee will be refunded if Travel Unlimited is unable to confirm.
> *Deposit at Time of Booking:* One week's rent upon confirmation; balance due thirty days before departure.
> *Minimum Stay:* Varies between one day and three weeks—details are on the company's information sheet.
> *Maid Service:* Included, from three days per week to daily.
> *Getting There:* All instructions and directions are provided at time of final payment.

The variety of accommodations, from apartments and B&Bs to canal boats and barges, makes this one of the most unusual companies included in this guidebook. Travel Unlimited's enviable reputation with travel agents ensures its good name with the public. The options (a week or two divided between a canal boat and a London apartment, and so forth) are appealing.

ORSAVA, INC.
P.O. Box 6175
Marietta, Georgia 30065
Tel: 404-578-9091

Approx. No. of Rentals: 2,200.
France: Aquitaine; Atlantic Coast; Brittany; the Dordogne and Lot river valleys; Normandy.
West Germany: Baden-Württemberg, Rhineland.
Switzerland: Canton of Uri—near Lucerne.
United Kingdom: Throughout England; some in Scotland and Wales.

Orsava is one of several U.S. agencies representing Hoseasons Holidays, Ltd. of England, which, in turn, is one of Britain's largest vacation rental companies. In addition to cottage rentals throughout England, Scotland, and, to a lesser extent, Wales, Hoseasons also offers boat rentals on the Norfolk Broads, renting anything from day cruisers and sailboats to cruiser-type houseboats for up to eight persons. It is also a good company from which to arrange passage on canal barges in Britain, France, Holland, and Denmark.

As with a few of the larger British companies (see Blake's Vacations, for example), Hoseasons has expanded its vacation rental operation into Continental Europe, principally for its British clientele, but certainly available to all. Its West German properties are mostly in rural "bungalow parks," not in towns. The Swiss rentals are apartments in a chalet in the town of Seelisberg.

> *Approach:* A descriptive, color-illustrated catalog will be sent. There is no fee.
> *Deposit at Time of Booking:* 50 percent of rent; checks and major credit cards accepted.
> *Minimum Stay:* In the United Kingdom, one week in June through September; three to four days in off-seasons. In other countries, usually two weeks in July and August, one week rest of year.
> *Maid Service:* Daily service is very rare; weekly exchange of linens and towels is usual.
> *Getting There:* This is a typical British operation principally for British vacationers who know the ropes, both in the United King-

dom and on the Continent, but North Americans are easily accommodated. All instructions and directions are given at time of booking.

Many of the rentals in Britain are in *holiday parks* (planned vacation developments), which, it seems to us, defeats for North Americans a primary purpose for visiting the United Kingdom. These rentals are often referred to as "purpose-built." Unless you want a rental in a vacation development, state that you prefer a farm or village cottage. The same applies to the West German properties, except there are fewer alternatives available from the United States.

We are not sure how closely the French and Swiss properties are inspected and overseen, but Hoseasons has a good reputation in England for offering modest accommodations at reasonable prices. One concern is that the strings grow long, stretching from U.S. agency to British agency to owners in other countries.

OVERSEAS CONNECTION
70 West 71st Street
Suite C
New York, New York 10023
Tel: 800-542-4007
      212-769-1170

Approx. No. of Rentals: 1,000.
France: Brittany; Côte d'Azur—Antibes, Cannes, Grasse Hills, Nice, Valbonne; Normandy; Savoy Alps (Haute Savoie)—Chamonix, Courchevel, Megève. Paris.
Italy: Amalfi Coast; Lake Como; Lake D'Orta; Riviera—Rapallo; Tuscany—Florence/Fiesole, rural areas. Islands of Capri, Elba, Sardinia. Milan, Rome, Venice.
Spain: Balearic Islands—Ibiza, Majorca; Costa Brava; Costa del Sol—Marbella, Puerto Vanuse. Barcelona, Madrid.
Switzerland: Gstaad, St. Moritz.
England: London.

During the five years of its existence, this ambitious agency has amassed a good selection of rental properties in the Caribbean and Florida, as well as in desirable locations in Europe. Although a large percentage of the rentals are upscale in standards and prices, there is also a fair choice of more modest ones, such as the comfortable $400-per-week one-bedroom apartment we had in Florence. Across the Tyrrhenian Sea on the Costa Smeralda of Sardinia, a luxury four-bedroom villa may be rented for about $7,000 per week. This illustrates the variety available. The Italian company the agency represents is not large, but it is well managed and takes a personal approach to the selection and overseeing of its properties. This also seems to reflect the way the owners of Overseas Connection, a young married couple, run their agency.

The luxury rentals in the French and Swiss Alps are in the most popular ski/summer resort towns. About a dozen properties, also in the upper-moderate-to-deluxe category, are on Ibiza in the Balearic Islands, with one or two on Majorca. The Costa del Sol rentals include modest apartments, villas in a cluster, and a few in the large luxury class.

Approach: This agency uses videotapes to present its portfolio of properties. Contact the toll-free number with your request for a specific country tape; you can either borrow it, or you can purchase it for $15. (American Express is accepted.) The properties shown on the tapes are accompanied by verbal descriptions and by a guide booklet that includes prices. Choose three or four properties as you watch the tape, then let the agency know your selections. This will begin the confirmation process. In the rare case that a property you have booked and paid for is cancelled, the agency will either refund your money or move you into an equal or better property at no added cost.

Deposit at Time of Booking: 50 percent; remainder plus the security deposit are due eight weeks before departure.

Minimum Stay: Côte d'Azur in July and August is one month; at other times two weeks. Balearics in July and August is two weeks; one week in other months. In Italy, two weeks. During low seasons, ask about one-week options. Paris and London: one week.

Maid Service: Varies. Let the agency know your requirements.

Getting There: Complete instructions and directions are provided at time of payment. There is always someone on the property to receive clients and handle problems, should they arise.

A new operation, called "Capitals of the World," concentrates on apartments in major cities for both corporate accounts and vacationers. The selection in Paris was the most complete at press time. This seems to be a tightly run, innovative agency, and the videotapes are an interesting departure from the standard catalogs.

PILGRIM'S WAY
P.O. Box 1307
Havertown, Pennsylvania 19083
Tel: 215-649-1868

Approx. No. of Rentals: 300.
United Kingdom: England—London; Scotland; Wales.

Pilgrim's Way is a small, personal agency that has informal relations with larger rental companies in Britain. Since moving to the United States, owner Anne Pilgrim has kept in close touch with her British homeland and can provide reliable advice on where to book cottages and apartments. She offers her clientele a wide choice of properties.

> *Approach:* Matching, some catalogs. Write or telephone with some idea of where you would like to locate and the range of the rent you are willing to pay. There is a $40 (U.S) booking fee, refundable if plane reservations are made by Pilgrim's Way. (Other services are available such as Britrail passes, car rentals.)
>
> *Deposit at Time of Booking:* 50 percent; balance is due two months before departure.
>
> *Minimum Stay:* Rural areas: one week, Saturday to Saturday; shorter periods in low seasons (see Chapter 13). For London, one week in high season, flexible arrival and checkout days.
>
> *Maid Service:* Varies. Rural rentals usually include only postrental cleanup, but in some cases more can be arranged. Service from three days per week to daily is common in the London apartments.
>
> *Getting There:* The agency provides maps and instructions upon payment of rent.

The agency combines small size, personal knowledge of Britain, and a large and dependable source of rental properties. Ms. Pilgrim's companies are well chosen and well respected. Her experience helps her obtain the best values for her clients.

RENT A HOME INTERNATIONAL
3429 Freemont Place No. 318
Seattle, Washington 98103
Tel: 206-545-4963

Approx. No. of Rentals: 25,000 (worldwide).
Austria: Throughout the country—Innsbruck, Salzburg, Vienna.
France: Throughout the country—Cannes, Nice, Paris.
West Germany: Baden-Württemberg; Bavaria. Cologne, Munich.
Italy: Throughout the country—Florence, Rome, Venice.
Portugal: The Algarve; Lisbon area.
Spain: Balearic Islands; Costa Brava; Costa del Sol. Barcelona, Madrid.

Switzerland: Throughout the country—Interlaken, Lucerne, Zurich.
United Kingdom: England, Scotland, Wales. London.

This very large agency, founded in 1984, represents dozens of rental companies and individual owners in Europe and the Western Hemisphere. Because the agency declined to provide the names or addresses of the European companies it represents, we were unable to make the contacts necessary to view properties.

> *Approach:* A brochure and registration form will be sent after you call the agency. The form asks for basic information on where you want to be and your general price range. Return the form with a *$50 registration fee.* Rent A Home will try to match your requirements and will send profile sheets for a variety of suitable properties. Upon deciding, inform the agency of your choices and the confirmation process will begin. If the agency cannot find the property you want, the fee minus communications expenses will be returned. If you book, the fee will be applied to the rent.
>
> *Deposit at Time of Booking:* 30 to 50 percent, depending on the property; the remainder is due eight weeks before occupancy date.
>
> *Minimum Stay:* One week, normally Saturday to Saturday.
>
> *Maid Service:* Varies. With such a large variety of properties, the best approach is to tell the agency your needs on the registration form.
>
> *Getting There:* All instructions are provided when the rent is paid.

Rental prices run from $300 to $3,000 per week (and up). The prices are shown in U.S. dollars on the profile sheets. Full travel services can be arranged.

RENT A VACATION EVERYWHERE (RAVE)
328 Main Street East
Suite 526
Rochester, New York 14604
Tel: 716-454-6440

Approx. No of Rentals: 1,200 (worldwide).
Austria: Throughout the country—Innsbruck, Salzburg, Vienna.
France: Throughout the country—Cannes, Nice, Paris.
Ireland: West counties.
Italy: Throughout the country—Florence, Rome, Venice.
Spain: Balearic Islands; Costa Brava; Costa del Sol. Barcelona, Madrid.
Switzerland: Thoughout the country—Interlaken, Lucerne, Zurich.
England: London and rural areas.

As with many of the companies that have properties scattered throughout Europe, it is difficult to get firsthand information about such extensive listings. It is important, therefore, that the agency be considered reliable. This firm enjoys a very good reputation in the business. Praise from competitors, and the absence of a fee to begin the search process, speak well for the agency (and it doesn't cost anything to find out more). The variety of properties is wide, mostly in the moderate and luxury categories, with rents from $450 to $6,000 per week.

Approach: Write or phone for information and a brochure, stating what locations are of interest and the rent range desired. Profiles, including prices, matching your requirements will be sent for consideration. If and when you select a property and its availability is confirmed, a deposit secures the rental.

Deposit at Time of Booking: 30 to 50 percent; balance due at least fifty days before occupancy.

Minimum Stay: One week for most rural rentals; three to four days for city apartments in low season.

Maid Service: Varies from none to daily; make your wishes clear in your initial statement of requirements.

Getting There: Complete instructions are sent when rent is paid.

Agency inspects about half the properties annually, relying on the European companies to inspect their own properties.

RENT IN ITALY
3801 Ingomar Street N.W.
Washington, DC 20015
Tel: 202-244-5345

Italy: Sicily; Tuscany—Florence, hill country, Siena; Umbria. Venice.

Mrs. Muoio runs a small, personalized agency representing three rental companies in Italy that, in turn, represent some three hundred property owners, mostly in the Tuscan hills, with a few in Umbria, and some who own apartments in Venice and large estates in Sicily. Rentals run the gamut in price, size, and comfort up to, and including, luxury villas with serving staff. We have not sampled her properties, but know that she knows the areas and inspects many of the units regularly.

Approach: She matches your requirements. Write or phone with dates, number in party, type, general location you are seeking, and your price range. Information will be forthcoming.

Deposit at Time of Booking: 30 to 50 percent; balance due at least four weeks before occupancy.

Minimum Stay: One week for most rural rentals; three to four days for city apartments in low season.

Maid Service: Varies from none to daily to complete staff. Make your wishes clear in your initial contact.

Getting There: Complete instructions are sent when rent is paid.

We know little about this small agency, so read all the material carefully. Often the personal touch is very helpful and assures a knowledge of the properties beyond that of a very large company that must rely on the European companies it represents.

RIVIERA HOLIDAYS
31 Georgian Lane
Great Neck, New York 11024
Tel: 516-487-8094

Approx. No. of Rentals: 2,000.
England: London only.
France: Riviera (including Côte d'Azur)—Antibes, Cannes, Eze-sur-Mer, Juan-les-Pines, Villefranche-sur-Mer; Paris.

As the agency's name implies, most of this agency's rental properties are along the Riviera. They range in size from studios to three-bedroom apartments, and in price from about $350 to $2,700 per week. Villas with from two to four bedrooms are also available, normally renting by the month in July and August and for shorter periods at other times.

No information was provided on the Paris and London apartments.

Approach: Upon contacting the agency, you will receive a letter of introduction, a sample list of properties (with prices), and a questionnaire. From the straightforward questionnaire the agency will try to match your requirements with what is available. No fee is charged for this.

Deposit at Time of Booking: 25 percent; balance of rent must be paid eight weeks before occupancy.

Minimum Stay: One week in apartments; one month in villas in the high season.

Maid Service: Except for postrental cleanup, maid service is not included (but it can usually be arranged). The question is asked on the questionnaire.

Getting There: All instructions are provided at time of rent payment.

The towns where properties are available are all the popular Riviera resort spots, but it is especially important to know before booking exactly where the property is located. Although the section on the Côte d'Azur in Chapter 6 will help, get all the details from the agent. Avoid apartments facing the busy section of the seafront boulevard (which has different names between Cannes and Nice); ask the agent.

SUSAN T. PIDDUCK, CUENDET AGENT
1742 Calle Corvo
Camarillo, California 92010
Tel: 805-987-5278

Approx. No. of Rentals: 1,500.
Italy: Elba; Sicily; Tuscany—Arezzo, Chianti, Florence, Lucca, Pisa, Siena; Umbria—Assisi, Orvieto, Perugia. Rome.

This small, very personalized agency is one of two North American agents for the large Swiss-Italian rental organization Cuendet & Cie. Cuendet's headquarters in a rural area near Siena blends ancient surroundings and modern technology: late-generation IBM computers installed in a great old stone building with a telecommunications room operated by a delightful multilingual staff. Cuendet offers the largest single collection of properties in the Tuscany/Umbria region, perhaps in Italy overall. The principal focus is central Italy, where many of the ancient stone country houses that dot the hill country have been converted into vacation rentals (see Chapter 9). Cuendet is a very professional and progressive organization, demanding good standards from the properties it represents.

Susan Pidduck is personable and helpful, providing information not only about Cuendet rentals but also about Tuscany, especially the Florence area, where she has lived. Her useful personal notes about traveling in Italy and about Florence accompany the catalog.

Approach: The key to the Cuendet operation is its catalog, a full-color 200 + -page compendium of properties filled with facts about Tuscany and Umbria. The catalog costs $12, but even if you don't book a Cuendet rental it is worth the money for its view of the countryside and its introduction to the variety of properties. From the catalog, pick and rank several properties, then phone or write Susan Pidduck with your choices. The agency will notify you of availability within three days. Then you send the booking form, the deposit, and the $50 booking fee to the agent. This will secure your reservation. *No commission* is charged on top of the published prices.

Deposit at Time of Booking: 25 percent, balance due eight weeks before departure; you will receive a voucher to give the owner on arrival.

Minimum Stay: Prices are shown per week for a two-week rental; for one-week stays there is a 20 percent surcharge.

Maid Service: Usually not included except for postrental cleanup. May be arranged in some cases.

Getting There: Explicit instructions are provided upon payment.

There are many rules and instructions to wade through with Cuendet, but the availability of so many different properties is worth it. The catalog clearly establishes five "comfort" categories (and price ranges). The prices seem fair, as does the absence of an add-on commission. Most of the properties are in the modest-to-moderate range, with a scattering of more elegant and expensive villas, and even a few castles.

The written descriptions are brief but accurate. The catalog also contains information about the booking and renting process and, most important, a 30+-page price list. This assures that the rental prices for U.S. and Canadian clients are the same prices paid by Europeans. The only additional cost for working with the agent is a $50 flat booking fee; there are no hidden agent fees. For Canada, the agent is Der Tours (see the listing in this chapter).

SWISS TOURING, USA
5537 North Hollywood Avenue
Milwaukee, Wisconsin 53217
Tel: 414-963-2020

Approx. No. of Rentals: 200.

Switzerland: Most Alpine areas; towns of Beatenberg, Kandersteg, Montana-Vermala, Wengen, Zermatt; Canton of Ticino—Lugano.

Specializing in modest to moderately priced rentals in popular locales, Swiss Touring opens up the ski areas and summer mountain resort towns to travelers who prefer not to spend large sums for luxury chalets. With few exceptions, the properties are apartments in chalet-style buildings. Each town has its own characteristics, so despite the adequate descriptions in the agency's profile sheets, it is a good idea to study a general guidebook to Switzerland (Chapter 12 also gives some good information about locales).

Approach: Upon contacting this unpretentious agency, you will receive a sheaf of photocopied sheets, each sheet covering the rentals available in a particular town. Included are descriptions of the town, its location, the area, and a photograph of the chalet or building and a price list for each apartment. The first week's rent is always higher than the rent for subsequent weeks because it includes the one-time booking fee, a very straightforward approach.

Deposit at Time of Booking: Upon selecting the rental you want, plus an alternate or two, return the booking form with 50 percent of the rent. If none of your choices is available, the deposit will be refunded.

Minimum Stay: One week, Saturday to Saturday; two weeks between December 25 and January 7.

Maid Service: Prices include postrental cleanup and washing of linens (which are always included).

Getting There: Complete instructions are always provided upon final rent payment.

Swiss Touring, USA provides a personalized service—and knows its Swiss territory. All of the locations have been visited by the director, so ask her for advice. For spring through autumn visiting, it is hard to exceed Wengen and Kandersteg in the Bernese Oberland for beauty (see also Chapter 12).

TOUR-HOST INTERNATIONAL
141 East 44th Street
Suite 506
New York, New York 10017
Tel: 800-445-2690
212-953-7910

Approx. No. of Rentals: 500.
France: Burgundy; Normandy. Paris.
Italy: Lombardy; Tuscany; Veneto.
Portugal: The Algarve.
Spain: Balearic Islands—Majorca; Costa Blanca; Costa del Sol.
England: Rural areas. London.

A full-service travel agency, Tour-Host represents a number of European rental companies plus a collection of private villas in Italy. The Parisian properties are apartments in several individual buildings, and are in the moderate-to-luxury range. In London the rentals tend toward the upper scale in standards and price.

Approach: Matching; provides no catalogs. Call or write the agency with information on what you are seeking, where, the number in your party, and the price range. Agents will propose an array of choices and send profiles. There is no fee.

Deposit at Time of Booking: 30 percent, payable by check (or American Express with a 4 percent surcharge).

Minimum Stay: One week, Saturday to Saturday. In Paris, shorter terms are available; in London, shorter terms in the off-season months only.

Maid Service: Varies. Let the agency know your requirements.

Getting There: Complete instructions are provided upon final rent payment.

We have not sampled this agency's properties, but know that the British company it represents, British Homes & London Flats, has a good reputation and handles selected upscale properties.

TWELVE ISLANDS AND BEYOND
4451 MacArthur Boulevard N.W.
Washington, DC 20007
Tel: 800-345-8236
      202-342-1248

Approx. No. of Rentals: 750.
Portugal: The Algarve.

This small agency has been in the vacation rental business since 1982, specializing in properties on the Greek islands and in Turkey (these properties are not covered in this guide). More recently it has ventured into Portugal, specifically the Algarve, where it represents some 350 properties, mostly upscale villas, but others that are modestly priced.

Approach: Write or telephone for a catalog and brochure. Make your selection and advise the agency, which will then contact its agent in Portugal and let you know of availability. There is no fee.

Deposit at Time of Booking: 50 percent.

Minimum Stay: Normally one week, usually Saturday to Saturday.

Maid Service: Included from three to six days per week in many of the deluxe villas; by arrangement in others.

Getting There: All instructions and directions are provided at the time the final rent payment is made.

This agency has close ties (but not a corporate relationship) with Twelve Islands and Villa Ventures, two British companies with very good reputations. The U.S. agency seems very straightforward, responds quickly, and charges no fee for finding a place for you. A good agency for Greece, but not the best for Portugal.

UTELL INTERNATIONAL
10606 Burt Circle
Omaha, Nebraska 68114
Tel: 800-448-8355
      402-498-4300

Principally a large hotel booking service used by the travel trade, Utell also deals with the public. No services except the booking can be expected, and no fees are involved. The company is included in this guide because it can book several apartment hotels in Europe directly, among them Fountain House in Bath, England, and St. James Court in London. Fountain House offers deluxe apartments in a desirable location three blocks from the center of Bath. St. James Court, in the Buckingham Gate area of Westminster, London, is an elegant accommodation. Although a studio apartment runs about $2,000 per week and a one-bedroom runs about $2,500, contrasted to the rates of a five-star London hotel these prices are a bargain. Daily rents are available.

VACANCES EN CAMPAGNE
P.O. Box 297
Falls Village, Connecticut 06031
Tel: 800-533-5405
      203-824-5009
      212-838-4045

Approx. No. of Rentals: 250.
France: The Dordogne; scattered elsewhere.

Of three agencies operated by Carl Stewart, Vacances en Campagne (Vacations in the Countryside) is the French branch, its sister firm is Vacanze in Italia. Both firms are owned by English Country Cottages of England. Thus, Vacances en Campagne does not represent a French company, but a British one. For anyone planning to rent a place in Europe, the advantage is that locations in more than one country can easily be arranged through a single contact. The parent company is one of the best in Britain (see Heritage of England, listed above in this chapter) and operates Vacances en Campagne with the same high standard. The difference is that far fewer properties are offered in France, and these tend to be in the more expensive categories. They are, nevertheless, well selected in terms of quality and are in locations that capture the essence of the region. The rentals in the Dordogne are as tranquil and picturesque as the Dordogne itself.

>   *Approach:* Send $5 for an excellent catalog, make a selection or two,
>   and ask the agency to confirm availability. No booking fees.
>   *Deposit at Time of Booking:* 50 percent.
>   *Minimum Stay:* One week, Saturday to Saturday. Shorter periods are
>   possible in some properties between October and June.
>   *Maid Service:* Usually not available except for postrental cleanup.
>   Make sure towels and linens are available (in some cases for an
>   extra charge).
>   *Getting There:* All instructions and directions are provided at the
>   time the rent payment is made.

Although we do not know the U.S. agency well, and it has been slow to send materials and respond to our inquiries, we do know the British company to be very reputable, careful in its property selections, and fair in its pricing policies. Perhaps the slowness from Connecticut indicates that business is brisk. The agency can provide rental cars and rail and flight information.

>   VACANZA BELLA
>   2443 Filmore Street
>   Suite 228
>   San Francisco, California 94115
>   Tel: 415-821-9345

Approx. No. of Rentals: 350.
Italy: Amalfi Coast—Positano; Tuscany—Florence, hill country, Siena; Umbria—hill country, Perugia, Todi. Rome.

A small, personally run agency, Vacanza Bella combines the resources of a large Italian rental company with an excellent assortment of individually selected and represented properties. Those in the latter group are not necessarily expensive, but they tend to be out of the ordinary. One example is a small number of farmhouses, villas, and castles in southern Tuscany, a region well off the regular tourist trails. A group of young people formed an agency called Veridea to breathe new economic life into the declining region while restoring some of the areas fine old country buildings. They have done an excellent job, and the prices are well below those in more popular areas.

The larger company, Florence-based Solemar, has several agents in the United States. A very well run organization, it lists a good selection of properties ranging from modest apartments and small houses to large, elegant villas and estates.

Approach: For the individually selected properties, you'll receive a set of descriptive pages and a price list. Contact the agency (it's best to do this by telephone) with your selection, and a packet of photos and more complete descriptions will be sent to enable you to make a final decision. There is no fee. For the larger listing, ask for the catalog, then follow the same procedure. In both cases, once you reach a decision, return the booking form and the check for a deposit. If the booking is confirmed, the deposit is applied to the rent; if not, the deposit is refunded.

Deposit at Time of Booking: 50 percent of the total rent. Balance is due upon receipt of invoice, at least sixty-five days before occupancy.

Minimum Stay: Usually one week.

Maid Service: Normally not provided except for postrental cleanup, but in some cases it can be arranged directly with the property owner.

Getting There: All vouchers and instructions are provided upon payment of rent.

This combination of properties, personally selected by agency owner Daniel Morneau and the owners of Solemar, offers prospective clients a good selection of categories, locations, and prices. We like the inclusion of the price lists with the initial descriptive material.

VACANZE IN ITALIA
P.O. Box 297
Falls Village, Connecticut 06031
Tel: 800-533-5405
　　　203-824-5009

Approx. No. of Rentals: 250.

Italy: Adriatic coast—Apulia; Tuscany—Florence, hill country, Siena, few on Tuscan coast; Umbria.

Of three agencies operated by Carl Stewart, Vacanze in Italia is the Italian branch; its sister firm is Vacances en Campagne, which handles rentals in France. Both firms are owned by English Country Cottages of England. Thus, Vacanze in Italia does not represent an Italian company, but a British one. For anyone planning to rent a place in Europe, the advantage is that locations in more than one country can easily be arranged through a single contact. The English company provides very good properties in Britain (see Heritage of England, listed above in this chapter) and operates Vacanze in Italia with the same high standards. The difference is that far fewer properties are offered in Italy, but there is a good selection and variety, and it appears that location is as important as style.

> *Approach:* Send $3 for a catalog, make a selection or two, and ask the agency to confirm availability. No booking fees.
> *Deposit at Time of Booking:* 50 percent.
> *Minimum Stay:* One week, Saturday to Saturday. Shorter periods are possible in some properties between October and June.
> *Maid Service:* Usually not available except for postrental cleanup.
> *Getting There:* All instructions and directions are provided at the time the rent payment is made.

Although the U.S. agency has been slow in getting materials to us, we are well acquainted with the British company and know it to have a good reputation; it is careful in its property selections and fair in its pricing policies. We have also heard good things about the U.S. agency, so perhaps its slowness indicates how popular and busy it is. The agency can provide rental cars and rail and flight information.

VACATION HOME RENTALS (VHR) WORLDWIDE
235 Kensington Avenue
Norwood, New Jersey 07648
Tel: 800-633-3284
      201-767-9393

Approx. No. of Rentals: 3,000+.
Austria: Tirol—Innsbruck; Vorarlberg. Salzburg, Vienna.
France: Côte d'Azur—Antibes, Cannes, Nice, others in countryside; the Dordogne. Paris.
Italy: Sicily; Tuscany—Arezzo, Florence, hill country, Siena; Umbria—Gúbbio; Maratea. Rome.
Portugal: The Algarve.
Spain: Balearic Islands—Ibiza, Minorca; Costa Blanca; Costa del Sol.
Switzerland: Alpine towns in the Bernese Oberland; Ticino; Valais.
United Kingdom: Rural English counties. London. Scotland—Edinburgh.

For an agency this large, with rental properties throughout Europe and in much of the Western Hemisphere, Vacation Home Rentals (VHR) Worldwide is remarkably personalized. Concurrently, it is very professional and prides itself in fair pricing policies. There are no add-on fees or commissions beside the $25 fee to cover the necessary expenses for determining availability and making the booking. The selection is wide, the locations and properties are carefully chosen, and rents run the gamut from $300 to $20,000 per week.

Approach: As do most of the larger agencies, VHR matches your requirements with properties in its portfolio. By letter or telephone, describe where you want to locate, approximate dates, number in your party, and a price range. The agency will send you a collection of well-written profile sheets from which to choose. More information is usually available on particular properties if desired, after your selection has been narrowed to one or two. After deciding, send a check for $25 along with the reference number of the property; you will receive confirmation within a few days.

Deposit at Time of Booking: 50 percent; an invoice will be sent for the balance due. Payment in full must be made sixty days prior to occupancy.

Minimum Stay: One week in most properties; two weeks in some prime locations, such as the Riviera, during peak months of July and August. London and Paris apartments, and English country cottages, can often be booked for less than a week in low seasons.

Maid Service: Varies widely. The information is included on the property profile sheets.

Getting There: All instructions and directions are provided at time of payment of rent. If key is sent in advance, there is a refundable deposit.

The agency is refreshingly open and straightforward in its rental and pricing policies and procedures. Although corporate accounts are welcome, the principal focus is renting individually owned homes to vacationers and other travelers. This is a thoroughly professional organization.

VILLA LEISURE
P.O. Box 209
Westport, Connecticut 06881
Tel: 203-222-9611

Approx. No of Rentals: 950.
France: Côte d'Azur.
Portugal: The Algarve.
Spain: Costa del Sol—Marbella.

Most of this agency's rentals are in the Caribbean and Mexico, with a few in the more popular tourist spots of Europe. Its brochure suggests calling a travel agent and mentioning Villa Leisure. Although Villa Leisure does take bookings from the public directly, using a travel agent is probably the best approach if the company's negligible response to our efforts to obtain information is any indication. The price list shows dollars per person per day, which gives an interesting "hotel-type" perspective, but it must be interpreted carefully. The figures are based on full occupancy of two persons per bedroom. Thus, the $55 shown in the column for a two bedroom villa in Portugal turns out to be $1,540 per week (4 persons × $55 × 7 days). Since this equals two double hotel rooms at $110 per night, it isn't bad, especially considering that the villa provides a kitchen, a living room, and greater space; but be sure to work the figures out.

We visited only the Portuguese properties, and found them attractive, new, immaculate, and altogether pleasant. They are in a large tourist development, Carvoeiro Clube, described in the chapter on Portugal and in this section under the listings for agencies Villas & Apartments in Portugal and Villas International.

Approach: Write or telephone for a brochure and price list, then advise the agency what you are interested in (or take the brochure to your travel agent).

Deposit at Time of Booking: 35 percent within seven days of confirmation; balance due sixty days before occupancy.

Minimum Stay: Two weeks in summer season, one week during the off-seasons.

Maid Service: Available at extra charge; normally included in rentals in Portugal.

Getting There: All instructions are provided upon payment of rent.

The properties seem well selected, and the prices for the rentals in Portugal are fair, certainly in keeping with others charged in Europe.

VILLAS & APARTMENTS IN PORTUGAL
Janino Bastos Advisory Service
500 East 83rd Street
New York, New York 10028
Tel: 212-535-3262

Approx. No. of Rentals: 400.
Portugal: The Algarve; Lisbon area—Cascais, Estoril, Praia das Maçâs (near Sintra), Sesimbra.

Mrs. Janino Bastos has assembled a very nice variety of villas and apartments in key locations in Portugal. Because of the popularity of the Algarve as a tourist mecca, properties in the south-central coastal region near Lisbon are especially interesting (and are more difficult to find). With the exception of apartments in the fishing village of Sesimbra (forty-five minutes south of Lisbon), the rentals in this area are private homes. In the Algarve they range from modest to elegant privately owned villas, and apartments in the towns.

In addition to representing private properties, this small, versatile agency is one of two in the United States representing Carvoeiro Clube, a very large complex near the Algarve town of Lagoa. Everything from town-house-style apartments to three- and four-bedroom villas with private pools and a maid are available (see the discussion of Carvoeiro Clube in Chapter 10).

> *Approach:* Write or phone for a brochure that briefly describes the properties. Call to ask for details of any you are interested in, and more comprehensive information will be sent, including prices. Once you have decided on a property, returning the booking form and deposit, and you will be notified of confirmation.
>
> *Deposit at Time of Booking:* 25 percent; balance due six weeks before occupancy.
>
> *Minimum Stay:* One week.
>
> *Maid Service:* Daily in Carvoeiro Clube rentals; by arrangement in most other properties.
>
> *Getting There:* Instructions are provided at time of paying rent. Although a rented car is an important asset in Portugal, a taxi is sent upon request to Faro International Airport for guests of Carvoeiro Clube. For some of the Lisbon-area rentals, a car is needed (see Chapter 10).

This rather personal and informal small company offers an excellent choice of Portuguese properties. The price lists are in U.S. dollars and conform to the European prices, indicating that there is no add-on commission.

VILLAS INTERNATIONAL
71 West 23rd Street
New York, New York 10010
Tel: 800-221-2260
212-929-7585

Approx. No. of Rentals: 25,000 (worldwide).

Austria: Burgenland; Carinthia; Salzburg—Salzburg; Tirol—Innsbruck, Kitzbühel, St. Anton, Seefeld; Upper and Lower Austria; Vorarlberg—Bregenz, Lech Valley, the Montafon villages. Vienna.

France: Atlantic Coast; Auvergne; Bordeaux; Brittany; Burgundy; Côte d'Azur—Antibes, Cannes, Hill country, Juan-les-Pins, Nice; the Dordogne; Languedoc; Loire Valley; Midi/Pyrenees; Normandy; Provence. Biarritz, Marseilles, Paris and Île de France; other main cities. Island of Corsica.

West Germany: Baden-Württemberg; Bavaria; North Sea Coast.

Ireland: Counties Cork, Donegal, Galway, Kerry, Limerick, Mayo, Sligo, Tipperary. Dublin.

Italy: Adriatic coast; Alps—Cortina d'Ampezzo, Valle d'Aosta, Val Gardena; Amalfi Coast; northern lakes—Como, Garda, Lugano, Maggiore; Riviera—Portofino, San Remo; southern provinces; Tuscany—Florence, Lucca, Pisa, Siena, Tuscan hills and coast; Umbria—Arezzo, lakes, Perugia. Islands of Capri, Sardinia, Sicily. Milan, Rome (and environs), Venice (and environs), Verona, Vincenza.

Portugal: The Algarve; central-west coasts—Costa da Prato, Costa Verde. Cascais, Estoril, Lisbon (and environs).

Spain: Balearic Islands; Canary Islands; Costa Blanca; Costa Brava; Costa del Sol—Marbella; Costa Dorado. Alicante, Barcelona, Madrid, Valencia.

Switzerland: Bernese Oberland; Valais and all cantons. Crans, Davos, Geneva, Grindelwald, Gstaad, Interlaken, Klosters, Lucerne, Locarno, Lugano, Montana, St. Moritz, Zermatt, Zurich.

United Kingdom: England—all countries. London (and environs). Scotland—Hebrides; Highlands and Lowlands. Edinburgh. Wales—all areas.

As can be seen from the long list of locations with rental properties available (which does not include the Cyprus, Malta, or Western Hemisphere lists), Villas International is the largest North American rental agency handling foreign properties. To the prospective client, an advantage of this is the availability of such a large selection, often in locations otherwise not represented by agents in the United States or Canada. Two possible disadvantages are, first, the lack of personal attention and, second, the probability that agency personnel have not personally visited many of the properties and do not inspect them periodically. As for the first concern, this operation is sophisticated enough that clients do not become lost in the process, and the staff members who answer the telephones and work with inquiries are pleasant, helpful, and personable. The second suspicion is true—Villas International personnel rarely know anything about specific properties from firsthand contact. This agency relies on the companies it represents to carry out that function, which means that the foreign companies must themselves be reliable. Those we have personally contacted do seem to be responsible, with good property selections and a keen interest in the North American market. Epsecially impressive are the excellent companies in Austria (see Chapter 5), on the Côte d'Azur of France (see Chapter 6), and in England, principally those in Cornwall and the Heart of England and those handling the luxury apartments in London. Although the economy apartments are adequate for the *relatively* low rents (for London), there is no guarantee of their location except in general terms (see also Chapter 13).

> *Approach:* Villas International uses a matching process. Tell the agency what country or area you are interested in, when you want to travel, how many people will be in the party, and give them an idea of the rent range. Agents will send photocopies of property profiles. Notify them of one or more selections, ranked; they will advise you of availability within a few days, and will send an invoice. There is no fee *unless* your request is withdrawn, in which case $25 is charged to cover their expenses.
>
> *Deposit at Time of Booking:* Normally 30 percent, with balance due two months before occupancy.
>
> *Minimum Stay:* One week, except two weeks in peak season in some prime locations (French Riviera, for example). City apartments are often available for periods of less than one week.
>
> *Maid Service:* There is no single rule among the thousands of properties. Tell the agency of your requirements and they will be met.
>
> *Getting There:* All instructions are provided upon payment of rent.

Many of the European companies represented by Villas International are also represented by other agencies in the United States, so not all the properties are exclusive. Therein lies the secret to this agency's success: a vast pool of properties consolidated at one address and toll-free number—it simplifies planning and booking. The smart traveler, however, will want to do some comparative shopping. Investigate a few of the other agencies offering properties in the country you are interested in (see the listings in each country chapter).

WAYSIDE TRAVEL
10101 Fifth Kolin Avenue
Oak Lawn, Illinois 60453
Tel: 312-423-2113

Approx. No. of Rentals: 250.
England: Cotswolds; Hereford; Shakespeare Country; Thames Valley; Wiltshire.

In this case the Heart of England refers to "olde" England, an area of rural pleasure and rustic charms sought by visitors from around the world. The properties are in a most desirable area and are especially popular with North American tourists. Also inquire about the cottages at Buckland Estates, near the town of Broadway in the north Cotswolds. Special activities (hunting, Shakespeare plays, and so on) can often be scheduled.

> *Approach:* Write or phone for a catalog. After deciding on one or two properties plus an alternate, contact the agency (telephone contact is best). While agents are determining availability, complete and send the booking form with a deposit check. Confirmation is returned with an invoice for the balance due.
>
> *Deposit at Time of Booking:* One-third of the rent.
>
> *Minimum Stay:* One week in summer, Saturday to Saturday as usual; three days possible in low season.
>
> *Maid Service:* Seldom available; postrental cleanup included in rent, but renters must leave place neat.
>
> *Getting There:* Instructions are sent after final payment is made.

Children are welcome in almost all properties. This British company is a smooth, personalized, and efficient operation. We were very impressed with the properties we visited, obviously carefully selected by the previous owner of the company—a gentleman of high standards—or by a member of his staff. The U.S. agency is headed by an airline pilot, a friend and associate of the English founder. Good service and fair prices can be expected.

WILLIAMS & CO.
2841 29th Street N.W.
Washington, DC 20008
Tel: 202-328-1353

Approx. No. of Rentals: 250.
United Kingdom: England, Scotland, Wales.

This small agency is a representative of the distinctive British company Blandings, which specializes in renting those large, stately houses that dot the British countryside and are usually well hidden behind the woods and acreage bordering the estate. Some of these magnificent homes are available in their entirety, including full staff; some come with maid service only. Others offer elegant apartments in a grand house or other building on the estate property. Although these homes tend to be large, they vary considerably in size and rental price. On the low end, a gracious Cotswolds four-bedroom country house runs around $1,700 per week; a Scottish castle that will accommodate twelve runs about $7,600 per week, including a full staff boasting a Cordon Bleu chef. As we note elsewhere, Britain offers very good value when prices there are contrasted with prices of better rentals on the Continent.

The agency also handles another level of rental houses, more modest in size and price (in the $400-to-$600-per-week range), but nonetheless very carefully chosen for style, character,and surroundings.

> *Approach:* Send for a brochure; it does not show all of the properties, but does illustrate the types available and their general locations. From this, let the agency know (telephone contact is best) what you are interested in. More details will be sent to meet your requirements. After deciding, call again; you will be notified of availability within twenty-four hours. The property will be held for one week, during which you must return the booking form and deposit.
>
> *Deposit at Time of Booking:* One-third of rent (plus cost of desired staff). Balance due within fifty-six days of occupancy.
>
> *Minimum Stay:* One week.
>
> *Maid Service:* Available in many properties at additional cost. May not be available for smaller rentals.
>
> *Getting There:* Complete details are given at time of payment.

Special services (from shooting parties to a hunt or a champagne picnic in an antique Rolls-Royce) can be arranged when renting some of the larger properties. Inquire. This is a very pleasant and personal agency to work with; Vera Williams knows Britain and the properties she represents.

WILSON & LAKE INTERNATIONAL, INC.
333 York Street
Ashland, Oregon 97520
Tel: 800-545-5228
    503-488-3350

Approx. No. of Rentals: 250.

United Kingdom: England—All counties; London and environs. Scotland—Highlands and Lowlands, Hebrides; Edinburgh. Wales.

Wilson & Lake International is a small company that was formed in 1981 mainly to offer literary tours in Britain, then expanded into offering small specialty tours of all sorts, from Scottish fishing to sacred sites, from London theater to searching for antiques. It encourages the idea of staying in guest houses, B&Bs, and rental cottages, villas, and flats. The owner knows Britain, especially the tours, through personal experience. One of the two British companies represented here, it is well regarded and selective in the choice of its properties; the other is actually an estate in Berkshire, near Reading, which offers apartments in the main house as well as cottages. Wilson & Lake International is not a travel agency, but can arrange air and ground transportation.

> *Approach:* Matching and catalogs. Upon request will ask for information about where, in general, you want to be, size and style of rental desired, price range, dates. Descriptions of a selection of appropriate properties will be sent. If a catalog is desired, one will be sent, along with a booking form.
>
> *Deposit at Time of Booking:* One-third of the rent. Full payment thirty to sixty days before departure.
>
> *Minimum Stay:* One week in summer and holiday periods, Saturday to Saturday as usual; three days possible in low season in rural areas of Britain and in some London apartments, especially in low or shoulder seasons.
>
> *Maid Service:* Seldom available in rural properties, but usually provided in city apartments.
>
> *Getting There:* All instructions and directions are sent after final rent payment is made.

A personalized company with a good history. The president, Helen Lake, is a true Anglophile who knows Britain well. However, the company's main interest is not rentals.

WORLD-WIDE HOME RENTAL GUIDE
142 Lincoln Avenue
Suite 652
Santa Fe, New Mexico 87501
Tel: 505-988-5188

This is not an agency. World-Wide publishes a directory of rental properties (most in the United States and the Caribbean) that are listed for a fee.

Some of the rentals are individually owned, and a few are listed by rental agencies such as those covered in this guidebook.

The "World-Wide Home Rental Guide" is published semiannually and is available by subscription. Properties can be listed for approximately $100 per one-third page, photo included. The publisher does not guarantee the accuracy of the listings, and has no connection to those who list. The directory does, however, enable private owners to list their properties so renters and owners can make direct contact. Typically, about twenty private properties in Western Europe are listed, and half a dozen U.S. agencies advertise in the guide.

4

Transportation in Europe

♦

If you want to set up a home base in a European country or region instead of following a multicountry itinerary and staying in hotels, the choices and economics of transportation need to be examined.

In each country chapter, one or more "Location and transportation" sections describe the local rail and highway systems and note whether a car is essential or only convenient. For virtually all of the rural properties, having a car is important. Cottages in the English countryside, chalets in the Swiss and Austrian Alps, farmhouses in the hills of Italy, villas above the French Riviera and in the Balearic Islands are, by their nature, away from main transportation arteries. This does not necessarily imply that they are all remote or isolated. But even those rentals that are just half a mile from a railroad station require some getting to, either by foot or, if the station is in a town of any size, by taxi or bus. The more distant the property is, the more complex it is to get there, which means that more time must be spent figuring out bus and train schedules—and meeting them. Sometimes this is simple and practical, and sometimes it is not. It is not only a matter of convenience; the question is: Can you go where you want, when you want?

♦ PUBLIC TRANSPORTATION

If you prefer not to rent a car, it is important to choose a property located near public transportation. When deciding on a property outside of a city, be sure to tell the agents that you will not have a car. If selecting from a catalog, read the location details carefully, and confirm with the agent that train or bus service is available.

In most of Europe, public bus service is limited to local or regional service, and schedules and routes are available locally. By contrast, rail schedules and routes are available in any station, and usually in tourist information offices as well. Train schedules for all of Europe are compiled in the *Thomas Cook Continental Timetable*, available in Europe in Thomas Cook travel agencies and larger bookstores. (By mail in North America, contact Forsyth Travel Library, P.O. Box 2975, Dept. TCT, Shawnee Mission, Kansas 66201; tel: 800-367-7984 toll-free for orders using MasterCard or Visa.)

While weighing necessity and convenience, you should consider the various options for rail travel and car rental. Because there is such a variation in prices, especially in the car rental and leasing business, sound trip planning includes getting several quotes from several companies, under different approaches. One fact, however, is fundamental: Whether you plan to travel by rail or car, *always make your transportation arrangements before leaving for Europe.* This is for economic reasons as well as convenience.

Prices for Rail Travel

The decision here is between purchasing a rail pass or buying tickets as needed. This, of course, depends on whether you plan to travel and explore extensively or stay fairly close to your home base. To travel freely, even throughout a small country such as Austria or England, a pass is usually the most economical choice, especially if you plan to cover all of the country, or tour larger countries such as France and Italy.

The following table shows the prices for three rail-pass options. Prices are in U.S. dollars, per person, for unlimited travel for the duration shown. EurailPass is good only in Continental Europe and on certain ferries; Britrail is good only in the United Kingdom. The first figure for Britrail is the price for first-class coaches, the second is for second-class. Prices may change from year to year with currency exchange rates. These passes *must be purchased in the U.S. or Canada* before departure.

Duration

	15 days	*21 days*	*1 month*
Eurail	$340	$440	$550
Britrail	$250/$179	$370/$259	$470/$339

Britrail also offers the Flexipass, for visitors who plan to travel less often or less consistently. The two options are any four of eight days at $210/$149 and any eight of fifteen days at $310/$219 (the prices are first-class and second-class, respectively, and may vary from year to year).

♦ CAR RENTAL/LEASING

There are three types of organizations for renting a car in Europe. One type consists of regular rental companies such as Avis, Budget, Hertz, and National. Another comprises agencies that represent European and international car rental companies (including those based in the United States). A third group directly or indirectly represents automobile manufacturers in France. All these organizations present the consumer with a complex and confusing array of prices and programs. For the same type of car in the same country, there is a wide variation in rental price. For example, excluding the value-added tax (VAT), which prevails in Europe, we found the rental price per week of a subcompact Ford Fiesta in England to range between $115 and $238 (U.S.). A similar vehicle in France ranged from $156 to $272, depending on the company, while in Italy the spread was only from $177 to $219. The prices include liability insurance, but not collision coverage, which runs anywhere from $7 to $25 per day depending on the car; an alternative is to post a large deposit (from $500 to $1,000 or more), usually made by credit card. If there is no collision or other damage, the charge is not put through and your receipt is returned. If a collision occurs, each country has a different maximum liability, between $2,000 and $3,000 plus tax. Up to this maximum can be charged to your credit card.

This variation of prices clearly suggests that with a bit of comparison shopping, considerable money can be saved. This does not mean comparing only the big four (Avis, Budget, Hertz, and National) that have operations in Europe, but also their smaller competitors, which, like independent insurance agencies, can offer the best prices from among several rental businesses. Some of these companies state that they will match or better any price you have been quoted, so do not hesitate to tell them if you have been offered a lower price than they offer. The names of and contact information on these agencies are listed at the end of this chapter.

Value-Added Tax

All car rentals throughout Europe are subject to a VAT in addition to the base rental price. The amounts are substantial, and vary from country to country. From highest to lowest they are: France, 28 percent; Belgium, 25 percent; Austria, 21 percent; Italy, 18 percent; Portugal, 16 percent; Great Britain, 15 percent; West Germany, 14 percent; and Spain, 12 percent. The tax is applied to the rental price and mileage charge (if any). The only escape is for persons who take a car for twenty-one days or more (six months maximum) and enter into a purchase/buyback program offered by the auto manufacturers of France: Renault, Peugeot, and Citroën.

◆ CAR PURCHASE/BUYBACK PROGRAMS

These programs are available only in France, although after being picked up at any of several locations in France the vehicle can be driven into any European country. All arrangements are made before departure in a single package including full liability, comprehensive, and collision insurance.

Basically, you sign a contract to buy a new car of your choice, stipulating when and where it is to be picked up and when and where it will be returned. The price, including all insurance, is shown on the document (there is *no tax*). On the same document the company— Renault, Peugeot, and Citroën—executes an agreement to buy the car back on the date, and in the place, you have specified. The amount the company will pay is also shown on the document. You, the buyer, pay the *difference* between the purchase price and the buyback price. We took this approach in 1984 when we needed a car in Europe for eleven months (there is now a six-month limit). We picked up a new Renault 11 in Paris, traveled some 28,000 miles throughout Continental Europe, Scandinavia, and the United Kingdom, and returned the car in Brussels.

Having been pleased with the Renault operation, we repeated it for an eight-week period during 1988. First we called agencies to obtain their price lists. (Start this process at least two months before departure.) Because the total prices for a variety of models by specific time periods—twenty-two days, thirty-two days, thirty-seven days, and so forth are on the agency schedules or brochures, the exact cost is always clear. In our case, the financial terms looked like this:

Total price of car (including touring documents and insurance)	$11,350.00
Repurchase price	9,697.00
Cash payment (price minus repurchase)	1,653.00
Delivery charge if other than free city*	————
Return charge if other than free city*	————
Others	————
Total cash payment	$1,653.00

*Each company has a list of cities in which there is no charge for pickup and return. There is usually no extra charge for pickup at one free city and return at another.

For the first month in England we had a regular rental, arranged with A1 Fullers in London, and learned in the process that there is no advantage to booking direct with a European car rental agency. Because most British rental companies do not allow their cars to be taken to the Continent, we dropped the rental off in London took the train to Dover and the ferry to Calais. At the ferryport, we took possession of a new Renault 21. For the eight-week period the all-inclusive price per week worked out to $206.62. Fuel and oil were extra. The car was a mid-size sedan that got well over thirty-five miles per gallon. Prices have increased and the dollar has dropped since the time of our transaction, but under this program, a Renault 5 would currently run about $200 per week, tax and insurance included; the larger Renault 19 would cost about $285. By comparison, a Renault 5 or similar car in France can be rented from the major companies (Avis, Hertz, etc.) for between $235 and $275 per week, plus 28 percent tax and an addition $7 per day collision insurance, for a grand total of $350 to $400 per week. There are some seasonal variations with the regular rental companies, and you should always ask about discounts through such organizations as AAA and AARP. Nevertheless, for periods in Continental Europe exceeding three weeks, it is hard to beat purchase/buyback programs. Even when your destination is in another country, if you plan to stay a month or more, it could be worthwhile to pick up a purchase car in the French free-delivery city nearest your destination and drive on. Although you may need a car for less than the full twenty-two-day minimum, it could be cheaper to pay for the minimum period, rather than to rent at the regular price. These programs are slightly less convenient than simply picking up a car at an airport or railway station, but the savings could be significant—and you are the temporary owner of a brand-new car. Among the vacation rental agencies, B. & D. de Vogüe offers the Peugeot program, and Europa-Let offers the Renault Eurodrive program. Auto Europe provides excellent service on the Renault program (as well as regular low-cost rentals); Foremost Eurocar and Europe by Car are the other Renault agents. Renault USA can be contacted directly (although, strangely, may charge more than its agents). The Peugeot program is principally available through France Auto Vacances, and the Citroën program through Auto Europe and Europe by Car. Obviously, there is crossing of the lines among all three, but different companies offer different free French cities for pickup and return, so look over all three programs. Addresses for these companies are shown at the end of this chapter.

◆ PRICES: CAR VERSUS RAIL

There are so many variables that comparison is difficult, but the least common denominator provides a guide. For Britain, it is possible to rent a typical subcompact (Ford Fiesta) for about $150 per week plus 15 Percent VAT ($173 total.) Add an average of $7 per day for collision insurance and the total is $222 per week. A second-class Britrail Flexipass to travel eight days out of fifteen is the closest time comparison, and the price is about $220. If, however, there are two in your party, the Flexipasses come to $440, while the car is still $222. Obviously, the larger your party, the greater the savings in having a car. There is, of course, the cost of fuel—no small thing in Europe—but nevertheless, the car is more economical and more convenient. Fifteen-day regular Britrail passes for two total about $740; two weeks' rent on a Ford Escort should not exceed $460, including VAT and insurance, plus fuel.

On the Continent, the difference is not quite so marked, but a Renault 5, Peugeot 205, or compact Citroën should not run over $215 per week in France, VAT and insurance included (less for periods longer than three weeks). The total for two weeks' rental is $550, while two-week Eurail passes for two total $680. These prices will change over time, but they provide a basis of comparison.

An additional cost in driving is the toll freeways, especially in Italy (*autostrada*), France (*autoroute-peage*), and Spain (*autopista*). The amount adds up quickly, but there are always auxiliary routes if you are not in a great hurry.

Contact Information
For Eurail and Britrail: Any travel agency.
For U.S.-based car rentals, leasing, and purchase/buyback programs in Europe, the principal sources include:

AUTO EUROPE
P.O. Box 1097
Camden, Maine 04843
Tel: 800-223-5555 (U.S.)
      800-342-5202 (Maine)
      207-236-8235
      800-458-9503 (Canada)

Renault, Peugeot, and Citroën purchase/buyback programs and regular rentals

B. & D. DE VOGÜE TRAVEL SERVICES
1830 South Mooney Boulevard
Suite 113
Visalia, California 93277
Tel: 800-727-4748
    209-733-7119

Peugeot purchase/buyback program (for vacation rental clients)

CENTRAL RENT-A-CAR (U.K.)
Agent: New Haven Travel
        900 Chapel Street
        New Haven, Connecticut 06510
Tel: 800-243-1806 (U.S.)
    203-772-0060

CORTELL INTERNATIONAL
17310 Red Hill Avenue
Irvine, California 92714
Tel: 800-228-2535 (U.S.)
    714-724-1003

DRIVING ABROAD
420 Lexington Avenue
New York, New York 10017
Tel: 212-687-9240

Peugeot purchase/buyback program

EUROPA-LET, INC.
P.O. Box 3537
Ashland, Oregon 97250
Tel: 800-462-4486
    503-482-5806

Renault Eurodrive purchase/buyback program

EUROPE BY CAR
One Rockefeller Plaza
New York, New York 10020
Tel: 800-223-1516 (U.S.)
    212-581-3040

Renault, Peugeot, and Citroën purchase/buyback programs and regular rentals

> EURORENT RENT-A-CAR SERVICE
> 3332 N.E. 33rd Street
> Fort Lauderdale, Florida 33308
> Tel: 800-521-0643 (U.S.)

> FOREMOST EUROCAR
> 5430 Van Nuys Boulevard
> Van Nuys, California 91401
> Tel: 800-423-3111 (U.S.)
>   800-272-3299 (California)

Renault, Peugeot, and Citroën purchase/buyback programs and regular rentals

> FRANCE AUTO VACANCES
> 420 Lexington Avenue
> Suite 2560
> New York, New York 10170
> Tel: 212-867-2625 (call collect)

Peugeot purchase/buyback program

> GENERAL RENT-A-CAR
> P.O. Box 21547
> Fort Lauderdale, Florida 33325
> Tel: 800-463-8990

> ITS AND TOWN & COUNTRY CAR RENTAL
> 3332 N.E. 33rd Street
> Fort Lauderdale, Florida 33008
> Tel: 800-521-0643 (Continental Europe)
> Tel: 800-248-4350 (U.K.)

> KEMWELL
> 106 Calvert Street
> Harrison, New York 10528-3199
> Tel: 800-678-0678
>   800-468-0468 (Canada)
>   914-835-5454

RENAULT USA, INC.
650 First Avenue
New York, New York 10016
Tel: 800-221-1052

Renault purchase/buyback program

The major "regular" car rental agencies that offer European rentals are:

AVIS
800-328-6262
800-268-2310 (Canada)

BUDGET
800-472-3325

HERTZ
800-654-3001

NATIONAL (Europcar)
800-CAR-EURO

5

Austria

◆

◆ THE AGENCIES

AARP Travel Service (Vienna)
Four Star Living, Inc. (Burgenland—Vienna; Tirol)
Grand Circle Travel, Inc. (Baden—near Vienna)
Idyll, Ltd. (Salzburg Province)
Interhome, Inc. USA (throughout Austria)
Rent A Home International (some areas and cities)
Rent a Vacation Everywhere (RAVE) (some areas and cities)
Vacation Home Rentals (VHR) Worldwide (throughout Austria)
Villas International (throughout Austria)

◆ THE COUNTRY

This chapter covers vacation rentals available throughout Austria and in the cities of Innsbruck, Salzburg, and Vienna (Wien). Austria is by no means large, but traveling its east-west length is a long day's drive, even on the autobahns, between Bregenz at the west end and Vienna near the eastern border.

In any case, Austria is not a country to hurry through, for in summer or winter a rich variety of things to do and see can be found.

We traveled Austria from west to east by car, then drove south into Italy, visiting vacation rental companies and properties in the principal regions and cities that draw visitors throughout the year. Summer visitors are hikers, climbers, walkers, glacier skiers, and sightseers, along with lovers of music, the arts, and history. In winter, Austria is a sports

• Prague
CZECHOSLOVAKIA
LOWER AUSTRIA
• Vienna (Wien)
• Linz
Baden •
Munich
UPPER AUSTRIA
WEST GERMANY
Eisenstadt •
Lake Constance
(Bodensee)
• Salzburg
AUSTRIA
• Bregenz
VORARLBERG
ARLBERG
Kitzbühel •
BURGENLAND
Seefeld •
• Zell am See
LIECHTENSTEIN
MONTAFON
• Innsbruck
SALZBURG
STYRIA
(STEIERMARK)
HUNGARY
Bludenz •
TIROL
Schruns •
EAST TIROL
CARINTHIA
(KÄRNTEN)
• Graz
SWITZERLAND
• Lienz
Cortina d'Ampezzo
Villach •
• Klagenfurt
ITALY
YUGOSLAVIA
• Lubljana

paradise, offering an amazing array of ski areas, ranging from modern resorts to valley villages. Thus, most areas have two high seasons in terms of crowds and elevated prices—July to September and again in winter. Because the periods of peak, high, middle, and low seasons vary throughout the country, check the property catalogs carefully, or determine from the agent exactly the dates of the various pricing seasons for the property you are interested in. There can be a very marked difference in rental prices—rates drop by 50 percent or more in low seasons, and often along with other incentives such as "rent three weeks, get one free," and reduced rates for groups.

BEST TIMES OF YEAR TO VISIT. If you're not a skier, the best time to visit, considering weather, number of tourists, and lowest prices, are mid-April through early June, and October. From November through early December, although the warm days of autumn are over and the skiing has not begun, there are no crowds, low rates apply, and the changing seasons lend even more beauty to the mountain scenery. Hikers tramp the high country, bikers ride the mountain roads and trails, and anglers fish the Alpine lakes, returning each evening to their valley or mountain town apartments or hotels. If you plan to visit rural areas during this period, tell the agent you want a place above the valley fog. If the agency is dealing with a knowledgeable company, it will know where best to suggest. The peak ski season and highest prices are in the internationally well known resorts from mid-December through New Year's weekend, followed by lower rates in January; rates go higher again from mid-February through March.

GENERAL INFORMATION ABOUT RENTALS. The terms *holiday house, chalet,* and *bungalow* are the names applied to separate dwellings to be occupied by only the booking party. References to a *holiday flat* or *apartment* mean that there are other units in the building. The style of most rural or village apartment buildings is what Americans think of as chalet style—peaked but gently sloped roofs, balconies, and shuttered windows. Sheets, towels, and linens are usually provided, but check to be sure. Although relative to the total cost they are not a large item, heat and electricity are not usually included in the rent, so ask your agent for details.

Rental periods run from Saturday to Saturday, but other times can be arranged during low seasons. Rents are often reduced for stays of over three weeks, and there are some reductions for older persons and larger parties. Some bargains are possible, especially in off-seasons; be sure to ask about the possibilities.

WHERE TO STAY: Vacation rentals are available throughout the country, but it makes sense to locate reasonably near the places that are of special interest to you. If you want to explore the entire country, plan to rent in two locations. From spring through fall the Vorarlberg, Tirol, or Salzburg provinces offer numerous good rentals in the west, and Carinthia, Styria, and the Vienna area are best for an eastern or southeastern stay.

Choices for a skiing vacation are almost as numerous, but additional factors should be considered. Many of the ski resorts are communities created to cater to skiers and are basically clusters of hotels, apartments, ski shops, gift shops, discos, and restaurants. As an Austrian friend noted, these communities "have no life of their own." He meant that outside of the ski season, or when summer tourists are not riding the gondolas, the towns virtually close down. They lack a permanent population and usually have little history. Prices of accommodations, meals, lift tickets, and entertainment are higher than those in villages in which skiing and tourism are important but not the entire economy. The resort towns are the glamour skiing spots, and what you wear may be as important as how you ski. Resort hotel and restaurant managements often discourage commuters—skiers who stay in the less pricey valley towns and drive or take the bus to the resort town ski runs for the day. As average skiers of modest means, we'd not only prefer staying in a live town, we'd also capitalize on the great slopes that rise around such towns, usually far less crowded than those of the more fashionable resorts.

As for the cities, Salzburg is a good choice, and although Vienna is an important city in which to spend some time, it could be visited from a rural home base located almost anywhere in eastern Austria. Innsbruck is an easy city to deal with, but it can also be visited from an apartment or chalet situated somewhere in the Tirol, Vorarlberg, or Salzburg provinces.

◆ THE REGIONS

We explored the five regions that are the principal destinations of visitors to Austria. These regions were also recommended by the national tourist authority, and by American and Austrian friends who live there. We visited before the ski season, but viewed the regions from the perspectives of both skiers and summer travelers.

Vorarlberg Province

ENVIRONS AND ACCOMMODATIONS. This westernmost province has it all: Lake Constance (Bodensee), Liechtenstein, and Switzerland on the west border; the high valleys, peaks, and villages of the Bregenz Woods, which rise eastward from the lake toward the great mountains and ski resorts of the Arlberg; and the valley of the Montafon, with its historic villages, Alpine meadows, great peaks, streams, and lakes.

We stayed in the Montafon region in a pleasant apartment in the village of Schruns (pop. 4,000), one of perhaps two-hundred vacation rental properties in Vorarlberg Province, most of which are handled by Villas International, representing PEGO. The oldest and most personally managed rental company in Austria, PEGO has its main office in Bludenz, Vorarlberg. Owner Peter Godula and his staff know the area and the properties very well.

The twelve villages scattered along the River Ill in the Montafon region have an aggregate permanent population of 17,000, and anyone of them is an ideal place to stay in either summer or winter. Dozens of gondolas, cog railways, and chair lifts rise from the valley floor into spectacular mountains, making the area not only one of Austria's best ski areas but also affording access to the peaks and high country meadows and lakes to summer hikers and climbers. Although there are good ski schools, and even tennis schools, this is not one of the high-fashion resort areas; it is more relaxed, more real, and more modestly priced.

The favorite hotel and café of Ernest Hemingway, who enjoyed skiing in the Montafon Valley, are still pointed out to visitors to the village of Schruns. You won't go wrong staying in any of these villages; just specify the Montafon. (See "Location and transportation" below).

Elsewhere in Vorarlberg are apartments in small villages in the Alpine meadows of the Bregenz Woods (Bregenzerwald), beautifully located for lovers of nature, scenery, and tranquillity, all generally modestly priced, and a few in the high Arlberg country toward the east. The latter are best for skiing holidays rather than summer visits. Although there are properties in the area of Lake Constance and along the Rhine, we recommend the Montafon Valley or Bregenz Woods (not the city of Bregenz) areas.

LOCATION AND TRANSPORTATION. Vorarlberg occupies extreme western Austria. The main cities are Bregenz and Bludenz, but don't miss the ancient and interesting town of Feldkirch. Within a few hours by car or train are Innsbruck to the east, Zurich (Switzerland) to the west, and Munich (West Germany) to the north. Mainline rail service is excellent, and there is even service connecting the mainline at Bludenz and

Schruns, about halfway up the Montafon Valley. A car is not essential, but it opens up vistas otherwise not accessible. Driving time between Montafon villages and the high Arlberg ski resorts is about an hour. If you want to be near a railroad station, be sure to specify this.

PRICES. Rents run the gamut in Vorarlberg, and are dictated not so much by the quality and size of the accommodation as its location. For example, our three-room apartment near the center of Schruns (a four-star hotel equivalent) runs about $500 per week in high ski and summer seasons (December, March, and July through August) and $240 in the low season months of January, April, May, and October. It accommodates four persons (two on a studio bed in the living room), but even if occupied by one couple, the cost is $71 per night in high season and $34 per night in low season. This price is average for the province, but is less than you would pay in the winter resorts of the Arlberg area. By comparison, a double room in the four-star Hotel Illpark in Feldkirch is about $110 per night. In Lech, one of the fashionable ski resorts in the Arlberg, most hotels require at least *demi-pension* (two meals) in high season; in five-star hotels this runs from $240 to $600 per night for two. Even at half that during off-season, the smallest room is much above the price of the apartment in Schruns.

ADVANCE BOOKING TIME. For December, July, and August—six months. For January, February, and September—four months. For the rest of the year—up to two months.

Tirol

ENVIRONS AND ACCOMMODATIONS. Tirol, the most well-known region outside of Austria, adjoins Vorarlberg on the west, and shares with it the mountains and ski areas of the Arlberg; to the east is the province of Salzburg. Tirol is described as the heart of the Austrian Alps. Although it is hard to pick out a single most spectacular area, what with all of the mountain scenery in Austria, Tirol must be it.

Chalets, holiday houses, and apartments can be found in virtually every village and town in Tirol, with more dotting the high meadowlands. The largest selections are offered by PEGO and its U.S. agent, Villas International, followed by Interhome, but all the agencies (except AARP and Idyll) should be contacted for information about properties here.

Because it is better known internationally than neighboring Vorarlberg, and because Innsbruck has been the site of two Winter Olympics, Tirol attracts more foreign visitors than other parts of the country, except

Vienna. With this long-running popularity have come more crowds and elevated prices during high seasons.

At the suggestion of an Austrian friend we stayed in an apartment, one of six in a large chalet-style building, in the center of the resort/spa village of Seefeld. At an altitude of 4,000 feet, the town lies in a wide mountain-ringed saddle on a plateau high above the broad Inn River valley and is only twenty minutes from Innsbruck. The Nordic races of the Winter Olympics were run here, evidence of the village's importance as a winter sports center. The terrain that makes it a fine area for cross-country skiing also makes it perfect for summer activities such as hiking, golf, horseback riding, bicycling, tennis, swimming, or just loafing. Alpine chair lifts and gondolas can take you to country even higher and to scenery even more spectacular. Seefeld is just one of many such villages in Tirol—it's hard to go wrong wherever you decide to stay. Apartments are also available in Innsbruck, a beautiful, small, but international city, central to all the Tirol. Study a map and a good guidebook on Austria, and obtain material from the listed agencies.

LOCATION AND TRANSPORTATION. The major town is Innsbruck. Within a three-to-four-hour drive or train trip are Zurich and Bludenz to the west, Salzburg and Linz to the east, Munich to the north, and Bolzano (Italy) to the south. The main east-west autobahn and the mainline railroad between Zurich and Vienna run through the center of Tirol. Spur rail lines serve many villages, so if you are not planning to rent or lease a car, find out from the agent about rail service to the community in which you'd like to stay.

PRICES. All other factors being equal, prices in Tirol run a little higher than in the Montafon Valley and Bregenz Woods areas of neighboring Vorarlberg Province. As usual, prices in resort villages are higher. Villages in the Arlberg and close to Innsbruck command generally higher prices. For example, Seefeld, where we stayed, fits both criteria for higher prices: It's a summer and a winter resort, and it's close to Innsbruck. Our small, stylish, nicely appointed flat (a four-star equivalent) rents for about $420 per week in summer and winter high seasons, $300 in winter low season (January and March), and $200 in spring and fall low seasons (May and October). As this illustrates, if you are looking for modest prices, go in the off-season months. If you are considering a hotel in the area, plan on spending $500 to $1,000 for a week's stay, plus eating all meals out. If you will have a car and are looking for more remote tranquillity, tell the agent that you want to be in a smaller, nonresort village or a rural chalet or apartment. A simple two-bedroom holiday house, perhaps on a high country farm, can be rented for $200 to $250 a week year-round. You can count on its being neat and clean.

ADVANCE BOOKING TIME. Summer and winter high seasons—six months. For mid-seasons—four months. Low seasons (January, March, May, and October)—up to two months.

Salzburg Province

ENVIRONS AND ACCOMMODATIONS. East of the Tirol lies this large province, most of it mountainous, except near its northern border, where the mountains give way to the rolling hills of West Germany. Despite the beauty of the lake country and the rugged Alpine core, it is the city of Salzburg that attracts the majority of visitors. Birthplace of Mozart, Salzburg is a center for music, art, and learning, as well as a city of spring and summer festivals (Easter, Whitsuntide, Mozart Week). It is an outstanding city in which to stay, not only because of its own character but also because it is a good base for day trips into the surrounding area.

To the east of Salzburg, just a matter of an hour or so by car, bus, or rail, lies an area of mountain lakes and lakeside villages well worth making excursions to, or staying in for a week or so. Whether you stay in Salzburg and travel to the countryside or vice versa is entirely a matter of personal choice. The province and the city are dotted with rental accommodations, available through all the agencies listed at the beginning of this chapter, except for AARP Travel Service and Great Circle Travel (Seefeld only).

West of Salzburg, Zell am See is an ideal town to stay in and just east of Salzburg, it is hard to go wrong in selecting any of these unspoiled lake region villages. The best resources seem to be Villas International (representing PEGO) and Interhome, with rentals in no fewer than eight villages in the area.

Traveling south from Salzburg toward Werfen, the Salzach River valley narrows as one moves deeper into the Alps, changing from an open pastoral area in the north to a more narrow valley, squeezed by the mountains. There are four villages in which Idyll, Ltd., has apartments, each typical of the area and of Austria: neat, charming, and old. Kuchi and Golling are in the lower, wider part of the valley; Werfen and Bischofshofen are more Alpine, but both are very scenic. The towns are small enough that a rental car is not essential, and all are on a mainline railway, served often by trains to and from Salzburg. Idyll's properties here are part of a program in which one or two weeks are spent in an apartment in Austria and one or two weeks are spent in another country (usually the United Kingdom). For more information, see the listing for Idyll in Chapter 3.

LOCATION AND TRANSPORTATION. The main city is Salzburg (pop. 150,000), reached within two hours by car or train from almost anywhere in the province or from Innsbruck. Major cities within five hours' drive include Vienna, Munich, and Linz. Toward the south, a visit to Austria's southern regions of Styria and Carinthia is worthwhile, and round-trip journeys of three days or so to the Ljubljana (Yugoslavia) or Trieste (Italy) make for a complete change of scene.

The main east-west autobahn between Zurich and Vienna runs through part of Salzburg Province and through West Germany for a hundred miles or so. However, because the other main highways are all excellent, there is no need to stay on the autobahn. Many villages are served by rail, so if you are not planning to rent or lease a car, find out about rail service from the agent.

PRICES. Rents vary widely, and are generally higher in the city of Salzburg. We stayed in a modest, well-located, one-bedroom apartment ten minutes by car or bus from the heart of Salzburg, for which the rent is about $375 per week year-round. A typical apartment in the lake region for two to four persons runs about $320 per week in July, August, and the Christmas season, and $220 per week the rest of the year. If you stay in the city of Salzburg, bear in mind that it is old and unusual, like so many cities in Europe; don't let the outside appearances of most of the apartment buildings concern you.

ADVANCE BOOKING TIME. Summer and winter high seasons—six months. For mid-seasons—four months. Low seasons (January, March, May, and October)—up to two months. Salzburg during Easter and festivals—six months.

Carinthia (Kärnten) and Styria (Steiermark)

ENVIRONS AND ACCOMMODATIONS. These southeastern regions are the least known by North Americans, probably because skiing has brought world fame to Vorarlberg and Tirol; Mozart, music, and history have made Salzburg a world destination; and sophisticated Vienna has a wealth of good reasons to be one of Europe's most popular cities. Yet these regions encompass the southern slopes of the Alps, and Carinthia is even influenced by the marine climate of the Adriatic Sea. They indeed have the reputation of being the warmest and sunniest regions of Austria, although still offering rugged mountain beauty, excellent skiing, and some of the most fascinating cities, villages, castles, and churches in Austria. But in addition there is the virtue of early springs; long, warm, and sunny summers; and extended autumns, especially in Carinthia.

Although Graz, the chief city of Styria, is the second largest city in the country, the entire area seems unhurried, uncrowded, and un-discovered. Prices of virtually everything—from hotels to restaurant meals to holiday chalets to groceries—are less expensive than in the provinces to the north. Maybe it's the influence of Yugoslavia along the southern border.

The most appealing area in which to have a home base in Carinthia is in the lake country in the vicinity of the capital city, twelfth-century Klagenfurt. Many of this area's rentals are on one or another of the many lakes, and those that aren't are near one. Fish from the Wörther See, Faaker See, Ossiacher See, and other lakes in the area are the specialties on the menus in the restaurants along the lakeshores, as well as being amply available in local markets.

Styria is a less popular destination, a bit less spectacular than Carinthia, with lower mountains and fewer pasturelands and wooded forests, but it is a good area for laid-back vacations with many interesting itineraries.

The best source of rentals in these regions seems to be Villas International/Pego, followed by the Swiss company Interhome.

LOCATION AND TRANSPORTATION. The main city of Carinthia is Klagenfurt and the main city of Styria is Graz. Especially pleasant lake district communities are Villach, Magdalenensee, Seeboden, Weissen See (an Alpine lake with good summer swimming), Spittal, Velden, Maria-Wörth (warmest weather, best sunshine), Falkertsee (for winter skiing as well as summer), and Pörtschach. Within a four-hour radius by highway or rail from the approximate center of the two regions are the cities of Vienna to the northeast, Salzburg to the northwest, Innsbruck to the west, Ljubljana and Jesenice (Yugoslavia) and Trieste (Italy) to the south. If you are planning to drive deeper into Italy, perhaps relocating your home base, and if you enjoy unusual mountains and don't mind tightly winding roads, and if the weather is decent, we suggest that you go via Lienz (East Tirol), south to Cortina d'Ampezzo (Italy) and across the passes through the Dolomites to the *autostrada* south of Bolzano. A detailed map will also show a remote road through the mountains to Venice.

Mainline railways intersect at Villach, servicing the cities noted above. There is extra service between Villach and Klagenfurt, but not all the smaller communities are served. There is public bus transportation, but a car is preferable.

PRICES. Because this part of Austria tends more toward being a summer vacation area (although there are lesser known but excellent ski resorts), the high season is usually summer, peaking in July and August; some properties are unavailable between November and March. The best time to go is in May or between late September and late October, when rates are more modest and areas are less crowded. For example, a pleasant typical lakeside apartment for four in the Carinthian lake district runs about $225 per week in those months and $550 per week in the peak months of July and August. As a general rule, in the mountain villages in ski areas, the peak season is December; mid-season is November, February, and March; and low season is usually November and January.

ADVANCE BOOKING TIME. Summer and winter high seasons—six months. For April through May and October—two months. For January through March and November through December—up to two months.

Vienna and Vicinity (Lower Austria and Burgenland)

ENVIRONS AND ACCOMMODATIONS. Vienna has been written about in everything from spy novels to books on history, art, architecture, music, and politics—even in dozens of travel guides. The only thing left to report is how to find a city apartment or a home base chalet or flat in the vicinity. *Vicinity* means close enough to make easy day trips to the city, which means one of the easternmost of Austria's nine states, Lower Austria, or Burgenland. The advantage of staying somewhere outside of Vienna is purely economic; there is no particular excitement in the landscape, which is mostly an area of low hills, flatlands, vineyards, farms, and market towns.

All of the agencies shown at the beginning of this chapter, save Grand Circle, have rentals in Vienna; some, especially Interhome and Villas International (representing PEGO), also have properties in the surrounding area, within an hour by car or rail from the center of Vienna.

AARP Travel's apartments in Vienna are in a single building, and can only be rented as part of an overall tour package, combined with a stay in an apartment in London. Your needs are carefully looked after by the resident owner or manager, and the programs cater mainly to travelers fifty years of age and up.

Grand Circle Travel's apartments are at Baden, twenty miles south of Vienna, and can be rented only as part of an inclusive, semi-independent "Live Abroad" package, principally for senior citizens.

As for Baden, it is an ideal out-of-Vienna location, and standard rentals can usually be arranged through several other companies; ask the agent, or scan the catalogs you receive.

LOCATION AND TRANSPORTATION. Vienna, due south of Warsaw, is the easternmost major city of Western Europe (except Athens), and with the proper papers a journey to Prague (Czechoslovakia) or Budapest (Hungary) is only a four-hour trip by car or train. Salzburg is four hours to the west, and a day trip south into the province of Styria and the city of Graz and return is feasible. Vienna is on mainline rail routes to all major cities and the towns in between. In the area, it's easy to travel to and from most of the towns of Burgenland and Lower Austria. Among all the regions of Austria, this area least requires a rented or leased car.

PRICES. Among major European cities, Vienna has prices among the lowest overall. This does not mean that rates for accommodations and food are low, just that they are considerably less than those in Paris, London, Zurich, and Rome, all else being equal. Rents in the outlying towns are not particularly lower than those in Vienna, but you get much more for the shilling. A two-bedroom house for four persons on a farm near Halbturn or half of a rural duplex for four in Schwarzenbach (very near Vienna) rents for $300 to $400 per week. Apartments in the city are usually in big-city apartment buildings, and typically rent for $350 to $400 per week for a studio or one-bedroom flat, with deluxe apartments in the $500-to-$700-per-week range. There is very little seasonal change, but often rates are lower in the high season months of July and August when all the citizens of Europe seem to have gone elsewhere on "holiday." When dealing with an agent, ask if there are seasonal rates.

6

France

♦

♦ THE AGENCIES

AARP Travel Service (Cannes, Paris)
At Home Abroad (Avignon country, Côte d'Azur, the Dordogne; some in Brittany and Normandy)
B. & D. de Vogüe (throughout France; Paris)
Blake's Vacations (throughout France)
Chez Vous (southwest France: Dordogne, Lot, and Garonne valleys)
Coast to Coast Resorts (throughout France)
Eastone Overseas Accommodations (throughout France; Paris)
Europa-Let, Inc. (Riviera/Côte d'Azur, southwest France; Paris)
Families Abroad, Inc. (Provence, Riviera, southwest France; Paris)
Four Star Living, Inc. (throughout France; Paris)
France Grandes Vacances (Riviera/Côte d'Azur, Atlantic Coast)
The French Experience (throughout France; Paris)
French Home Rentals (southwest France; some Côte d'Azur, Provence)
Hometours International (Paris)
Orsava, Inc. (throughout France)
Overseas Connection (Côte d'Azur, Savoy Alps; some in Brittany and Normandy)
Rent A Home International (throughout France)
Rent A Vacation Everywhere (RAVE) (Côte d'Azur; Paris)
Riviera Holidays (Côte d'Azur; Paris)
Vacances en Campagne (Brittany, Loire, Normandy, southwest France/ Dordogne)
Vacation Home Rentals (VHR) Worldwide (southern France, Maritime Alps, Côte d'Azur; Paris)

Villa Leisure (Côte d'Azur)
Villas International (throughout France; Paris)

♦ THE COUNTRY

Equaling, or perhaps surpassing, the United Kingdom in number and variety of vacation rentals, France offers something for everyone—from simple, inexpensive rural houses (*gîtes*) to elegant châteaus, from all kinds of apartments in Paris to villas along the French Riviera and chalets in the ski resorts of the Alps. Unlike Austria or Switzerland, this is not a country that can reasonably be explored from a single home base. Either plan rental periods in two separate areas or decide where you wish most to visit and settle there. In any event, it is safe to say that wherever you decide to stay there will be a rental property available.

BEST TIMES OF YEAR TO VISIT. It is almost impossible to state the best times of year to visit—it depends on where you want to be and what you want to do. However, the proclivity of the French to take vacations in August and, to a far lesser extent, in July suggests some patterns if you must visit in summer. The coastal and mountain vacation areas are crowded in July, and especially in August, and prices are at their peak. The cities, however, are vacated by their citizens during those months and are left to the tourists. As the head of the largest rental agency in Paris told us, these months are good times to visit the city because hotels and apartments have lost many business clients to the beaches. However, another Parisian wondered who would want to come to Paris if the French were gone and only the tourists were left. Our view is that a visit to France—in fact, to anywhere in Europe—should be avoided in August. Fall and spring are the best times; and as for skiing, avoid December, and go in January instead.

GENERAL INFORMATION ABOUT RENTALS. In the French rental business the term *villa* means a detached house that may, but not necessarily, be above average in quality, size, and amenities. We often think of a villa as being located in pleasant suburbs or in a resort or holiday area. In common usage in France (and elsewhere in Europe), the term can mean a freestanding house, large or small, and it can be either a private, single-family place or a large one divided into several apartments. The important thing is not to let the term conjure up an image of what it is not; rather, the description and standard need to be weighed just as with any other rental property. In Alpine villages and ski resorts, the term *chalet* usually applies to a villa distinguished by sloping roofs, balconies, and shutters. *Bungalow* is a term often applied to a single-family dwelling, and is the word to use if the place you want is a modest, freestanding, private house. *Apartments* and *flats* are the same as in the United States and Canada, and the words are used interchangeably. Technically a flat is all on one floor, so if for any reason you must have a one-floor apartment, be sure to avoid confusion by specifying what you mean. Apartments in villas, chalets, and châteaus, as well as in the larger buildings we often think of, are available. *Château*, originally meaning a feudal castle, has come to mean an exceptionally large, and usually elegant, country home. A *gîte* (pronounced "zheet") is a privately owned farm or rural village house, thousands of which are now furnished and equipped for short-term renting.

Among rental properties available in France, it is the 20,000 or so *gîtes* enrolled in the organization called Gîtes Ruraux de France that, as a group, are unusual. Along with *gîtes* that are not included in the organization, they offer the possibility of truly experiencing French rural life, not only from the habitation itself, but from doing the marketing, buying farm and dairy products from the owners or the neighbors, and in myriad other ways.

The *gîtes* tend to be modest in character and in price, a virtue that, along with the exposure to rural tranquillity, makes them desirable and popular rentals. There are literally thousands of them, and the history of their availability for rent is interesting (and bears upon renting one).

THE GÎTES RURAUX DE FRANCE: With decreasing rural populations and the concurrent abandonment of farms and village homes, France needed to take steps to avoid the ultimate dissolution of traditional rural life and the rich cultures of centuries past. A way of life was threatened, and somehow needed to be restored and maintained. At the same time, there was the fear that tourism, a means of revitalizing rural areas, would indeed mean uncontrolled modern development, as is evident in the high rises and fashionable hotels and resorts along the Mediterranean coast. Controlled development of tourism was the key, and the answer was the establishment of an organization that brought together the French government, local and regional authorities, and representatives of rural property owners and agricultural interests.

Named the Fédération Nationale des Gîtes Ruraux de France, this quasi-governmental nonprofit organization ensures that the cultural riches of rural France, and its attractions—from the cliffs of Brittany to the vineyards of Bordeaux and the peaks of the Alps—are available to travelers without the usual alteration of the countryside.

Owners of rental *gîtes* who belong to the federation accept its rigid standards and, in exchange, are assisted in many ways by the federation.

The standards are set forth in the charter, and include such requirements as:

1. The best of welcomes is to be offered, and everything must be done to make the guests' stay agreeable.

2. Minimum fittings and furnishings (include electric light in all rooms, a sink with running water and an indoor lavatory with flush toilet and ventilation, shower, and washbasin; and shuttered or curtained windows. Walls must be painted or papered, and floors must be covered with tiles or easily cleaned materials. The interior must be kept clean and in a perfect state of hygiene. Each bedroom must contain at least a full-size bed, a table, two chairs, a wardrobe, and preferably a closet and wall cupboard; the kitchen must contain the fixtures necessary for a family, cooking facilities, a sink, closet, and wall cupboard. Shopping must be made easy for the renters.

3. Limited quantities of water, electricity, and heating fuel must be included in the rent.

4. The front of the house must be decorated with care.

5. The toilet must be well situated, well lit, ventilated, and hygienically installed.

6. The premises will be thoroughly cleaned and ventilated after each occupancy.

7. Prices will be established in advance, and will include everything. These prices must be filed by each _gîte_ owner with the respective Relais Departmental des Gîtes, and subsequently adhered to.

8. The sign GÎTE DE FRANCE supplied by the federation shall be affixed to the _gîte_.

There are a few other regulations, and all are pretty well observed, but be forewarned that these are standards for relatively humble rural houses and cottages, not country villas or châteaus. The range of quality and comfort can be determined by observing the federation ratings—from one to three ears of corn (heads of wheat, from the North American view), much as hotels are rated by stars.

Booking a gîte, part 1: One of the benefits (or, perhaps, obstacles) that _gîte_ owners derive from the federation is a reservation process handled through regional booking offices (Relais Departmental des Gîtes) located throughout France. Unfortunately, this makes booking a very complex process, especially from across the Atlantic.

First, write the French Government Tourist Office closest to you (see Appendix C), request the list of Booking Service Offices of the Relais Departmental des Gîtes Ruraux de France, and find the one that serves the region you plan to visit. Second, notify that office that you want to rent a _gîte_. Specify the community or area you want to be in, the rating (one, two, or three ears of corn), the dates of your arrival and departure, the number of adults and children in your group, and that you need bed sheets and house linens. Enclose an international reply coupon (available at U.S. and Canadian post offices). After a time you *might* receive a suggestion of three possible *gîtes*. Write back to the same Relais, stating that you wish to rent. Reference the properties in the order you prefer and confirm the dates and number in your party (don't forgot another international reply coupon). If one of the *gîtes* is available, you will receive two copies of a rental agreement showing the owner's name and the amount of deposit required, in French francs. Obtain a draft in French francs from your bank in the exact amount stipulated, made payable to the *gîte* owner, and send it with one signed copy of the rental agreement to the Relais department. A final obstacle is that the correspondence and contracts you will receive will be in French; it is also possible that your request in English will not be answered at all (depending on the office to which you write). Fortunately for owners and vacationers alike, there is another way.

Booking a gîte, part 2: The alternative is to book a *gîte* through one of the agencies that specialize in these rural French properties. This may be more costly than booking through the federation, but the agency people have gone through the effort of finding good properties, preparing descriptions, and making them known to the traveling public. They are the ones, too, who have to deal with the world of currency fluctuations and getting your funds translated to francs and into the right hands. We think it's worthwhile to follow this route *unless* you are in France during the off-season without accommodation and can simply find a *gîte* on your own. In that case work out the details of the rental (the owner will be bound by the same rules that apply on rentals through the regional office), or walk into one of the booking offices in a Relais department and make the arrangements on the spot.

The best agencies for booking a *gîte* are (in descending order) The French Experience, B. & D. de Vogüe, At Home Abroad, Vacances en Campagne, Chez Vous, France Grandes Vacances. Others are Blake's Vacations, Coast to Coast Resorts, and Orsava, Inc.

WHAT IS AND IS NOT SUPPLIED: In most Paris apartments, all bed linens and towels are supplied, and utilities are included, as they are in most deluxe properties. In moderately priced apartments and villas, be sure to determine if these are included; it is not a universal policy. In most farm and rural properties, *gîtes*, and others, linens and towels are rarely included, but can be arranged for in advance (through your agent), possibly at an additional charge. A *coffeepot* to the French may be either an espresso maker or cone filter, but it is not predictable which one. If you are coffee drinkers, carry instant coffee for emergencies (but buy a small filter cone, filters, and coffee just in case).

THE SEASONS AND PRICES: In France, as it is throughout Europe, *high season* is usually considered to be the summer months. *Middle* or *shoulder seasons* occur during spring and autumn, and *low season* is during the winter. However, large tourists crowds and prices of rentals, hotel rooms, and restaurant meals do not always conform to the calendar seasons. For example, the high season for large crowds and prices on the French Riviera is in summer, peaking in August, but in the ski resorts of the French Alps, such as Chamonix, Megève and Courchevel, the high season is midwinter, peaking in December. Some areas that are popular as ski resorts and also as summer resorts may have two periods of higher prices.

To deal with the presentation of seasonal prices in brochures and price lists, rental agencies representing properties in more than one town or region almost always head their price list columns with *High* conforming to summer, *Middle* conforming to spring and autumn, and *Low* in winter. You may find, however, that a price for a particular property may be higher in the Low column than it is in the High. The reverse is also found, and usually means that the property is in an area where summer is either so hot or so rainy that few tourists visit, so the demand and prices are low. Thus, the vagaries of pricing affect southern latitude beach areas as well as winter resorts. It is important, therefore, to look closely at rates, surveying prices for all the seasons, and pay special attention to some of the seasonal idioscyncrasies of such areas as the Riviera. Christmas and Easter seasons, for example, tend to show upward price spikes in the southern climes.

◆ THE REGIONS

For purposes of identifying areas of interest to vacationers, France is variously divided into anything from ten to twenty-five regions. This guide carves the country into the nine most prominent vacation destination areas.

One of the great advantages to renting a home base is that the surrounding area can be thoroughly explored, but it is also important to feel free to roam beyond your immediate surroundings. This means, of course, that it is not necessary to choose one style of vacation to the exclusion of others. A trip to Paris from Brittany or Burgundy isn't that difficult, nor is a visit to Pisa or Florence from the Côte d'Azur, or an excursion into Spain from the Languedoc or southwest France. But again, don't forget that France is a relatively large country, from 600 to 700 highway miles (975 to 1,150 km) between the north and the south and almost that far between east and west, so choose carefully the area you want to be in (or rent in two locations).

Paris and Environs
(Île-de-France)

In Paris, as in any major city, prices are high and, in general, you get what you pay for. That is, if you rent an apartment (or hotel) for a modest cost, you'll be in a modest accommodation; more often than not, Parisian standards for "modest" are something less than those in North America. Yet simply being in Paris is worth a great deal, and older buildings—with high ceilings, narrow hallways, small kitchens, unusual elevators, and oddly adapted twentieth-century bathrooms installed in eighteenth-century buildings—are all part of the scene. On the other hand, it is difficult to find in the United States or Canada the elegance of some of the Parisian apartments available for short-term rent.

ENVIRONS AND ACCOMMODATIONS. The Île-de-France encompasses a region rich in outstanding attractions within easy day trips from central Paris and accessible by bus, train, and car (although a car is usually more trouble than it's worth if you are staying in the city). Plan trips to Fontainebleau, Versailles, Dampierre, Melun, and Chartres. High-speed trains make Brussels, the Loire Valley, the Normandy coast, and even Bordeaux accessible on excursions of two days or so.

Although there is an attraction to staying near Paris, staying *in* Paris, if even for a week, is one of the important experiences in a visit to France. One problem for first-time visitors is deciding where in the city to stay.

There are apartments available in almost every arrondissement (district) of the city, and their locations bear as much upon the rent as do the size and standards. To determine where you want to stay, study a good Paris map and a reputable Paris guidebook that describes the various areas of the city; that is, what they are like in terms of style, age, and atmosphere. You will see that the famous points of reference—the Eiffel Tower, the Arc de Triomphe, the Louvre, Montmartre, the Church of the Sacré-Coeur, Pompidou Center, Notre Dame Cathedral—are spread widely throughout Paris, but because the metro (subway) and bus systems are very good, you need not make a decision based solely on being near one of these landmarks. So, since you can easily visit one part of the city from another, the important thing is to select an area where you'd like to be on a day-to-day basis.

If it is to be your first visit, or if you are not committed to some special place from a former visit, the best approach is to let someone who knows the city decide for you, within the parameters you set.

In either case, outline your interests: Do you prefer to stay in old Paris or new? Are you more interested in shopping in the flea markets and antique stores or in the designer boutiques and fashionable stores? Do you want to be close to some of the finer restaurants, or will the more modest ones do? Do you prefer to be in an area popular with North Americans and other tourists, or would you enjoy a more "Parisian" part of Paris? Do you plan to concentrate your time along any special lines, such as historic art, modern art, music and opera, architecture, palaces, and other notable places? None of these preferences exclude the others, but a definite leaning helps an agent find the best location for you, or helps you choose an area from a Paris guidebook. The final factor is your ideal budget (and an absolute maximum rent you are willing to pay).

Be careful about selecting a location simply because you have heard of it—the chances are that everyone else has, too, making it "touristy" and high priced. For example, if you stay just off the Champs Elysées near the Arc de Triomphe in the 8th arrondissement, you will find a premium locale rich with shops and stores and restaurants, close to one of the Prisunic department stores (which also sell groceries), theaters, an easy walk from the Seine and the Eiffel Tower, and near bus and metro stations. But, because of these factors, and because tourists know the names Champs Elysées and Arc de Triomphe, rents in the 8th arrondissement are high, as are prices for very ordinary food in the very ordinary tourist restaurants that line the boulevard. Apartments farther out, in the 16th arrondissement, for example, or in less well known areas, will run 20 percent to 40 percent below those in the 8th, all else being equal. Again, unless you know Paris, see how reputable agencies match locales and prices to your preferences.

LOCATION AND TRANSPORTATION. Paris is the hub of France; all roads and railway lines run there, creating a city difficult to drive in, but overall making it easy to go anywhere else. A car is unnecessary and the public transportation system is usually quite adequate, even if you are going outside of Paris proper. If you will have a car, be sure to advise the rental agency that you must have some sort of parking available.

PRICES. Hotel room rates in Paris are high, with two- and three-star hotels running from $100 to $150 per night, four-star hotels at $200, and five-star hotels beginning around $250. Thus, despite apartment rents beginning at $450 per week for a modest studio, around $600 for a well located studio or one-bedroom, and ranging up to $2,000 per week for the more elegant apartments, rentals remain a bargain at about 60 percent of the rate at a hotel of comparable standards, and rentals offer much more room. Also, because of the high prices of restaurant meals, much money can be saved by eating at least some meals in the apartment. We found grocery stores easy to locate and food prices comparable to those in most U.S. cities.

ADVANCE BOOKING TIME. Although the turnover rate of apartments is faster than that of rural properties, there is an ever-increasing demand, and many foreign corporations are renting apartments for their personnel rather than putting them up in expensive hotels. Our recommendation, therefore, is that you book at least three months, preferably four, in advance for any time of year except midwinter.

THE AGENCIES. Paris Sejour Reservations (PSR) is the largest rental company in Paris, and we are impressed not only with its overall operation but also with its ability to work with American clientele. The PSR agent in the United States is B. & D. de Vogüe, a reputable organization that specializes in apartments in Paris. Five very good agencies you should also contact are Europa-Let, Families Abroad, Rent A Vacation Everywhere (RAVE), Vacation Home Rentals (VHR) Worldwide, and Villas International. And for a small but very nice selection, contact French Home Rentals, which will send good descriptions of the properties and their locations.

Brittany and Normandy

ENVIRONS AND ACCOMMODATIONS. These are the provinces of northwestern France, Normandy meeting the English Channel to the north, and Brittany jutting into the Atlantic. The region's coast is punctuated by craggy cliffs and white sand beaches, with an interior of wooded hills and farmlands. All of Brittany and Normandy can be explored from a base anywhere in this region, although we recommend travel by a rented or leased car; there are too many fascinating places here that are out of the way of easy rail or bus access. Bus and rail are adequate if your accommodation is reasonably close to a town or city, but be sure to ask the agency prior to booking.

A round-trip visit of two or three days to Paris is feasible, but the chances are that there is so much to see and do here that you may not want to take the time. Even a day or two in England, and especially on the Channel Islands of Jersey and Guernsey, can easily be managed from Brittany, with ferries running out of Roscoff, Saint-Malo, and Cherbourg.

Vacation rentals are scattered throughout the region, and tend to be individual cottages, private homes, and *gîtes ruraux.*

Because the months of July and August are pleasantly warm (while the south tends to be hot), the coasts and their beaches are a magnet for vacationers, especially the French and British. May, June, and September through October are ideal months to visit; the coastal crowds are not too large. But if you can't visit during those months, be sure to book ahead at least four months, preferably more. The relative scarcity of properties that can easily be reserved from this side of the Atlantic adds to the problem, so plan ahead and book early, and don't discount going in winter—it's a mild climate year-round.

Especially desirable are the north coastal towns of Brittany's Côte d'Emeraude in the vicinity of Saint-Malo, followed by some of the inland market towns and *gîtes* in the farm areas. As for Normandy, there are scattered rentals available, mostly along the beautiful peninsular coast; the western area will provide interesting days of exploration, from Mont-Saint-Michel to the city of Rouen. The region's proximity to England makes the idea of a vacation divided between France and England worth considering. The east of Normandy is not as physically beautiful as the west, and given the other possibilities in France, one might need to have a special, perhaps personal, reason to select this as a destination.

PRICES. Prices are moderate, peaking in the high season (July and August), but dropping considerably in the low seasons (May, June, and September to early October). During winter the rates drop even more: a one-bedroom cottage can be rented for about 1,400 French francs per week, and a typical house for four for about 1,900 French francs (Fr.).

ADVANCE BOOKING TIME. For July and August—six months. For May, June, and September, through October—two months. For the rest of the year—up to one month.

THE AGENCIES. The best information and selection are from Bowhill's of England, through its U.S. agent B. & D. de Vogüe, and from The French Experience and Vacances en Campagne. Also contact Blake's Vacations, Coast to Coast Resorts, and Orsava, Inc.

The Loire Valley

ENVIRONS AND ACCOMMODATIONS. The broad Loire River valley wanders almost the breadth of France and is often called the garden of France. Although many rentals, especially *gîtes,* are available in the

upper valley (south of Paris), most are concentrated in the region between the city of Orléans and the Atlantic. Due to its mild climate, this is
a good area to visit in spring and fall, as early as April and as late as
October. It is a valley of châteaus where Parisian gentry go to relax and
play, a valley of remarkable cities (such as Tours and Angers) and of
castles and fortresses (such as Chambord and Chaumont-sur-Loire).

In addition to the *gîtes*, scattered villas, and apartments, nearly two
dozen elegant châteaus in the Loire Valley between Vichy and Nantes
belong to an organization called Château Accueil (welcome), an association of château and manor house owners who offer a glimpse of *La vie de
Château* by renting guest rooms and apartments in their estates. These
are available elsewhere in France, but the Loire Valley offers the most.
(For more information, see the listing for B. & D. de Vogüe, the U.S.
agent, in Chapter 3.)

This is one of the most delightful areas of France to spend a few
weeks in, ideally during the shoulder seasons. And to savor the Loire in
its entirety, consider renting somewhere in the lower valley (west of
Orléans) for a week or so and somewhere to the south of Orléans for a
second week.

LOCATION AND TRANSPORTATION. From a rental anywhere in this
region of the Loire it is easy to explore not only the entire area but to visit
Paris, the Île-de-France, and the Atlantic coast area by highway or rail.
(We suggest the train if you go into Paris proper.) Although local public
transportation is available, the Loire is best explored by car, especially
because most of the rental properties are rural.

PRICES. Because the Loire Valley is so large and so diverse, an area,
where small towns are scattered among farm areas, rural *gîtes* sit isolated on their farms, and elegant châteaus rise in wooded areas of large
estates, rental prices vary greatly. A simple one-bedroom rural house
(*gîte,*) for example, should rent for no more than $200 per week in the
summer months, slightly less in spring and autumn, and as low as $125
in winter. Expect a range of from $350 to $650 per week for a very
comfortable country home and around $1,000 per week for an apartment
in a château. At the high end of the spectrum, there are a few large,
staffed châteaus available that rent for many thousands per week, with
prices often dependent on length of stay and the staff and amenities you
require.

THE AGENCIES. The best information and selection for the Loire
Valley are from B. & D. de Vogüe, Vacances en Campagne, Vacation

Home Rentals (VHR) International, and The French Experience. Also contact Blake's Vacations, Coast to Coast Resorts, and Orsava, Inc.

Southwest France
(the Dordogne, Lot et Garonne, Tarn et Garonne)

ENVIRONS AND ACCOMMODATIONS. Foreign lovers of the Dordogne River valley might decry its inclusion in a single region with the Lot, Garonne, and Tarn River valleys, but indeed they are all tributaries of a single watershed draining into the Atlantic by way of the vast estuary of the Gironde, on whose shores lie the vineyards of Bordeaux. This is an area of rolling countryside rising toward the east, with lakes for summer swimming, forests of pine and oak, vineyards and wineries, farms and market villages with produce to sell, and Romanesque churches and ancient fortified towns. It is a region popular with those who love tranquillity, Frenchman and foreigner alike. Toward the south, into Tarn et Garonne, the villages are frequented by fewer tourists and remain even less touched by modern civilization than those elsewhere in the area.

Rental properties, usually individual stone or stuccoed houses, range from simple to modest, with a few in the near-deluxe category. The rentals are liberally scattered throughout this region, and where you locate is probably less important than the nature and character of the property itself, unless you have no car and must find a place near one of the three railway lines that cross the area. The entire region can be enjoyed better by having a car.

LOCATION AND TRANSPORTATION. The principal city of the area is Cahors, and within an easy one-day round-trip toward the southeast are Toulouse and, a bit farther along, the walled city of Carcassonne. Toward the southwest, again a matter of only a few hours' travel, are the Bay of Biscay and the coastal cities of Bayonne and Biarritz. The latter especially is a living monument to the resort pleasures of the nineteenth and early twentieth centuries. With a car, a round-trip of several days' duration can include the eastern Pyrenees and the principality of Andorra.

PRICES. Prices are moderate, peaking in the high season (July and August), but dropping considerably in the low seasons (May, June, and September to early October). During other months off-season rates drop even more, and a one-bedroom cottage can be rented for about $225 per week, a typical house for four for about $300.

ADVANCE BOOKING TIME. For July and August—six months. For May, June, and September through October—two months. For the rest of the year—one month.

THE AGENCIES. For information on properties in this area, contact At Home Abroad, B. & D. de Vogüe, Chez Vous, Blake's Vacations, Europa-Let, Families Abroad, France Grandes Vacances, The French Experience, Interhome, Vacances en Campagne, Vacation Home Rentals (VHR) Worldwide, and Villas International.

The West and the Atlantic Coast

ENVIRONS AND ACCOMMODATIONS. From the southwest corner of France where it meets Spain and the sea, north to Finisterre, the peninsula of Brittany, the Atlantic Coast and its beaches seem to be the part of France for family holidays, where swimming, boating, surfing, and lying in the sun are the principal activities. But all of western France is steeped in some of the most significant events of European history. The signs of this are still very much in evidence, from the scenes of battles with the British at Poitiers to the outstanding Norman architecture of the cathedrals of Angoulême, Luçon, Poitiers, and Saintes, and the château-fortress built by England's Henry II that dominates Niort.

Boating on the inland waterways of the Poitou marshes near Niort and eating at the restaurants famous for mussels, oysters, and fresh fish specialties are all part of the region's appeal. And for visitors with a vacation rental, utilizing the fine array of seafoods and locally grown produce in your own kitchen, accompanied by the wines of Anjou and Saumur, can be another happy pastime if you tire of sight-seeing.

There are many rentals along the 375 or so miles (600 km) of coastline, many near the shoreline to capitalize on the white sand beaches, and some in rural areas or in scattered villages.

LOCATION AND TRANSPORTATION. A week could easily be devoted to the Atlantic Coast, especially north of the Gironde estuary, beginning with Royan, a new city built on the ruins of the old, which was destroyed by Allied bombing of an entrenched German garrison in World War II. Although there are properties available south of the Gironde River, excursions throughout the region of Poitou-Charentes are most rewarding; along with clean beaches and offshore islets, the area offers visitors fields and forests, vineyards, farms, and ruins from pre-Christian and Roman times. The coastal city of La Rochelle, and the important inland cities of Niort and Poitiers merit excursions. Some pleasant coastal towns include Carnac, La Baule, Erquy, and Sables d'Olonne.

The mainline railroad follows the coast, serving Biarritz, Bayonne, Bordeaux, Saintes, Rochefort, La Rochelle, Nantes, and on to Brest at the end of the Brittany peninsula. Four spur lines connect the mainline with Royan, Sables d'Olonne, La Baule, and Quiberon. If you do not plan to have a car, tell the agent you must locate in or near a town with rail service; the area is well connected so this should not be hard to do. If you prefer a more rural area, or a *gîte* rental, we suggest having a car.

There are two ways of approaching a stay in this area, one being to time your visit with the spring or, better, fall shoulder season and drive around looking for a well-located rental rather than booking ahead. But if you must travel in summer, think of this area as you would any popular beach area of North America. And book well ahead.

PRICES. Between September 15 and early June the rental rates are low, yet many of the accommodations are fairly large private villas. Typical is $500 to $600 (3,100 Fr to 3,800 Fr) per week for a villa for six to ten persons; the rent will be double those figures in July and August. Smaller places are available, but the choice is limited. Nevertheless, renting a good-size private villa for well under $100 per night is indeed a bargain—but you should avoid the two high season months. As everywhere, a *gîte* can be rented from $150 to $300 per week.

ADVANCE BOOKING TIME. For July and August—six months. For May, June, and September through October—two months. For the rest of the year—up to one month.

THE AGENCIES. B. & D. de Vogüe, Blake's Vacations, France Grandes Vacances, and The French Experience.

Languedoc–Roussillon

ENVIRONS AND ACCOMMODATIONS. This long region stretches from the Spanish border and the Pyrenees eastward along the Mediterranean coast almost to Marseilles. Surprisingly, despite the obvious appeal of much of the area, in our many journeys there we have run across relatively few Americans. As a region for coastal resorts it seems only recently to have been discovered, and the difference over the four years between our last visit and the one we took for this guidebook was amazing. Outside the quiet old town of Sète, the port for the long-route ferries to Tangier and the Balearic Islands, new resort communities featuring clusters of white stuccoed apartments and villas shimmer in the Mediterranean sunshine. Yet even now agents list only a very few properties in the region, and most of them are inland, in the valleys of the upper

Tarn and lower Rhône rivers. This is just as well, because the beaches are always accessible by day trips, and the greater beauty of the area and its splendid cities are not on the sea.

LOCATION AND TRANSPORTATION. The major cities of Languedoc–Rousillon are all worthy of extended visits, as are many of its ancient smaller towns. Among the former are the walled city of Carcassonne to the west; Narbonne, Béziers, and Montpellier in a line along the curve of the coast; Nîmes, up the Rhône Valley; and Alès on the northwestern edge of the region. One could easily and happily spend a week or two in this region, ideally renting a place in a village fairly close to one of the main cities noted above. Outside of the region, but within range of an overnight stay are the major cities of Marseilles, Avignon, and Aix-en-Provence.

For a special longer journey, consider a voyage to Spain's Balearic Islands on one of the large ocean ferryliners out of Sète. Trasmediterranea (Spanish) and COMANAV (Moroccan) both operate excellent ships from spring to fall; the fare is modest, so book a cabin and take a first-class ticket. (To book, contact S.N.C.M., agent, 4 Quai d'Alger, Sète, France; tel: (67)74-70-55.) The dock area is small, so the ticket office is easy to find. Toward the west and south, a visit to Barcelona by rail or car is reasonable from this region of France.

Three north-south rail lines intersect with the east-west coastal mainline (Geneva—Barcelona) at Béziers, Nîmes, and Tarascon, providing service to even some of the smaller towns. A car will enhance your exploration of the entire region, but if you are not planning to have one, be sure to tell the agent that you need to be near a railroad station.

PRICES. Rates vary depending on location, season, and type of rental. The properties all tend to be large and very nice, commanding generally higher prices than, say, those on the west coast. A simple one-bedroom house is about $300 per week in off-season and $600 in peak season; top properties in terms of location, style, and standards begin at $700 per week in low season and $1,000 to $1,500 in high season. Most houses in this category will accommodate six or more persons.

ADVANCE BOOKING TIME. For July and August—six months. For May, June, and September through October—three months. For the rest of the year—two months.

THE AGENCIES. B. & D. de Vogüe, Blake's Vacations, The French Experience, Rent A Home International. Also contact Coast to Coast Resorts, Vacation Home Rentals (VHR) Worldwide, and Villas International.

Provence and the Riviera
(Côte d'Azur)

ENVIRONS AND ACCOMMODATIONS. Between the Languedoc region and the border of Italy lies what is probably the most famous and varied region of France, so much so that it can rightfully be divided into three areas of different topography and climate. To the northeast are the Maritime Alps, an area of mountains, lakes, and villages. Toward the west the mountains soften, then give way to the broad valley of the Rhône. Underlying the two is the coast of Provence, the Riviera, of which the section from Saint-Raphaël east to the Italian border is officially designated as the Côte d'Azur.

THE RIVIERA: In spite of the crowds who pack the area in summer and late into the fall, in spite of the high rises that compete with each other for a glimpse of the Mediterranean, in spite of the yachts that pack the harbors at Saint Tropez, Cannes, Nice, and Villefranche-sur-Mer, in spite of stony beaches, and in spite of the high prices of virtually everything, the Riviera continues to draw people, newcomers and old-timers alike. Part of the reason is the climate, pleasant almost year-round; part is the physical beauty of the area; and part is the Mediterranean class and style of the area's cities and towns. The result is a distinctive ambience, difficult to explain but apparent to all, those who live there as well as those who only visit. Even if you don't go to one of the casinos, or if you don't go to horse races, or if you can't afford night after night of the tariff at the elegant restaurants, they contribute to the atmosphere, as do the things that are free: sunshine, the sea, strolling through the seaside and hill towns, shopping for nothing in particular, picnicking, and people-watching.

This area can be reached with ease from any of dozens of home base locations, but, because accommodations in this tourist-impacted area are on the expensive side, it is important to sort things out before deciding. Three basic questions are: Can persons of modest means spend any time on the Riviera? If so, how? And can those with larger budgets find luxury and comfort without paying usurious prices? The answer to all three is certainly yes, but a basic understanding of this complex area helps. Three factors dramatically affect rental prices on the Riviera: location, season, and style.

Location—the first tier. Refer to a good map of this area, and begin to think of the Riviera as three distinct environments. The cities and towns that border the sea form the first tier: Menton, Monte Carlo, Beaulieu, Villefranche-sur-Mer, Nice, Cagnes-sur-Mer, Antibes, Cannes, and, farther southwest, Sainte-Maxime and Saint-Tropez. Near the center of this string of cities and towns, between Nice and Antibes, there is a sweep of hotels, apartments, and restaurants along thirty-five or so miles (60 km) of the Bord de Mer, a broad seaside boulevard that changes its name as it runs through one city or another (Promenade des Anglais and Quai des États Unis in Nice, and Boulevard de la Croisette in Cannes, for example). As desirable as it may sound to have an apartment directly on the Mediterranean, virtually all of the buildings from Nice to Antibes face the sea across this crowded boulevard. Many of the grand hotels and apartments there were built at a time when carriages, or at most a few automobiles, traveled the streets. Now, the noise level is high, and you have the choice of keeping the windows closed or enduring the sound. People who know better don't stay along the Bord de Mer; it is for the unsuspecting first-time visitors. East of Nice, however, from Villefranche-sur-Mer to Menton, the cliffs rise more abruptly from the sea and the high-speed boulevard does not intervene; the same is true from La Napoule west to Saint-Tropez.

Therefore, the key, if you prefer an apartment in any of the "first tier" seaside cities or towns, is to choose one that does not front on the Bord de Mer where it is a wide boulevard heavy with traffic. You should make this clear to any agent. In Nice, stay in the "centre" or "hors centre" in the areas of La Conque and La Mantega or, for less expensive apartments, toward Saint-Roch. In Cannes, the expensive hotels and apartments are along the Boulevard de la Croisette, and prices drop significantly a few blocks away in La Cannet and Super Cannes. In Saint-Tropez prices are high and can be avoided by staying back from the seafront, or across the bay in Sainte-Maxime.

Also in this first tier are small communities, often like suburbs, in which rental properties tend toward the elegant, and that offer visitors quiet luxury and four-star standards at much less than a comparable hotel. (See "Prices," below). In these towns the rentals are often privately owned vacation homes of well-to-do Europeans that, for ten or eleven months of the year, are managed by rental agencies. The most prominent of these coastal communities are Beaulieu, Saint-Jean–Cap Ferrat, Ville-franche-sur-Mer, Villeneuve Loubet, Cap d'Antibes, Juan-les-Pins, Golfe Juan, La Napoule, Saint-Raphaël, and Sainte-Maxime, any of which are delightful. Unusual among them is Villeneuve Loubet, which principally comprises a newer planned resort community of privately owned villas set in several hundred acres on the highlands immediately above Antibes (the agent is France Grandes Vacances). A town we stayed in and liked is Cagnes-sur-Mer, about halfway between Nice and Antibes; it is unusual in its unpretentiousness (and modest prices). Look for an apartment at least a block back from the Bord de Mer (contact Europa-Let or France Grandes Vacances).

Location—the second tier. The hills that rise just back from the sea and parallel the coast not only contribute to the pleasant climate of the Riviera, they also provide a setting for villages that perch on hilltops and even larger towns that spill amazingly down the slopes. The rentals are mostly in rural settings, often with broad views of the Mediterranean and the first-tier cities below. Many are apartments in individual villas, some are complete individual villas, others are less elaborate bungalows. A few are available in the towns themselves. These hill locations are very desirable, away from the press of population and the tourist throngs that crowd the coastal band, yet accessible to the beaches and the cities below. Rentals in the areas of Vence, Mougins, and Grasse should be of special interest; just ask the agents to provide specific information on the hill properties of the Côte d'Azur. The fields around Grasse, incidentally, provide the bulk of the flowers for France's perfume industry.

EFFECT OF THE SEASONS: As in most resort areas, especially those such as the Riviera, where there are thousands of hotel rooms, apartments, and villas, prices of accommodations vary greatly with the seasons. *Minimum stays* are also affected, sometimes requiring a month for a private villa, but more often a two-week minimum, in the peak season, dropping to one week at other times. The peak season is July and August; shoulder seasons are June and September; and low season is the rest of the year (October through May). There are some variances to these, but they generally apply. The price difference, coupled with the crowds in the peak season, makes clear that the best times of year to stay in this area are April through June and September through October. The weather in spring and fall is usually mild and delightful; September can be very warm, ideal for swimming, sailing, and surfing.

EFFECTS OF STYLE: This is the third consideration, and it means simply that there are spots along the coast that are considered to be more stylish, or fashionable, than others. All else being equal as far as accommodations are concerned, prices are higher in these more fashionable areas; they are where people go to see and be seen. They are hard to sort out, but any agency should be able to match your requirements accurately. If you prefer to be in a known fashionable community or area, make it clear what you are looking for; if not, make this clear also. Nothing will suffer if you prefer the latter. For example, an apartment or private villa in less expensive Golfe Juan is just as nice as one of equal standards in Juan-les-Pins, a mile up the coast. Saint-Tropez is thought of as more fashionable than Sainte-Maxime; the part of Cannes near the luxury hotels is more fashionable than the Le Cannet district. If you do not know the Riviera, the key is to compare the property descriptions and prices in the catalogs carefully, and be specific with the agents about what you require. Of course, some of the most quietly fashionable areas are also the most desirable: Cap d'Antibes, Villefranche-sur-Mer, Saint-Jean–Cap Ferrat, Eze-sur-Mer.

LOCATION AND TRANSPORTATION. From the Riviera, all of Provence can be explored—from Avignon, Aix-en-Provence, and the port city of Marseilles in the west to the interesting towns of Digne and Sisteron in the north. Day trips into Italy are easy, to nearby San Remo, and even to the city of Turin. From the commercial harbor at Nice there are inexpensive port-to-port daily sailings from June through September (three to four sailings per week in winter) to the island of Corsica and its ancient towns of Bastia and Ajaccio and the resort town of l'Ile Rousse. It is a seven-hour voyage, and you can arrange a car rental on Corsica before departing from Nice. If you just want to take the round-trip and lay over for a few hours, make Bastia the destination. (Contact any travel agent on the mainland or the offices of the shipline, S.N.C.M., at the port for schedules and tickets.)

The mainline railway between Paris and Genoa runs along the coast, with locals stopping at almost every town along the Riviera. Northbound out of Nice the line runs to Digne, Grenoble, and then on to Lyon or Geneva. There are also buses that serve the hill towns as well as towns along the coast. Again, the way to explore at ease is by car.

PRICES. A brief note about prices is usually enough in most country chapters, but due to the large seasonal differences and the sometimes elevated prices of properties in the Riviera area, a more comprehensive sampling here gives a better idea of what to expect.

The following examples are of average prices listed by various real estate agents (*agences immobilières*) along the Riviera and by local tourist offices and the Comité Régional du Tourisme. They are approximate, intended to show the order of prices, not exact figures, and are expressed in French francs. Just check the newspaper for the current rate of exchange and convert the francs to dollars. When comparing the prices shown here with any quoted by U.S. agencies, bear in mind that the former do not include the cost of overseas phone calls, foreign currency bank drafts, guarantees, and other services normally provided by a U.S. agent. A few sample hotel room prices are included to give an idea of what they run.

The locations of the studio and one-bedroom apartments are in and around Menton, Nice, Cannes, and the hill cities of Grasse and Mougins. The luxury villas sampled are in residential areas of Cap d'Antibes and Cap Ferrat. Many include swimming pools and most are on or within an easy walk to the sea.

The ratings for the apartments and villas are equated to three hotel-type ratings: ★★★★ = Top Class; ★★★ = Comfortable; ★★ = Standard. The first figure shown is French francs; the second is U.S. dollars at an exchange rate of 6.3 francs to the dollar, the exchange rate at the time of writing. The longer the rental period, the lower the weekly rate.

Studio Apartments (approximate price per week, usually including electricity)

	July & August		June & September		Rest of Year	
★★★★	3,150	$500	2,200	$350	1,500	$240
★★★	2,000	$320	1,300	$210	1,000	$160
★★	1,600	$260	1,000	$160	900	$140

One-Bedroom (approximate price per week, usually including electricity)

	July & August		June & September		Rest of Year	
★★★★	3,500	$555	2,200	$350	1,800	$285
★★★	2,500	$400	1,700	$270	1,200	$190
★★	1,800	$285	1,000	$160	700	$115

Private Villas (prime locations)

Standard 2 bdrm, 1 bath, yard, sea view, standard furnishings
   July & August—$4,000/mo. (1-mo. minimum)
   June & September—$550/wk. (2-week minimum)
   October through May—$375/wk. (1-week minimum)
Luxury 4 bdrm, 3 baths, terrace, pool, gardens, beautifully furnished
   July & August—$12,000/mo. (1-mo. minimum)
   June & September—$1,500/wk. (2-week minimum)
   October through May—$900/wk. (1-week minimum)
Luxury 7 bdrm, 5 baths, terrace, large pool, gardens, elegant furnishings
   July & August—$28,000/mo. (1-mo. minimum)
   June & September—$4,000/wk. (2-week minimum)
   October through May—$2,500/wk. (1-week minimum)

After visiting these properties we were told by the agent that we could not see their prime property, an eleven-bedroom estate on the sea that was booked through 1991 by an American family; the peak season rent for this property is $67,000 per month, and it *is* available in 1992.

A sampling of hotels revealed quite a variety of room rates, depending on the same factors that apply to vacation rental properties. The figures given here are for summer high season, so if you are booking between October 1 and May 30, large discounts apply. The two figures are for the least and most expensive double rooms, *per night.*

Antibes ★★★	400/560	$64/$90	($450 to $630 per week)
Cagnes-sur-Mer ★★★	300/400	$48/$64	($336 to $450 per week)
Cannes ★★★★	550/900	$88/$143	($616 to $1,000 per week)
Cannes ★★	300/400	$48/$64	($336 to $450 per week)
Grasse (Hills) ★★★★	440/800	$70/$127	($490 to $890 per week)
Nice ★★★★	550/900	$88/$143	($616 to $1,000 per week)
Nice ★★★	350/550	$56/$88	($382 to $615 per week)
Nice ★★	220/320	$35/$51	($245 to $357 per week)

This sampling gives an idea of the variety of hotel rates, and although there are so many variables that an accurate comparison between hotels and apartments is hard to make, these and other figures indicate that a ★★ hotel room runs about the same as a ★★★ apartment; or, put another way, the cost of apartments runs from 10 percent to 40 percent less than the cost of hotel rooms of equal standards. Given the high cost of restaurant meals, just preparing breakfast and a few other meals at home will make a marked difference in the overall cost of staying on the Riviera; the difference is, of course, greater in the winter and shoulder seasons. At the top end, from October to May you can rent a private 5-bedroom (or more) luxury villa with gardens and pool at about the rate of a one-bedroom suite at the Cap Eden Roc Hotel.

ADVANCE BOOKING TIME. For July and August—six months. For May, June, and September—3 months. For the rest of the year—up to 1 month.

THE AGENCIES. For obvious reasons there are many U.S. agencies that represent companies in Provence, especially on the Riviera, and even represent a scattering of private owners. If you plan to arrive in this area in the peak months, or even after mid-June or before mid-September, it's a good idea to book through one of these agencies before departing. But be careful; there seems to be a heady atmosphere when rental prices escalate as though the price is no object when renting a private villa in Cap Ferrat or Cannes. Competition is heavy among the many companies with offices on the Riviera as well as among the agencies in the United States. When the demand for rentals is high, the prices are high—but in the off-seasons there are many empty apartments, and a few francs rent income is better than none. Therefore, if you plan to arrive any time between mid-September and early June (except around Christmas and Easter), you should have no problem going without reservations and finding an apartment, bungalow, or private villa. Simply check into a hotel for a day or two (they are also available at lower rates) and contact a local Office de Tourisme, or go to one of the many agencies you'll spot. (Some addresses are listed in Appendix C.)

The U.S. agencies that have a large selection of properties in the area of the Riviera are At Home Abroad (mostly deluxe); B. & D. de Vogüe (moderate to deluxe); Europa-Let (modest to deluxe); Families Abroad (moderate); Four Star Living (mostly deluxe); France Grandes Vacances (modest to deluxe); Interhome (modest to moderate); Overseas Connection (mostly deluxe); Rent A Home International (moderate to deluxe); Rent A Vacation Everywhere (moderate to deluxe); Riviera Holidays (modest to deluxe); Vacation Home Rentals (VHR) Worldwide (modest to deluxe); Villa Leisure (modest to deluxe); and Villas International (moderate to deluxe). Several of these agencies also offer properties elsewhere in Provence: At Home Abroad, B. & D. de Vogüe, France Grandes Vacances, Villas International.

Savoy and the Savoy Alps
(Haute Savoie)

ENVIRONS AND ACCOMMODATIONS. This is the mountain country of France, an area lying north of Provence and between the valley of the Rhône on the west and Switzerland and Italy on the east. Not only is this the ski and winter sports area of the country, it is one of the most popular destinations for summer visitors who love hiking or driving through mountains and spending time in Alpine towns. Summer is the time to visit Aix-les-Bains and nearby Annecy, partly for their beautiful settings and partly because they are towns that are fun to be in. For the gourmet, the place to visit is Bourg-en-Bresse, a town of fine restaurants.

Despite warm weather pleasures, it is nevertheless winter in the Alps—and the ski resorts such as Chamonix, Val d'Isère, Courchevel, and Megève draw the dedicated skiers, people-watchers, and the rich and famous.

Most of the vacation rentals in the region are either rural or in the mountain towns, and although they tend to be less expensive than those on the Riviera, they are on the high side for France overall, and quite expensive in the fashionable winter resorts. In general, the chalets and apartments in large chalets are of top-class or deluxe standards. Chamonix is the town for Mont Blanc skiing, with cable cars running to within 2,000 feet of the 13,000-foot summit. Megève is another favorite, especially for those who prefer an older village for their home base, and Courchevel offers ninety lifts and a great variety of slopes. Most rentals in these towns can best be described as modern-rustic apartments, usually two to six in a chalet. They tend to be attractively furnished, comfortable, and warm; that is, they are apartments that fit into the Alpine surroundings, designed for relaxation after a day of skiing the slopes or hiking the mountain meadows.

LOCATION AND TRANSPORTATION. The major cities within a round-trip of a day or two from anywhere in Savoy the Savoy Alps are Lyon to the west, Grenoble to the south, Geneva and Lausanne (Switzerland) to the north, and Turin (Italy) to the east. Railways connect all the major towns in the area, with mainlines running between Lyon and Geneva to Aix-les-Bains and Turin. Other lines connect Aix with Annecy, Saint Gervais, and Chamonix. Many of the smaller Alpine towns, however, including Val d'Isère and Courchevel, are well off the main rail lines and highways, and if you are not planning to have a car, be sure to get specific instructions from the agent on how to get to the community and the rental property.

PRICES. In the summer peak season (July and August) a comfortable studio or rural *gîte* in most areas of Savoy will run between $200 and $300 per week, and a one-bedroom apartment between $300 and $400. Between September 15 and mid-June, you'll pay about 40 percent to 50 percent less. In the winter resorts, expect to pay between $400 and $650 per week for a deluxe studio and $500 to $1,000 for a one-bedroom, depending on the location. Larger deluxe private chalets or 3-to-4-bedroom apartments can run up to $2,000 per week, but obviously can accommodate large groups. Unfortunately, there are few simple and inexpensive rentals in the resort towns, especially for booking from overseas.

ADVANCE BOOKING TIME. For July and August (summer peak)—six months. For December and March (winter peak)—six months. For June and September (summer shoulder)—two months. For January and February (winter shoulder)—two months. For the rest of the year—up to one month.

THE AGENCIES. The best way to book, since Europeans seem to know their way around the mountain resorts and there are relatively few properties in the catalogs, is to contact U.S. agencies B. & D. de Vogüe, Overseas Connection, Four Star Living, Interhome, Rent A Home International, Vacation Home Rentals (VHR) Worldwide, and Villas International for their current materials, specifying your needs and price range.

Other Regions

To the north of Savoy lie northeast France and the winelands: Burgundy, Champagne, Franche-Compté, and Alsace. To the west is central France, the area of the valleys of the Rhône and the upper Loire. Oddly, despite the richness of the lands, villages, and cities of these regions, North American and British agencies list remarkably few vacation rental properties there. Perhaps one reason is that there is no principal destination, no special city or attraction of sufficient interest to foreigners that they would be willing to stay for a week or two. This suggests that these large regions are devoid of tourists, which, of course, they are not, although there are far fewer North Americans visiting the great cathedrals at Metz and Reims than there are sunning on the beaches of the Riviera.

If you wish to stay in, and explore, these regions, the best approach is by car and the best times are spring and autumn. In fact, late spring is ideal if you want to travel through the mountainous Massif Central of central France. At these times, there is very little competition for accommodations, and any city or regional Office de Tourisme will provide a list of apartments and cottage rentals.

Another approach is to contact The French Experience, a U.S. agency that can book a *gîte* in virtually any area you wish. Other agents with properties scattered in these two regions are B. & D. de Vogüe, Interhome, Vacances en Campagne, and Villas International.

7

Federal Republic of Germany

◆

◆ THE AGENCIES

Coast to Coast Resorts (Baden-Württemberg, Rhineland)
Four Star Living (Baden-Württemberg, Rhineland; scattered else-
where)
Idyll, Ltd. (Rhineland)
Interhome, Inc. USA (Baden-Württemberg, Bavaria, Hesse, Rhine-
land)
Orsava, Inc. (Baden-Württemberg, Rhineland)
Rent A Home International (Baden-Württemberg, Rhineland; Co-
logne)
Villas International (Baden-Württemberg, Bavaria, North Sea Coast)

◆ THE COUNTRY

With an area slightly smaller than the state of Oregon, the Federal
Republic of Germany (West Germany) is a long and narrow country,
stretching from the North Sea and the border with Denmark south to
Switzerland and Austria. The distance between Hamburg, the largest
northern city, and the Swiss border near Basel is about 555 miles (900
km), so it is not a country that can easily be explored from one central
location. But it is not only its size that makes two home bases necessary,
it is also the diversity of things to see and do.

Much of the countryside, from the high Alps of the south to the
rolling forests of the north, is very appealing. But it is the multitude of
unique cities and towns, as well as the famed castles, that brings history

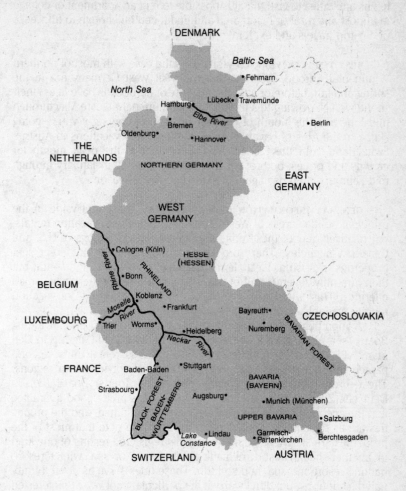

to life in West Germany. Fortunately, there are so many very worthwhile towns and cities to visit that it is possible to rent an apartment or cottage in almost any rural or resort area and find it central enough to fill weeks of day trip travels and explorations.

BEST TIMES OF YEAR TO VISIT. As is the case with most of northern Continental Europe, the best times to visit West Germany are in the spring and fall, before or after the majority of Europeans have taken their "holidays." Narrowing this further, the optimum periods are May through mid-June and the month of October (except, of course, if you're going skiing in the Alps of Bavaria). As is true for winter vacations in Austria, Switzerland, and the French Alps, December is the peak month for crowds and prices, both of which generally drop off in January through mid-February, then rise again until the end of the season.

GENERAL INFORMATION ABOUT RENTALS. The countryside in the principal holiday areas of West Germany is dotted with vacation rentals, but relatively few of these units are offered in the catalogs of U.S. and Canadian agencies. There are at least nine agencies that represent properties in Austria, West Germany's small neighbor to the south, but there are only seven for all of Germany—and most of them have small offerings. This is not to say that there are not thousands of vacation rentals available—only that they are more difficult to find and book.

A good beginning is to contact the nearest German National Tourist Board (see Appendix C) and ask for the booklet "Self-Catering in Germany." In it you will find listed several hundred rental units, accompanied by photographs and descriptions, nicely divided into regions. These properties are listed with the German Tourist Board (DZT— Deutsche Zentrale für Tourismus) in Frankfurt, a pretty good guarantee that the accommodations are spotless, well maintained, and the properties are as described in the catalog. You will also note that most of the properties are shown as being in officially registered resorts of one kind or another: health resort, climatic health resort or spa, winter resort, bathing resort and spa, and so forth. These titles serve as good thumbnail descriptions, but don't worry if the particular spot you are interested in is not "officially registered." Unless you are very familiar with the country, work with a good guidebook to West Germany to link the booklet's geography to the guidebook's detailed description of the various areas. These rentals *cannot* be booked through the German Tourist Board offices in North America. The details on how to book are in the booklet, but, basically, it is a process of either directly contacting the Accommodation Reservation Service of the DZT in Frankfurt or working through a regular travel agent. The commission paid to travel agents on these properties is small, so the difference in rent between booking through a travel agent and the DZT in Frankfurt direct should be correspondingly small. We suggest that you book through a travel agent—*after* you have studied the government's booklet and have some idea on prices and the choices of locations.

For rentals that are more individual, such as private homes and apartments in private buildings, the best selections are available through Four Star Living, Interhome, Rent A Home International, and Villas International.

The properties of Coast to Coast Resorts and Orsava, Inc., which represent Britain's Hoseasons, are mostly in vacation developments—clusters of cottages or bungalows built for the express purpose of vacation renting. Principally for German vacationers, they are nonetheless popular with other Europeans, and the developments usually feature a clubhouse, a community swimming pool, tennis courts, and other amenities.

Idyll, Ltd.'s "Untour" (see Chapter 3) offers an interesting assortment of accommodations along the Rhine River, appealing for first-time visitors to West Germany. These are described below in the section on Rhineland.

◆ THE REGIONS

Although West Germany comprises ten *Länder* (states), for the purposes of finding a home-base vacation rental from which visiting and touring can best be carried out, it is easy to divide the country into five regions: Northern Germany, Rhineland, Hesse, Baden-Württemberg, and Bavaria. From the list of agencies at the start of this chapter, it can be seen that the majority of rentals are available in the Rhineland and Baden-Württemberg areas, followed by one agency each with properties in Bavaria and on the North Sea coast. For some reason, no properties are now listed for the state of Hesse. We think that the spotty distribution of rentals offered through U.S. agents is more a matter of a yet-to-be developed resource than a reflection of some conscious selection of the most popular or interesting regions of West Germany. Fortunately, the gaps left by the private agencies are filled by the properties listed with the German Tourist Board in its catalog. These properties, although not relatively large in number, are located throughout all the regions.

WHERE TO STAY. If the length of a planned visit between May and late October is limited to two weeks, and you want to find a single locale most central to the greatest diversity of things to see and do, then the southern Rhineland or northern Baden-Württemberg are good choices. If more time is available, two-thirds of it should be alloted to the southern Rhineland and the two southern regions and one-third to the north. For a winter vacation, go to the area of southern Baden-Württemberg, or especially southern Bavaria, along the Swiss and Austrian borders, respectively.

Northern Germany

ENVIRONS AND ACCOMMODATIONS. This region is less frequented by North Americans than the better-known areas to the south. The coastal area of West Germany, its Continental beaches and ocean resorts, and those beaches of the offshore Frisian Islands (especially the East and North Frisians), are popular with vacationing Germans, as are the sea resorts and towns of the Baltic. The countryside ranges from flat to rolling, much of it forested and dotted with lakes, in addition to the actual beach areas and coastline. Toward the south, the region rises into the Weser Hills and, to the southeast of Hannover, the Harz Mountains, both areas of forests, lakes, and holiday resorts.

Both the coastal vacation areas and mountains are too similar to parts of North America to be particularly magnetic destinations, but as vacation rentals they are spacious and relatively inexpensive home bases from which to visit the important cities and towns of the region. Where you locate specifically is dependent on whether you prefer mountains or sea, because the whole region can be explored readily by day trips and a few overnighters.

The North Sea coast is flat with long stretches of beach, often swept by wave and wind from fall through late spring. Our personal preference is the coastal region from the Baltic Sea coast along the Bay of Lübeck, from Fehmarn south to Travemünde.

LOCATION AND TRANSPORTATION. The North Sea resort areas are central to several very important and interesting cities, each of which is easily worth more than a day of exploration. The most interesting of these are the garden city of Oldenburg; Bremen, Germany's oldest and second largest port, and one of the former major cities of the Hanseatic League; the towns along the estuary of the Elbe River from Cuxhaven to Hamburg; and Hamburg itself. This is West Germany's second largest city, and although much of it has been reconstructed since World War II, it retains large-city charm and many of its Renaissance-style buildings and is especially noted for the St. Pauli quarter and its lusty nightlife. From Hamburg there are three to four sailings weekly of large ocean ferryliners bound for Harwich (England), a twenty-hour voyage on vessels featuring excellent food, pleasant cabins, and a delightful journey along the Elbe River estuary. It is a wonderful two-day voyage at very modest cost. (Contact any travel agency in Hamburg, or the DFDS shipline offices at the dock.) To the southeast of Hamburg, the medieval town of Lüneburg is worth the twenty-five-mile trip and serves as a starting point for exploring the Lüneburg Heath, a vast reserve of wildlife and flora.

The Baltic Sea resorts center around the city of Lübeck, a picturesque and historic collection of twelfth- and thirteenth-century buildings along the River Trave. Ten miles downriver from Lübeck is Travemünde (literally, mouth of the Trave), a beautiful old resort town where pine forests meet the river and the sandy beaches along the sea. It is a place to come to relax and enjoy the food and the water, yet is close to its companion city of Lübeck. Travemünde is also one of the Baltic's major ferryports, with many departures daily by ocean ferryliners to Gedser (Denmark) and Trelleborg (Sweden). As is the case with the vessels that sail between Hamburg and England, it's almost worth the ride to enjoy the smorgasbord served on board.

Physically distant from this geographical region, but considered a part of it, is the city of Berlin, accessible by mainline rail and highway from Hamburg and Hannover.

The public bus system is good in this region, with many local buses that travel from town to town. Virtually every town of any consequence has rail service. Bremen and Hamburg are the hubs, with mainlines between them and going north into Denmark, east to Berlin, and south into the Rhineland. Because the principal sights of interest in this region are in the cities, and the resort areas are well served by bus or rail, having a car is more of a convenience than a necessity.

PRICES. The principal variable affecting price is the season. For example, a typical one-bedroom sea-view apartment in a modern complex runs about $250 per week from March to mid-May, $350 from mid-May to mid-June and again in September, and $480 from mid-June through August.

ADVANCE BOOKING TIME. For July and August—six months. For mid-May to July and September—two months. For the rest of the year—one to three weeks.

THE AGENCIES. The agency with the best selection of North Sea properties is Villas International; DZT also lists several larger resorts where accommodations are available.

Another approach to finding a rental, if you plan to visit between mid-May and mid-June or between mid-September and late October, is to contact the tourist authority in any of the towns you want to visit. Check into a local hotel for a day or two while working with the tourist office, and decide where you prefer to be.

Apartments in Berlin can be booked directly through the DZT or a travel agent. The apartment-hotel Berlin, a full-service accommodation, has one-bedroom apartments for $1,250 per week from April 1 to mid-November, $975 the rest of the year. For a studio, the rates are about $600 per week in the high season and $450 in the low season.

Rhineland

ENVIRONS AND ACCOMMODATIONS. The valley of the Rhine (Rhein) River runs for almost two-thirds of the north-south length of West Germany, from Lake Constance (Bodensee) and the Swiss and Austrian borders at the south, through the region of Baden-Württemberg northward, dividing Rhineland to the west from Hesse to the east, finally departing into the Netherlands in the northwest. The valley widens from south to north, and to the great river is added the waters of the Neckar, Moselle, Nahe, Saar, Main, and other smaller rivers that have served as a major transportation network for thousands of years. Along the route are everything from the famed vineyards of the Rhineland to castles, forests, towns, and cities that reveal their antiquity in a thousand ways.

The northern Rhineland has the concentration of population, and it is hard to tell when you leave the industrial city of Düsseldorf and enter the city of Essen or proceed on to Dortmund. But despite the population and industry, the rebuilt cities still hold the old within them and deserve a visit. Cologne (Köln) is the northern beginning of the Rhineland as foreigners think of it: hills, gorges, villages on steep slopes, ramparts and fortresses, ancient towns, barges and sight-seeing boats on the river.

Vacation rentals are plentiful in almost all parts of the Rhineland but, again, are not very well represented in North America by the commercial rental agencies. One very good approach, however, is through Idyll, Ltd. and its "Untours," a program in which the company helps determine the right location and type of accommodation, provides assistance in making flight reservations, initiates an orientation meeting with a staff person on arrival at Frankfurt, and books an apartment for three weeks (or more). The apartments are in villages along the section of the Rhine known as the Lorelei, between Koblenz and Bingen, where the hills rise steeply and much of the river flows through a wide gorge—with castles, of course, on the cliff tops. We found these towns (St. Goarshausen, St. Goar, Bacharach, Kaub) to be very pleasant, uncrowded and tranquil, perfectly situated to serve as a home base from which to discover the entire Rhineland, and to travel south into Baden-Württemberg and east into Hesse.

LOCATION AND TRANSPORTATION. With an area this rich in terms of castles, walled towns, ancient cities, cathedrals, and winemaking, as well as river trips and beautiful countryside, it is difficult to name all the important places to visit; a good guide and good maps are essential. Of special focus should be Cologne (Köln), if only for a visit to the cathedral; Trier, the oldest city in Germany, is a must, as are Worms and Koblenz and a trip to Aachen. A day or two spent in the Principality of Luxembourg is rewarding and easily accomplished from any of the rentals in the Rhineland. Longer, yet still feasible, is a trip south to Lake Constance, Zurich, and northern Switzerland.

Local bus service is good in this region, which is also crisscrossed by railroads, with mainlines following much of the Rhine along both its banks, one connecting Koblenz along the Moselle Valley with Trier and Luxembourg, between Cologne, Düsseldorf, Bremen, Hamburg, and to Aachen. Yet with all the public transportation available, the region lends itself well to exploration by car; a car is not essential, but it's very convenient to have one.

PRICES. As in the rest of West Germany, the main variable affecting price is the season—but prices tend to be higher in this region than in Northern Germany and Hesse, all else being equal. A typical modern studio in a small apartment house directly on the Moselle River near the town of Cochem, an ideal location, rents for about $225 per week from November 1 through March 25, $250 through June 28, and $285 from then to November 1. Even at peak season this is only about $40 per day, plus electricity and a small final cleaning charge. An equivalent hotel room (without kitchen) in Cochem is about $65.

ADVANCE BOOKING TIME. For July to mid-September—six months. For late March to July—two months. For the rest of the year—one to three weeks.

THE AGENCIES. Coast to Coast Resorts and Orsava, Inc., acting as agents for the British company Hoseasons, offer rentals in modern bungalow parks, two in the Mittelgebirge southwest of Cologne not far from the Belgian border, another in the Pfalzer Wald between the Rhine River and Saarbrücken, and a fourth farther south, in the Baden-Württemberg region.

Interhome, Inc. USA offers the largest selection of rentals, while

Four Star Rentals, Rent A Home International, and Villas International offer a scattered few. The DZT lists many in the Saüerland, Eifel, Wester-wald, Moselle, and Pfalz/Saarland areas of Rhineland, all central to exploration of the Rhineland, and all available for booking direct with the DZT office in Frankfurt or through most regular travel or rental agents.

Hesse
(Hessen)

ENVIRONS AND ACCOMMODATIONS. To the east of the Rhineland, including part of the Rhine Valley and on to the border with East Germany, lies the state of Hesse (Hessen), the least familiar (except for Frankfurt and its environs, where most of us land after the transatlantic flight to West Germany) area to North Americans.

One reason this area is not so well known is because of the magnetic appeal of the surrounding regions. Unlike Rhineland and Baden-Württemberg, Hesse has a relatively small number of castles and ancient towns. But there are still many, including the castle of Sababurg, the home of Sleeping Beauty, made famous by the Brothers Grimm. It is hill country, part of the Mittelgebirge, heavily forested and cut with rivers and small streams.

LOCATION AND TRANSPORTATION. We suggest that there may be regions of the country that can better fill the precious days of first-time visitors to West Germany. This is not to diminish the beauty of most of Hesse, or the interest of Wiesbaden, baroque Fulda, ancient Limburg, or the bright and beautiful Rhenish town of Rüdesheim. But if you cannot find a rental to your liking (due to the small selection available in the United States), this is a region that can reasonably be explored from a home base in the central Rhineland. If you visit during any month between late September and mid-June, it will not be difficult to find rentals listed at local town tourist offices and simply locate one you like.

Two north-south mainline railroads cut diagonally across Hesse between Frankfurt and Berlin, and most of the towns in the region are served. There are also town-to-town buses.

THE AGENCIES. The only U.S.-based company with a few vacation rentals in this region is Interhome Inc. USA; DZT also lists about half a dozen vacation complexes, most tucked away in quiet woodlands.

Baden-Württemberg

ENVIRONS AND ACCOMMODATIONS. This state occupies the south-western corner of West Germany. At its western edge is the Rhine Valley, from which the land rises toward the east into the hill country of the Black Forest (Schwarzwald) and then into the Swabian Alps, making it the country's most diverse and picturesque region. Despite its popularity as a tourist destination, both for Germans on holiday and for foreigners visiting West Germany, there are many areas that are off the beaten path; and in the spring and fall it is an ideal and uncrowded region to explore.

A land of castles and woods, of Alpine meadows and quaint towns, Baden-Württemberg offers the vineyards of the Neckar River valley, medieval abbeys, centuries-old health spas, the shores and waters of Lake Constance (Bodensee), and villages famous for their craftsmen working in everything from gold to clocks. In all, Baden-Württemberg is a delightful region in which to spend a few weeks.

During April, May, and early June, and from mid-September through October, you can drive through the region and find a cottage or apartment to rent for a few weeks quite easily, but a small percentage of everything that is available is represented by North American agencies. As seems to be the case throughout West Germany, many of the vacation rentals are apartments or bungalows in holiday parks built for this purpose, although there is also a fair selection of apartments in private homes and larger buildings. The important thing is to specify which you prefer. The advantages of the holiday parks are that they are usually less expensive and often offer such amenities as laundromats, swimming pools, and clubhouses. Rentals in private homes and smaller buildings usually offer more privacy and a better sense of the locale. However, because of all that there is to see and do in the region, it is likely that you will be spending most of your time away from "home." Regardless of which type of rental setting you stay in, you can count on comfort and cleanliness.

LOCATION AND TRANSPORTATION. It is difficult to find an unattractive town in this region; even the industrial city of Stuttgart, capital of Baden-Württemberg, is an ancient city surrounded by wooded hills. And although Heidelberg and Baden-Baden are the best known towns, both worthy of their fame and of extended visits, the entire region seems dotted with inviting places. Beyond the borders of the region, yet within reach for a stay of a day or two, are Basel, Lucerne, and Zurich (Switzerland); and to the southwest, a touch of Austria where it meets West Germany on the shore of Lake Constance near the walled island town of Lindau. To the west, a sample of medieval France (and some fine French restaurants) can be enjoyed at Strasbourg, one of the great cities of Europe.

The regional railway system is very good, with mainline service connecting all the major cities and serving many of the smaller ones, and extending into France, Switzerland, and Austria. The intercity bus system is fine as well, but there are so many interesting and picturesque out-of-the-way places in the region that having a car is more than just a matter of convenience—it will heighten your enjoyment of Baden-Württemberg and its environs if you stay off the autobahn).

PRICES. Along with those in the Rhineland to the north, prices tend to be higher in this region than elsewhere in West Germany, but are modest relative to the area's richness of things to do and see. Prices are definitely lower in smaller towns and in the countryside and higher in the most popular cities. A good example is a private apartment in the village of Bergach, a Black Forest town about an hour's drive south of Baden-Baden, offered by Rent A Home International. It is of moderate standard, comfortable but not luxurious, has two bedrooms, a living room with dining area and fireplace, bath, terrace with open barbecue and an equipped kitchen. It rents for about $440 per week in July and August, and $350 during other months (even less in winter); add a few dollars for linen rental. A one-bedroom apartment in a modern mountain apartment hotel near Weis-Stockmatt, just north of Basel (Switzerland), rents for about $460 per week in the peak months of July and August, $410 in the shoulder months, and $240 between October and March. A studio in the same building runs from $185 to $295 per week. That equals $27 to $42 per day; a modest hotel room in Heidelberg runs from $55 to $85 per night.

ADVANCE BOOKING TIME. For July to mid-September—six months. For late March to July—two months. For the rest of the year—one to three weeks.

THE AGENCIES. Coast to Coast Resorts and Orsava, Inc., acting as agents for the British company Hoseasons, offer rentals in modern A-frame chalets in a pleasant holiday park overlooking the village of Tennenbron, centrally located southwest of Stuttgart. The DZT also lists numerous rentals in its catalog. Rent A Home International and Inter-home USA offer the largest selection of rentals in private homes and apartments, and Four Star Rentals and Villas International offer a scattering.

Bavaria
(Bayern)

ENVIRONS AND ACCOMMODATIONS. Between Baden-Württemberg and the Czechoslovakian border north of Austria, lies Bavaria, the largest of West Germany's five regions. Bavaria offers the high Alps, summer hikes and winter sports in the south, the Bavarian Forest in the northeast, and a rich history everywhere, manifested in its towns and cities from Augsburg to Würzburg.

Upper Bavaria (Oberbayern) is the most scenic area of the region, encompassing the Alps it shares geographically with Austria. It is just a little over 40 miles (64km) from West Germany's famous ski resort of Garmisch to Innsbruck, Austria. Although travelers have a tendency to find a vacation rental reasonably central to the region they are planning to visit, the beauty of Upper Bavaria and the Allgäu argue strongly for locating in the southern Alpine area. This does not mean that the rest of Bavaria is hard to explore; it is only 180 miles (290 km) from Garmisch in the Alps across the region to Bayreuth near the northeast corner of the region. Along with the attraction of Upper Bavaria come higher prices than are generally found in central and eastern regions. We feel that the few extra dollars are comparatively little to pay for a place in this spectacular area.

Like neighboring Baden-Württemberg, much of Bavaria is a very popular vacation destination, for both Germans and foreign travelers, so accommodations are plentiful. There are fewer large holiday park developments here; the rentals tend more toward chalet-style holiday homes with four to ten apartments, or small private apartment buildings, usually rustic in appearance although modern in all respects.

LOCATION AND TRANSPORTATION. The major city is Munich (München), located in the central south, a city of 1.5 million people and rich in culture and history, good food, and nightlife. Many days can be spent wandering its museums, churches, shops, parks, restaurants, and theaters. Bayreuth becomes packed with Wagner fans during the annual Wagner festival in late July and August, but a visit there—along with Nuremberg, Bamberg, and Würzburg, the important cities of northern Bavaria—makes for an interesting and rewarding journey from your home base.

Despite the fact that they are jammed with tourists from mid-June through August, two places in the south attract visitors by the thousands—Füssen and Berchtesgaden. The former because it is near Neuschwanstein, Mad King Ludwig's castle, and the latter because of its beautiful setting and its history (you can see the remains of Hitler's former retreat). The great attraction in the vicinity, however, is the city 20 miles (32 km) down the highway: Salzburg (Austria). If you cannot find the rental you want in Upper Bavaria, an alternative approach is to select a rental in northern Austria. A look at a map will show five main highways (one an autobahn) across the border in the area between Innsbruck on the west and Salzburg on the east. There is a good selection of rentals in the northern Vorarlberg, Tirol, and Salzburg provinces of Austria (see Chapter 5, "Austria," for information on agencies).

Mainline railroads run between the major cities of Würzburg, Nuremberg, Munich, and Augsburg, extending to major cities of Austria, Switzerland, and other parts of Germany, with spurs serving Füssen, Garmisch-Partenkirchen, Berchtesgaden, and Oberammergau, among others. There are fewer lines in the east and through the Bavarian Forest, so a car is needed there. For example, Passau can be reached by train, but it is 6 miles (10 km) to the nearest chalet rental; you can take a taxi, but once you're there it's a long walk back for groceries.

In the south, the town-to-town bus system is very good, but if you truly want to explore the mountain roads of Upper Bavaria, it must be done by car.

PRICES. All rates vary seasonally, but most rentals are less expensive in eastern Bavaria and the Bavarian Forest areas than in the south, especially in or near the Alps. A typical, comfortable, one-bedroom apartment in a chalet-type apartment building in the Alpine resort areas of Garmisch-Partenkirchen costs about $280 per week year-round, except during the high months of July, August, December, and March, when rents are $420 per week. A similar apartment in a rural chalet in the Bavarian Forest near Passau rents for about $265 per week from late June through August, and $120 in the other months. Another typical Bavarian Forest rental is a 700-square-feet two-bedroom half chalet, which costs $385 per week in the high months and $220 during the other months. One reason for these very modest prices for modern, attractive accommodations in a beautiful part of West Germany is that the Bavarian Forest area is not heavily visited by foreign tourists.

ADVANCE BOOKING TIME. For July to mid-September—six months. For late March to July—two months. For the rest of the year—one to three weeks. *Ski areas:* December and mid-February through April—four months; November and Jan. to mid-February—one to two months.

THE AGENCIES. The principal U.S. agencies with rentals in Bavaria are Rent A Home International and Interhome USA, with most of their properties in Upper Bavaria. The DZT also has a good selection, and is your best bet if you are interested in eastern Bavaria and the Bavarian Forest—and in finding the most for your money. These registered properties are all attractive and, like those represented by private agencies, are mostly in chalets and town apartments rather than large holiday parks.

8

Republic of Ireland

♦ **THE AGENCIES**

Blake's Vacations (Counties Clare, Connemara, Cork, Kerry, Limerick)

Castles, Cottages & Flats of Ireland & the U.K., Ltd. (throughout Ireland—counties Clare, Cork, Donegal, Galway, Kerry, Leitrim, Roscommon, Tipperary, Waterford, Wexford)

Hideaways International (scattered castles and manor houses)

Lismore Travel (Counties Clare, Galway, Mayo. Tipperary; scattered elsewhere)

Lynott Tours (Counties Clare, Cork, Donegal, Limerick, Tipperary)

Rent A Home International (scattered)

Rent A Vacation Everywhere (RAVE) (scattered)

♦ **THE COUNTRY**

Ireland is principally rural, and vacation rentals (called "self-catering") provide the tranquillity of peaceful settings in farmlands, along remote coastlines, and near small villages. Many of the cottages—built especially as vacation rentals—are in small clusters situated in locations that enable visitors to explore the beauties of rural Ireland.

But is not just the physical beauty of Ireland that draws tourists. The term *beauty* often seems strangely applied; the western countryside can be as sere and barren as the hills of Tipperary are lush and green. Look across a sweep of stone wall–crossed fields toward a distant sea; the view is stirring because of the sense of isolation it evokes. But of course

158

Giant's Causeway

•Londonderry

DONEGAL

NORTHERN
IRELAND

Donegal•   Belfast•

FERMANAGH   •Enniskillen

Sligo•   CAVAN
MAYO   SLIGO   LEITRIM
•Westport   Cavan
CONNEMARA   Carrick
•Castlebar

ROSCOMMON

•Roscommon

GALWAY   REPUBLIC OF IRELAND

CONNACHT   Dublin•   *Irish Sea*

Galway•

Atlantic Ocean

CLARE

Ennis•
Shannon▲   TIPPERARY
International Airport
Limerick•   Thurles• Kilkenny
•Tipperary   KILKENNY   WEXFORD
LIMERICK

•Tralee   Wexford•
KERRY •   Waterford• •Rosslare Harbour
Dingle Bay   CORK   WATERFORD
•Killarney   Cork•
Bantry Bay •Skibbereen

there is real beauty: lakes and hills and even forests, meadows, flowers, castles, and quaint towns and fishing villages. Dublin's attractions include the old Custom House, the Four Courts along the River Liffey, and the spectacular National Gallery. And the people, visitors say, enhance the stranger's visit; we agree.

GENERAL INFORMATION ABOUT RENTALS. This is not a large country, so it is not impossible to explore a large part of it quickly from a single location. However, if you are planning to stay fewer than three weeks, you might want to divide your visit between the southwest and the northwest.

A preponderance of the rental properties—especially those in the small holiday clusters, but others as well—are near the west coast. Additional sites lie along the southeast coast between Wexford and Skibbereen in Counties Wexford, Waterford, and Cork.

For a day or two in Dublin it is not necessary to find a local vacation rental; hotels and B&Bs are numerous, and the city is accessible from almost any cottage rental area in Ireland. The distance between Dublin and the towns of western Ireland is not great; for example, Limerick to Dublin is 125 miles, Donegal to Dublin is 140 miles, and Killarney to Dublin is 190 miles, all easy and pleasant drives or a few hours by train (many departures daily).

As for those other eastern and southeastern cities—Wexford, Waterford, and Cork—industry and commerce are their focus. While these areas are not devoid of interest, they are not destinations that merit several days.

In addition to the more prevalent cottage parks, there are numerous independent private cottages, as well as apartments in castles and some of Ireland's most elegant country manors. These luxurious accommodations are collected under a company called Elegant Ireland, and can be booked through the U.S. agency Castles, Cottages & Flats. Lynott Tours handles a few sites, too.

The ITB (Irish Tourist Board) publishes "Self Catering," a comprehensive catalog that lists and briefly describes, alongside black-and-white photos, hundreds of properties throughout the country. Bookings *cannot* be made with ITB offices in the U.S. or Canada, but the catalog contains a booking form to send to any of several tourist offices in Ireland. For the independent traveler who is willing to make the foreign contact by mail or telephone, this is a way to get the most for your money; no intermediary agent is involved. The procedure is explained in the catalog, which is available from ITB offices in New York and Toronto (see Appendix C). Before you choose direct bookings, it is best to know something about Ireland and have a good idea of where you want to go, because the catalog does little to describe the actual properties, much less their locales. This can be overcome to some extent by studying a traveler's guidebook to Ireland and a good map.

A brief overview of the regions and the vacation rentals, along with a good guidebook, will help first-time visitors decide where best to stay, *unless* you are particularly interested in a specific activity such as golfing, fishing, or boating. In this event, book through one of the North American agencies and tell them exactly what you are looking for.

◆ THE REGIONS

We divide Ireland into quarters, and although properties are available in the eastern half, few of them can be booked through agents in the United States or Canada. One reason is that the east is not the half of Ireland North Americans want to visit. Further, all transatlantic flights between North America and Ireland terminate or originate at Shannon International Airport, not far from Limerick. (The exceptions to this are Aer Lingus flights, which stop at Shannon both ways on the Dublin–North America route). This automatically brings virtually everyone from our side of the ocean into western Ireland, and the region capitalizes on this. In fact, one of the most popular vacation rental plans, Rent-an-Irish-Cottage, centers on arrivals into Shannon, offering modern, country-style cottages from north to south in western Ireland. (The U.S. agent of this Irish company is Lismore Travel.)

The western half of the country interests visitors more than the eastern half because it is the most scenically attractive, offers a greater sense of remoteness, and seems more like our idealized view of what Ireland should really be like. And who is to say that it isn't? The crowds wandering the old streets of Killarney and Tralee during the high tourist season are now part of Ireland and, indeed, have helped share the nature of the towns themselves during the past few decades.

The exception to this preference for the west occurs if you are interested in either a hosted or an independent stay in a castle or in one of the elegant manor houses that dot the countryside. Their locations have been dictated by history, not by Shannon Airport. The castles stand at strategic defense points, many in the eastern lands. The manor houses are, of course, where the large estates were carved out during the past two or three centuries. Again, for those few that offer their elegant accommodations, don't worry about the location—it is the experience of staying in such a place that matters.

The Southwest Quarter
(Counties Clare, Cork, Kerry, Limerick, and northern Tipperary)

ENVIRONS AND ACCOMMODATIONS. In the southwest, from Skibbereen northward into Counties Kerry and Clare, the coastal areas are striking, the inland countryside is rolling and rocky yet green, and the main towns of Killarney and Tralee are lively and attractive. Many of the smaller villages are little changed from earlier times. Cork (pop. 160,000) is the main city in the south of this region, and although it is principally industrial, it certainly offers visitors much to do and see. It is easily accessible from anywhere in the southwestern counties, only 55 miles from Killarney, 75 from Tralee, and 75 from Shannon Airport. Because distances are not great, a vacation rental in any of the southwestern counties allows for easy exploration of the others.

In the north of this region, the main city is Limerick (pop. 70,000), the first large town seen by new arrivals at Shannon. Mostly of the Georgian period, it is also an industrial town, interesting for a short visit.

It is in the countryside that, logically, most vacation rentals are available, close to the smaller towns of the region that are so delightful to visit. The largest town of County Kerry is Tralee (pop. 13,000), an enjoyable place to while away a day or two, as is nearby Killarney. The fame of these places, like that of most Irish villages, certainly exceeds their size. (Killarney's population is only 7,500, and Tipperary is a market town of 5,000.) The region's many towns are not places to go to see; but, when you rent for two or three weeks, you share village life in the pubs, tea shops, and markets.

Southwestern Ireland is relatively small, and all its parts are accessible by day trips, so where to stay is a matter of personal choice. The Dingle Peninsula west of Tralee has a dramatic coastline and a good sense of rural Ireland; the Ring of Kerry, which is the next peninsula south from the Dingle, is also a desirable area, and includes the Killarney Lakes country. The best approach is to peruse the brochures and catalogs of the U.S.-based agencies, especially Castles, Cottages & Flats, Blake's Vacations, Lismore Travel, and Lynott Tours. While the first two specialize in cottage rentals, the latter two offer self-drive and self-conducted tours as well. If you prefer to pick your own property and deal with the owners directly or through the tourist offices in Ireland, contact the ITB for its self-catering catalog (see Appendix C).

LOCATION AND TRANSPORTATION. Ireland is not a country one usually thinks of as a jumping-off place to other destinations, but it is not difficult to cross the Irish Sea to England on ferryliners from Rosslare Harbour (near Wexford) and from Dublin. There are also port-to-port and round-trip sailings of about twenty-two hours' duration out of Rosslare Harbour for Cherbourg and La Havre (France), and out of Cork for Le Havre and Roscoff (Brittany) if you want a taste of something different. The ships are big, the cabins pleasant, the food good, and the prices very modest.

The mainline railroad runs the length of Ireland from Belfast (Northern Ireland) to Dublin and Cork, with connecting service to Killarney and Tralee; to Limerick and Shannon; and to Kilkenny, Wexford, and Rosslare. There is also a fairly good town-to-town bus system. But for the most part the rentals, whether independent cottages or units in cottage parks, are not accessible by public transportation. Further, the nature of the rural landscape and the coasts is such that without a car one is very hampered. Cottage rental agencies can set up vehicle rentals, usually for less than can be arranged independently. If you are booking your cottage independently, you will, of course, book your own car. But in any case economics dictates that you should reserve the vehicle before leaving home; the price of waiting until you arrive at Shannon or Dublin is high (see Chapter 4, "Transportation in Europe").

BEST TIME OF YEAR TO VISIT. Although Counties Clare and Kerry are on almost the same latitude as central Labrador, the south end of Hudson Bay, and Edmonton, Alberta, the Atlantic Gulf Stream keeps southwestern Ireland virtually free of frost. The result is mild temperatures year-round and the richest vegetation in the country—subtropical plants grow and flower in the more sheltered spots. The sea temperature is certainly not tropical, but summer swimming is possible.

The high season for tourists is early July to late August, the shoulder seasons are June and September, and low season is the rest of the year. Rental prices and crowded towns follow this schedule, so the optimum times are indeed the shoulder months, adding late April and May on the early end and until mid-October in the fall.

PRICES. Most of the cottages are designed for families or groups of four to six or more, very few for only a couple. If there are two in your party, think of it as having plenty of room. The prices, relative to hotel rooms of similar standards, are very modest.

A typical cottage on the sea runs from $150 per week in winter (November to April) and $250 in the shoulder months, to $350 to $400 during July and August. These are also the approximate prices of cottages on a river or lake. Simpler cottages, not on the water (perhaps farmhouses or one of the few apartments in rural houses), can be found for $100 to $250 a week.

Although most of the private rentals (through commercial agencies) adhere to a standard three-season price range, a ridiculously complex variety of seasonal and holiday prices is often used for cottages in the holiday clusters. This not only makes it hard for foreigners to figure out precisely when to go, but also makes it appear that the owners want to wring every possible *punt* (Irish sterling, as pound is to British sterling) out of the client. The following list is interesting not only in that it shows typical prices but also because it dissects the holiday periods as seen by Irish landlords, individual or corporate. This tariff box is average; it includes the kind of extra charges that are customary in Ireland (and often in Britain) and need to be watched for. The prices per week are for a two-bedroom cottage on the water. The prices in U.S. dollars are at a rate of .70 Irish punts (IR£) per dollar; for today's figures, multiply the current exchange rate to convert to U.S. or Canadian dollars.

Period	IR£	U.S.$
January 4 to May 3 (except Easter Week)	90	129
Easter Week	155	222
May 4 to May 31	125	179
June 1 to June 30	180	257
July 1 to August 31	225	336
September 1 to September 28	180	257
September 29 to October 25	125	179
October Bank Holiday (a 3-day weekend)	125	179
October 26 to December 20	90	129
Halloween Week	155	222
Christmas to New Year's	155	222
Off-season weekends & mid-week breaks	80	114
St. Patrick's Weekend	130	186
Electricity, 50p coin meter*		
Turf, extra*		
Bed linens available to overseas visitors, 8£/person/week*		

50p coin meter means that you need to have a pocketful of 50-pence coins when you arrive in order to feed the timer on the electric meter. (Some rental prices may include electricity.) *Turf* is peat to be burned in the open fireplaces. (Most modern cottages have central heating, so the fireplaces generate more atmosphere than heat. In simpler cottages, however, turf and the cookstove ["cooker"] are the only sources of warmth.) Be sure to confirm that you want linens and towels.

In the low season, and even in the early and later periods of the shoulder months, there is rarely a problem in not booking ahead. Simply walk into the Tourist Information Offices in Dublin or Limerick or at Shannon Airport, or telephone one of the seven "Self-Catering" reservation offices around Ireland upon arrival and book by Visa or Access Card. If you want to scout the region first, rent a hotel room for a day or two. You might not find the best choice of rentals in early June and early September, but you should have no trouble finding something suitable. (Do *not* try this between mid-June and September 1.)

ADVANCE BOOKING TIME: For July and August—six months. For June and September—two weeks to two months. For the rest of the year—up to two weeks.

The Northwest Quarter
(Counties Donegal, Galway, Leitrim, Mayo, and Sligo)

ENVIRONS AND ACCOMMODATIONS. The farther one travels northward from County Clare into Galway and Counties Mayo, Sligo, and beyond, the more barren and empty the country seems. It is capped by the coast of Donegal, surely the most ruggedly scenic and primitively stunning part of all Ireland. After Cromwell crushed the Irish revolt in 1641 and confiscated the estates of the Catholic gentry, the former landowners became peasants, saved from starvation by the fact that potatoes grew fairly well in the area known as Connacht. To the north, in Donegal, the land was so poor and the farm production so meager that the owners were pretty much left alone—they had little worth taking.

There are many parts of the northwest where Irish is still the main language spoken, and where even the popularity of the region among tourists has had a minimal effect on the language. Visitors seem somehow swallowed up in the vastness. There are fewer vacation rentals in the Northwest Quarter than in the southwest. The region is marked by rugged treeless mountains, moors, cliffs rising sheer from the sea, and isolated fishing villages. Weather is often inclement, especially in winter and at the change of seasons between spring and summer and summer and fall. But the late-summer winds that blow across the bogs and moors are scented with heather, adding to the mysterious beauty of it all.

All of the northwest can be explored easily from any point in the region, so the choice concerns the desirability of the immediate area rather than its general location. As is true in the southwest, most of the cottages offered by rental agencies are in clusters, usually fewer than ten cottages to a cluster, situated to take advantage of the sea or lakes. The best approach is to study the photos and descriptions in the brochures and select one or two that are most appealing. Castles, Cottages & Flats is the best source of cluster cottages, but few individual properties are offered except through the ITB (see Appendix C). The "purpose-built" cottages are usually newer and slicker than the private ones, but the private rentals are, of course, authentic.

LOCATION AND TRANSPORTATION. Despite the region's sense of relative emptiness and space, nothing is too far away from anything else. It is an easy four-hour drive from the village of Donegal to Dublin, less to Galway. From the airport at Shannon, it is about 55 miles north to Galway, and another 75 across the peninsula that comprises Connacht and Ballina. These distances demonstrate that virtually all the roads in the region can be covered in a few days.

It is possible to leave the Republic of Ireland by crossing the border of Donegal or Leitrim into Northern Ireland, and despite the Troubles, a long visit to Londonderry will prove to be most worthwhile. About 50 miles east of Londonderry is the Giant's Causeway, an expansive and interesting geological oddity of octagonal basalt columns, which has lured travelers for well over a century.

As far as the railways in this region are concerned, it is almost as though "you can't get there from here." One line runs from Dublin to Sligo, another from Dublin to Galway, and a third from Dublin to Westport, but there is no line north and south along the coast. It is not impossible, for example, to get from Shannon to Sligo, but it must be done by going across the country to Dublin first. A car is very a important thing to have in this region.

BEST TIMES OF YEAR TO VISIT. The winter climate of the North Atlantic begins to overwhelm the benign influence of the Gulf Stream in the northwestern counties of Ireland. To some travelers, the cold winds and scudding clouds add to the severe beauty and sense of isolation they come to Ireland for, but in terms of better weather, the best times to visit are in July and August. As these months usually offer the best weather, they are also the ones with the highest prices for accommodations and the most crowded with tourists. We recommend the months of June and September.

PRICES. See the price ranges for accommodations in the Southwestern Quarter.

ADVANCE BOOKING TIME. For July and August—six months. For June and September—two weeks to two months. For the rest of the year—up to two weeks.

Other Regions

Few cottages in the central and east coast counties are available through agencies in the United States or Canada, but a wide selection of individual, privately owned houses is listed in the publication available from the ITB in New York and Toronto. These rentals can be booked directly with the owners specified in the catalog, or through the tourist information offices.

RECOMMENDATIONS. We suggest that if you are planning your first visit to Ireland, especially for the summer months, it is best to make arrangements with one of the commercial agencies based in the United States or Canada. It will cost about 15 percent to 20 percent more than booking direct, but will help you avoid some possible pitfalls and will give you some avenues of recourse in case there are any problems.

The six-month advance booking time for a cottage in July or August is necessary. If you are able to travel in the shoulder seasons, September is the optimum month in terms of weather; spring can be delightful, but it can also be termperamental, especially in the north. On the other hand, the windblown low clouds and mists that come in from the North Atlantic top the cliffs of Counties Donegal, Sligo, and Mayo and scud across the rocky fields before shrouding the Slieve Gamph and Derryveagh mountains, enhance the stark beauty of the land.

ABOUT THE LANGUAGE. Although English is almost universally used, Irish is the official national language of the country. It is called *Ghaeilge,* which literally translates into English as "Gaelic," but in fact "Gaelic" refers to Scots Gaelic, and the proper term for the language in Ireland is, indeed, Irish. For the record, the sign MNA above the rest rooms is Irish word for "Ladies," not a mispelling" of "Men."

9

Italy

◆ **THE AGENCIES**

At Home Abroad (Amalfi Coast, Tuscany, Veneto; Lake Garda)
Cuendet-Posarelli Vacations (throughout Tuscany, Umbria; Florence, Siena; Sicily)
DER Tours (throughout Tuscany, Umbria; Florence, Siena; Sicily)
Eastone Overseas Accommodation (throughout Italy)
Europa-Let (throughout Italy; Rome; Islands)
Families Abroad, Inc. (Tuscany, Umbria, Veneto)
Four Star Living, Inc. (throughout Italy)
Hideaways International (throughout Italy; Sardinia coast; Amalfi Coast, Florence, Siena)
Hometours International (Amalfi Coast, Naples coast, Tuscany; Florence, Venice)
Interhome, Inc. USA (throughout Italy; ski resort areas of Alto Adige, Piedmont, Valle d'Aosta)
International Services (throughout Italy; Tuscany, Umbria, Rome, Naples, Venice, Palermo; Islands of Sardinia, Capri, Panarea, Ponza)
Italian Villa Rentals (Tuscany coast; Florence and environs; scattered elsewhere)
Overseas Connection (Tuscany, Umbria; Florence and environs)
Rent A Home International (throughout Italy; Amalfi Coast; Florence, Rome, Siena)
Rent A Vacation Everywhere (RAVE) (Lombardy, Tuscany, Umbria; Rome)
Rent in Italy (Tuscanny, Umbria; Florence, Lucca, Siena; Sicily)

Susan T. Pidduck, Cuendet Agent (Tuscany, Umbria; Florence, Siena; scattered elsewhere)

Vacanza Bella (Amalfi Coast, Lake Garda, southern Mediterranean coast, Tuscany, Umbria; Florence, Rome, Siena, Todi)

Vacanze in Italia (a few on Adriatic coast near Brindisi, Tuscany Hills, a few on Tuscan coast, Umbria; Florence, Rome)

Vacation Home Rentals (VHR) Worldwide (throughout Italy; southern Mediterranean coast, Tuscany, Umbria; Florence, Rome; Sicily)

Villas International (throughout Italy; Adriatic coast, Alps, Amalfi Coast, Calabria, northern lakes, Tuscany, Tuscan coast; Islands of Capri, Sardinia, Sicily; Florence, Milan, Rome, Venice)

♦ THE COUNTRY

"If you were to spend a month or so in a vacation rental, where would you go?" This is a difficult question, one often asked of us, and we have, of course, many favorite places and countries. But if hard-pressed for a reply, Italy would be very near the top of the list.

For centuries, Italy has invited travelers to savor its riches. Poets, novelists, essayists, photographers, and filmmakers have filled libraries, galleries, and cinemas with countless images of the land, the art, and the culture of this country. Guides and other books, materials from the Italian government Travel Office (ENIT), and brochures from travel agents should help you decide where to go, but there is so much to see and do—and the more the material, the more difficult the decision.

The country comprises twenty regions, or states, each with its capital, and each somehow different from the others in topography, climate, history, architecture, flora, cities and towns, and atmosphere. For example, on our latest visit we came into Italy from the northeast, driving in from south-central Austria to Cortina d'Ampezzo, then through the Dolomites westward to Trento. High in this land of amazingly craggy mountains (and craggy mountain villages) we were astonished to see a sign at an intersection of narrow roads that read VENEZIA—165, indicating that we were 100 miles (165 km) from Venice, a world so different from where we were that it was hard to believe that in a couple of hours we could be sipping an aperitif in the Piazza San Marco. This is a good example of Italy's contrasts: a countryside of hills, mountains, fields, and lakes reminiscent of North America, but also a less familiar world of pre-Roman and Roman ruins, historic cities, and stone farmhouses that were built before Columbus set sail.

Italy's configuration makes it difficult to see everything in a relatively short time. On a clear day, it is said, there is a place in the Tosco-Emiliano mountains northeast of Florence where you can see the breadth of the country, from the Adriatic Sea on the east to the Mediterranean on the west, a distance scarcely over 100 miles (162 km). But from Reggio at the toe of the boot, it is 440 miles (704 km) north to Rome, and another 450 miles (715 km) on to Como, in the lake country of Lombardy. From Reggio to Venice it is 750 miles (1,220 km), and another 100 miles (162 km) to Cortina d'Ampezzo. With such distances, a fundamental choice must be made by anyone planning to visit Italy: to see a little bit of many things, or to select one or two locations from which to explore some, but not all, of this fascinating country.

GENERAL INFORMATION ABOUT RENTALS. As can be seen from the long list of U.S.-based agencies that offer rentals in Italy, it is a very popular destination. And one problem facing would-be renters (how to choose an agent) goes hand in hand with another (choosing the property).

With such variables as size, standards, amenities, season, and location affecting price, it is difficult to sort out the impact of the commission or fee. Usually, the most reasonable fees are charged by three kinds of North American agencies. First, there are those that represent some owners directly and therefore are not adding their commissions to the already commissioned prices of a European company. Examples of this type are International Services and Vacanza Bella. The second category takes its commission from the company, not the client: Vactation Home Rentals (VHR) Worldwide, for example. The third category is made up of agencies that may charge a small amount for a catalog published by the company in Italy but include the company price list (in dollars, lira, or pounds sterling) with the catalog and charge a stated flat fee to make the booking. Examples of this third type are Susan T. Pidduck, Cuendet Agent and Cuendet-Posarelli Vacations.

Start planning early and gather all the information you can. Several U.S. agencies may represent a single company in Italy, so when you receive the same catalog from more than one source, check to see if the prices are the same. Some agencies charge more than others but offer more services. If you need these services you can evaluate their worth to you; otherwise, there is no need to pay for them.

Minimum rental periods are generally one week. Two-week minimums are common during July and August, and some city apartments can be let for three days during low season. The periods are from Saturday to Saturday, but because it is difficult to work out airline schedules and itineraries down to the last detail, consider arriving in the area of your rental a day early and taking a hotel room.

See Appendix B for addresses of selected rental companies in Italy.

PRICES. Despite the number of agencies, Italy has far fewer rentals than France or the United Kingdom, countries with comparable populations. Furthermore, most privately owned rural properties in those two countries—as well as in Austria, West Germany, and Ireland—are cottages, small homes, or bungalows. In Italy, for historical reasons, most rural houses built during the past few centuries are large. With bigger accommodations and fewer of them, rentals command relatively higher prices. Factor in a desirable location, plus the tendency of owners to commit considerable effort and funds to restorations, and it's easy to see why rental prices on the whole are somewhat higher in Italy than in other European countries. The trade-off is that the rentals, especially the rural ones, are often more attractive than those in other countries. This does not mean that there are no modest, or modestly priced, rentals in Italy, only that it is more difficult to find a simple cottage in the Tuscan or Umbrian hills, for example, than one in rural France or Britain.

To help put prices in perspective, a double room in the four-star Plaza Hotel Luccesi, a very nice small hotel on the River Arno in Florence, runs 271,000 lire per night in shoulder seasons (higher in July and August); that is 1,897,000 lire per week, the equivalent of about $1,460 (U.S) per week ($210 per night), Continental breakfast included. A room in the pleasant three-star Hotel Privilege, on the river ten blocks from the central Piazza del Duomo, runs about $800 per week. Remember, these are only standard rooms, not apartments.

One rental in which we spent a few days is a good illustration of price, style, cost of extras, and location.

The Fattoria degli Usignoli (see "Rural farm villas," below) has long been a vineyard and winery high in the Tuscan hills 20 miles (33 km) southeast of Florence, near the village of Reggello. The railroad station at San Ellero is 5 miles away (8 km) and there is a bus between it and San Donato, a tiny village a quarter of a mile from the *fattoria* gate. Nestled in the twenty-acre vineyard are the lavish estate grounds: lawns, paths, gardens, cypress trees, statuary, a large swimming pool, a tennis court, and a barbecue area for hosted evening parties once a week—all in a setting looking over the hills and the valley below. It is a working winery as well as a small, informal resort, and beneath the walks and gardens some of the ancient cellars have been converted into a café for guests who enjoy taking some of their meals "out." The main house, a three-hundred-year-old stuccoed stone building, has been beautifully restored and renovated, its two stories converted into a dozen apartments, from studios to two-bedrooms. Much of a large adjacent building, part of the winery operation from years past, has been artfully restored and converted to modern apartments. All are nicely designed and adequately furnished, complete with small fully equipped kitchens and modern bathrooms with showers. The Fattoria degli Usignoli is an unusual place that draws an international clientele. Hostess and owner (with her husband) Madame Sylvia Pincitore speaks English fluently with a Tuscan lilt as warm as her personality. Prices in the shoulder months (June and September) run from about 575,000 lire per week ($440 at 1,300 lire per dollar) for a small studio to 661,000 lire ($510) for a two-bedroom apartment. In May prices are about $380 to $490, peaking in July and August to about $660 to $830, and dropping during other months to a low of $310 to $410. This happens to be the top range for rural apartments; prices for simpler, yet comfortable apartments or small individual houses without a pool or other external amenities run from about $300 in the off-season to $500 in July and August for two bedrooms. (The apartments in the Usignoli main house are among hundreds of properties offered by the Swiss/Italian company Cuendet, and can be booked in the United States through Posarelli Vacations and Susan T. Pidduck, Cuendet Agent. In Canada, contact DER Tours. The apartments in the adjacent building are among many handled by Solemar, and are available through Villas International, Vacanza Bella, Hideaways International, and Rent in Italy (see the alphabetical listing of agents in Chapter 3 for more information).

Near Strove we visited another style of rental, also a farmhouse. This property was more like a small stone feudal castle; it had a cavernous vaulted living room, a large formal dining room, a well-equipped kitchen large enough for three cooks, five bedrooms, massive doors, a swimming pool, a tennis court (which had seen better days), and a sweeping view across the Chianti toward Siena. Not elegant, but imposing, it rents for about $1,750 per week in the peak months and $850 per week from October through May; it is Cuendet property.

A more modern rental was reminiscent of a large turn-of-the-century home in one of the better areas of San Francisco or Denver or Boston, except that it was ten minutes from the Duomo in central Florence and was set on an acre or so of land. The rent was about $1,000 per week. A modest one-bedroom, fourth-floor walk-up we stayed in two blocks from the Porta della Romana in Florence rents for about $400 a week, the price of a room in a two-star pensione. (Both of these, and other good properties in Florence and its environs, are offered by an excellent small company headed by an Englishwoman who has lived in Italy since the early 1970s. You can count on good rentals at fair prices from this company, represented in North America by Overseas Connection.)

A very interesting, modern, three-bedroom apartment (which includes the study in which Dostoyevski wrote *The Idiot*) in a thirteenth-century building on the central Palazzo Pitti square in Florence rents, from Cuendet, for about $1,000 per week—less than a single room in a four-star hotel.

Other properties run the gamut of prices: Vacanza Bella has a luxury four-bedroom home on twenty-two acres overlooking Lake Garda, near Bardolino, at $20,000 per month. It also has some unique properties in relatively untrammeled southern Tuscany in the $200-to-$500-per-week range.

Extras that you can expect to pay for, especially for rural rentals, are electricity and a postrental cleanup (around $10 per person). Linens and towels are often rented for a small fee. These charges are unusual in deluxe villas and in the cities. Also, a substantial refundable damage deposit is required in most Italian rental properties ($150 to $400, often payable in lire upon arrival), so be sure to study the rental terms and, if necessary, go to a bank to get lire before arriving at your rental.

TYPES OF RENTAL PROPERTIES. Basically, there are four types of vacation rental properties in Italy: rural/farm villas and apartments, deluxe villas/summer houses, purpose-built villas/apartments (mainly in beach resorts), and city apartments.

RURAL/FARM VILLAS AND APARTMENTS: Farms may well be the accommodations most popular with foreign visitors, certainly, these are some of the most desirable properties. They dot the countryside, especially the hills of Tuscany and Umbria, and are often surrounded by vineyards (many in the Chianti region produce some of Italy's best wines). Called *fattorie* in Italian, the farms of the past few centuries have generally been large, family enterprises, and the houses were built to accommodate many people and much activity. And they were built to last. The typical Tuscan, Umbrian, or Emilia-Romagnan farmhouse is large, stone, cube-shaped, and anywhere between one hundred and four hundred years old. A small one might have eight rooms and an area of 3,000 square feet, and a large one a dozen or more rooms and 6,000 square feet. Then there are the main houses of the larger estates, which assume palacelike proportions. And, of course, there are actual palaces and castles.

In recent years, in order to stem the abandonment of these great rural buildings and to help maintain the age-old hill country culture, the government has encouraged (and often supported financially) the restoration and renovation of scores of *fattorie*. Private owners, too, have expended large personal sums turning their great old properties into comfortable, often elegant, accommodations for rent. Some have apartments in the main building; some have individual stone houses, usually large; and some have clusters of apartments resulting from restoration of outbuildings. We were impressed with the style of the properties we visited and the way in which they have been modernized without losing their essential character. Even some of the larger rental companies, such as Cuendet, have helped and encouraged renovations in the hope of listing the completed properties. In this way they can insist that owners meet company standards.

By far the greatest number of these properties is in rural Tuscany, especially the Chianti area, followed by Umbria. They range from simple to grand; many are apartments in the main house, and many are independent villas set in estate grounds with a pool, tennis courts, and other amenities. In other words, don't let the term "farm" deceive you; just study the agency's descriptions carefully.

One final point to consider is that hotels in the hill towns, especially the smaller ones, are rare. If you want to spend a week or two (or more) in this unusual and tranquil part of the world—and be within easy traveling distance of such cities as Florence, Siena, Lucca, Pisa, Arezzo, and even Rome—then renting a villa, or an apartment in a villa, is by far the best and most economical way of doing it.

DELUXE VILLAS/SUMMER HOUSES: *Villa* simply means house, and it can be a small or large house; the term can even be applied to the farmhouses described above. It is possible to rent an apartment in a villa or an entire villa. Make sure that you and your agent are talking about the same thing, especially if you are dealing directly with a company in Italy. If you want a private, individual house, make this clear; don't leave it to chance that your interpretation of the word *villa* and theirs is the same.

The villas described here are private homes—or single-family dwellings, as we refer to them—located throughout Italy. Although many are the main buildings on farms, the majority of the deluxe villas are the vacation homes of well-to-do Italians or foreigners and are located in especially desirable areas such as the Ligurian Riviera, the Amalfi Coast, Capri, Sardinia's Costa Smeralda, near the lakes of Lombardy, and close to Lake Trasimeno in Umbria. They can also be the principal homes of owners who travel for a few months each year and engage a company to find renters and manage the property in their absence. They tend to be upscale in quality, location, and price, and some can be richly elegant, set in beautiful grounds, and come complete with a pool, tennis courts, and a resident staff.

PURPOSE-BUILT VILLAS/APARTMENTS: Along sections of both the Adriatic and Mediterranean coasts are beach resorts popular with citizens and foreigners alike. The rentals in these areas have been built specifically for vacationers, and in the off-seasons they are usually closed. Some are depressing in their sameness—row after row of motel-like stuccoed apartments—but others are very attractive clusters of individual small villas, often with terraces, lawns, gardens, and set around a pool. Another style is the modern low rise, and there are even some high rises, which are basically apartment hotels that can be found along the Mediterranean coast from Naples to Marbella (Spain).

CITY APARTMENTS: Compared to rural and village rental properties, there are very few city apartments available. But for anyone who plans to stay for a week or more in Rome, Florence, Naples, Venice, or other major Italian city, an apartment is certainly worth seeking out. Most of them are privately owned and are rented and managed by one or another Italian company that, in turn, has an arrangement with one or more of the agencies listed in this chapter.

A city apartment has two advantages over a hotel: space and price. Except in Italy's most deluxe hotels, rooms are rarely very large and prices have become high, even for modest rooms that a few years ago would have cost $25 to $40 per night. By contrast, even a studio apartment has more room for movement, and a one-bedroom seems spacious indeed. Unlike the practice in some rural rentals, linens and towels are provided in city apartments, and electricity is usually included in the rent. As for location, apartments in the cities are very much like European hotels—scattered about rather than concentrated in the city's center, but certainly available in central areas if this is your preference. Expect to pay from $400 per week for a centrally located studio, and around $600 for a one-bedroom. International Services and Overseas Connection offer very good selections.

Many city apartments are in ancient buildings, so don't be alarmed at outside appearances. And before you book, study a map of the city you plan to visit to make sure you will be where you want to be. Also, if you plan to have a car, it is essential that the agent describe the parking situation for the apartment under consideration. The central cores of some cities are already closed to traffic, and in others the parking problem is monstrous.

WHERE TO STAY—MAKING CHOICES. Too many Americans who visit Italy independently act as if they are on a tour, setting up an overly demanding itinerary that allows them only a few days in each of many principal cities or areas. Those who know something of Italy, or are more travelwise, yet have only a few weeks, limit the number of moves to one or two, or none at all, and concentrate on the northern half of the country or the southern half, but seldom both. The point is that a satisfying visit to Italy requires some hard decisions about where to locate; discriminating reading of travel books will help you make these decisions.

Those who ask us what country we especially enjoy also ask what region of Italy we favor. The answer depends, in part, on the time of year. The optimum situation, however, is to go in spring or fall, to have a car, and to divide the time you have between the north and the south. If you have three weeks, you might spend two in Tuscany or Umbria, and one in the south, perhaps on the Amalfi Coast, or in Rome or the lakes region north of Rome. Limited to two weeks, a place in the hill country of central Tuscany would be rewarding, or if you prefer to be a little farther off the beaten trail, locate in southeastern Tuscany or eastern Umbria; a visit to the lake country of northern Lombardy and the mountains of Piedmont would be possible from there.

BEST TIMES OF YEAR TO VISIT. This decision largely depends on what areas of Italy you plan to visit, but as we continually suggest, avoid the peak months of July and August and the peak prices and crowds that go along with them. Otherwise, Italy is a land of benign climate moderated by the Mediterranean and the Adriatic, which almost surround it, and along the northern border by the high Alps, which shield it from the winter cold of the rest of Continental Europe.

Nevertheless, midwinter in Venice, Padua, Verona, Bolzano, Milan, Turin, and other northern cities, as well as in the northern lake country, can be unpleasant, so if your plans are for November through February, stay south of Rome. The obvious exception is a ski vacation in the Piedmont, Valle d'Aosta, or Trentino–Alto Adige regions (winter peak is December, shoulder months are November and March, low season is January and February; the summer, as in other parts of Italy, peaks in July and August).

Considering rent prices, availability, crowds, and climate, the optimum months for visiting northern Italy are June, September, and early October. For central Italy, the Tuscany hill country, Umbria, Emilia-Romagna, Marches, Latium (Làzio), and Abruzzi regions beckon most strongly in May, June, September, and October, although the coastal region of Liguria and the Mediterranean coasts of Tuscany and Latium are appealing as early as April 1. In the southern third of the country, January daytime temperatures are typically in the 60s on the Amalfi Coast, in coastal towns from Naples to Reggio, and in Sicily and the western coast of Sardinia. The best times for this area are April through June and September through October. Also, it is usually delightful as early as mid-March and well into November.

TRANSPORTATION. Rome and Milan are the gateway cities for transatlantic flights, so if you are planning to stay in southern or central Italy you can fly to Naples from Rome, or to Florence from either Milan or

Rome; if Venice is your destination, departure is usually from Milan. Other flights to Florence and Venice can be made via Frankfurt or other principal international airports in Europe. An important consideration, however, is the means of transportation upon arrival, especially if you want to settle in a rural area but also hope to explore a major part of the surrounding country by taking day trips and a few overnighters. Although it is good, Italy's railroad system remains unfortunately susceptible to labor stoppages, which could mean anything from a one-day demonstration to weeks-long strikes. The regional and local bus systems seem to be less prone to disruption; indeed, one can usually get around well using a combination of bus and rail. Even the remote and tiny hill villages are served by bus, but the problem for visitors is that much precious time can be taken up in gathering information on local schedules and fitting your time into those schedules. A car solves this problem, only to create another.

It's more convenient to drive to and from most of the noncity rentals and to explore the country by automobile. But cars are virtually useless in urban Italy. This is simply a fact of life. In most of the main cities of interest—Rome, Naples, Florence, Bologna, Milan, Palermo—the central areas are closed to everything except taxis, buses, and commercial vehicles. (All drivers visiting Venice have to park their cars in large garages on the edge of the city.) These ancient cities were not made for cars, and no one is about to destroy the former to make room for the latter. For the sake of history and art, one learns to live with frustration, sealed-off city centers, and traffic congestion. For the visitor, it means combining modes of transportation.

With a car you are able to set your own pace, go to out-of-the-way areas and enjoy picnic lunches. You can stop, wander, and take photographs with no concern about when the last or only bus is due and where it stops. To avoid driving into a city, locate the railroad station in a village 6 or 12 miles (10 or 20 km) away, park the car, and buy round-trip tickets, usually for less than the price of city parking. (Some stations on spur lines are not in villages, but in the country; follow the distinctive electric power lines and watch for signs that usually read FDS or FERROVIE DELLO STATO, meaning "Railroad of the State."

Prices are usually lower and it is more convenient if you book a car for pickup in your destination city before departure from the United States or Canada. Some agents can arrange a car rental while booking a vacation rental. If your stay is going to be three weeks or longer, there can be considerable savings with one of the lease or purchase buyback programs of French automakers, either through one of their agencies or the company's office in the United States (see Chapter 4, "Transportation in Europe"). This means that the car will have to be picked up and returned in France. The pickup/return city closest to Italy is Nice. It is an interesting day's drive from there to Milan and the northern Lombardy lakes, the Ligurian coast, and even Florence and most of Tuscany, but it is a hard twelve-hour drive to Rome. Another option, if you have the time and are interested in seeing some of France, is to pick up the car in Paris and spend a few days driving to Italy; it can be turned in at a southern French city if you prefer.

♦ THE REGIONS

This guide breaks Italy into thirds: the northern region lies north of where the peninsula begins. The central region encompasses the area from about Bologna south to Rome, and from coast to coast. The southern region is south of Rome, and includes Sicily and Sardinia.

Northern Italy
(Emilia-Romagna, Friuli–Venezia Giulia, Liguria, Lombardy, Piedmont, Trentino–Alto Adige, Valle d'Aosta, Veneto)

This region, the broad top of the Italian "boot," can generally be divided into four areas. The first three are the western rim, comprising the Ligurian coast and Ligurian Apenines (mountains) stretching toward the north; the vast River Po valley, which runs west to east from the French and Swiss borders to the Adriatic Sea south of Venice; and the mountain country north of the Po, including the Lombardy lakes (Maggiore, Como, Lugano, Orta) and Lake Garda, which is divided among the regions of Lombardy, Veneto, and Trentino–Alto Adige. The fourth area is Veneto, which includes Venice itself and the little-visited coastal area east of Venice to Trieste and the border with Yugoslavia.

ENVIRONS AND ACCOMMODATIONS

LIGURIA: If time on the sea is in your plans, consider the Riviera di Levante, the eastern stretch of the Ligurian coast from just east of Genoa to Portovènere, which includes the justifiably well-known peninsula of Portofino. To the west of Genoa, the stretch known as the Riviera di Ponente is more crowded than the Levante. A populous strip of roads and streets linking high rises that battle for a view of the sea, the Riviera di Ponente now competes in prices with the French Côte d'Azur. The eastern Riviera, however, is less crowded, and the towns remain more separate from one another, making it a delightful area in which to spend a week or so, especially in the shoulder and low seasons.

The main city of Liguria is Genoa, which we find hard to manage. Important palaces, museums, and churches seem to be losing the battle for prominence in a high-density, high-speed, formerly splendid city. Despite its problems, Genoa is certainly worth a visit of a day or two, but not a week-long stay.

The passenger ships visible in the harbor are usually not cruise ships but port-to-port vessels that have numerous sailings weekly to cities in Sardinia and Sicily (and on to Naples, Rome, and Tunis). The fares are low, tickets can be purchased one-way, the food is good, the cabins are comfortable, and you can take a car if you wish. Check with any travel agent or Tirrenia Line office.

Advance booking time needed for July and August—six months. For May, June, and September—three to four months. For the rest of the year—up to one month.

The best selection of rentals on the Ligurian coast is from Four Star Living, Vacation Home Rentals (VHR) Worldwide, and Villas International.

VALLEY OF THE PO: Although the cities of this central area—Turin, Alessandria, Milan, Piacenza, Cremona, Parma, and Bologna—are all very much worth a visit, they are in reach of home bases in more attractive regions to either the north or the south of the hills and flatlands of this area. This probably explains why there are so few rentals available through North American agencies. In winter, and into spring, endless days of fog are the norm.

NORTH OF THE PO VALLEY: The regions of Valle d'Aosta, northern Piedmont, and Lombardy occupy the northwest portion of Italy and the western mountain country, with Valle d'Aosta encompassing the southern slopes of Mont Blanc and the northern Piedmont sharing the Lepontine Alps and the lake country with Switzerland. This is perhaps the most spectacularly beautiful part of the country, a magnet for skiers in winter and for hikers, walkers, cyclists, wanderers, and lake sailors in the summer. The country around Lakes Maggiore, Como, and Lugano is an idyllic area of water, mountains, and shorelines dotted with beautiful small villages and covered with subtropical vegetation: oleanders, magnolias, palm trees, citrus trees, tulip trees, cedars, and nut trees. It is a tourist-oriented area, with restaurants, hotels, villas, and lake steamers. From a home base in the area, visits can be made to the cities of Milan, Alessandria, and Turin to the south, and journeys can be made into Switzerland, from Geneva in the west to Interlaken, and St. Moritz if desired. Mainline railroads run through Stresa and Arona on Lake Maggiore, and they connect Como and Lugano on the route between Milan and Zurich.

May, June, and September are the best months to visit, followed by October; for skiing in Valle d'Aosta, December is the peak month for crowds and prices, January to mid-February the best period to go.

Advance booking time needed for July and August—six months. For May, June, and September—two to three months. For the rest of the year—one to two months. *Ski resorts:* for December, February, March— six months; for November and January—two to three months.

The agencies with the widest variety of rentals in the northwest area mountain and lake country are Hideaways International, Interhome USA, Rent A Home International, Vacation Home Rentals (VHR) Worldwide, and Villas International.

THE NORTHEASTERN AREA: This is a large and remarkably varied area, incorporating the eastern Lombardy region, Trentino–Alto Adige, and Friuli–Venezia Giulia. The first two regions share Lake Garda, the largest lake in Italy at thirty-two miles long and eleven miles wide. Mountains rise from the northwestern shore, and looking up the lake from the more densely populated south shore is almost like looking out to sea. Along the eastern shore are numerous villages and resorts, some very pleasant and some very touristy. The little town of Desenzano, one of the largest on the shoreline, is a treat to visit, and the food in its traditional restaurants is excellent. The climate is mild, but in the midwinter months the fogs of the valley can affect the southern end (to the benefit of the famous vineyards of Bardolino). The main city is Verona, and it is easy to visit Parma, Padua, Bologna, and Venice from anywhere in the area. The railroad mainline that connects Venice, Verona, and Milan runs through the lakeside towns of Peschiera and Desenzano, and there is town-to-town bus service, so a car is useful but not essential.

Most vacation rentals in the Lake Garda area are available through At Home Abroad; Interhome USA; International Services, Vacanza Bella, and Villas International.

A drive northeast from the Lake Garda area into the region of Trentino–Alto Adige is like going into another world, because the road that turns off the *autostrada* north of Trento to Cortina d'Ampezzo goes through the heart of the justifiably famous Dolomites. Rail service runs from Venice and from Padua as far as Calalzo, 20 miles (32 km) south of Cortina, and connects with a bus. But to get into the Dolomites, a car is essential.

Advance booking time needed for July and August—six months. For May, June, and September—three to four months. For the rest of the year—up to one month.

Contact Four Star Living, Interhome USA, International Services, and Villas International for information on rentals in the Trentino–Alto Adige region.

VENETO: The final region of the northeast, is separate by virtue of its capital city, Venice, where there are a few rentals available. A week would be ideal here, concentrated on the city, with a possible excursion along the coast to Trieste or even into Yugoslavia if you have a car. In Venice proper, however, a car is of no use, and all vehicles must be left in the parking garage on the Piazzale Roma.

We have not visited rental properties in the Veneto region, but from several other trips to Venice we are aware of the high price of hotel rooms, particularly in June and July, with only slight reductions in the shoulder months; $150 to $250 per night is not out of line for two-, three-, or four-star hotels, so a studio or one-bedroom apartment renting for under $800 per week would be a bargain. An apartment or villa outside the city proper will rent for much less, even in Mestre, across the lagoon on the mainland; it is easy to get into the city by bus or train from the surrounding area. If you are on a budget, ask the agents for prices for similar rentals in Venice proper and in the near environs and compare.

As for the best time to visit Venice, romantics would say anytime. But to better enjoy the city itself, from mid-April through mid-June and September and October are the best months to visit. From mid-June through August the weather is fine, but Venice is packed with tourists, and the midwinter months can be chilly, rainy, and possibly foggy.

Advance booking time needed for June, July, and August—six months. For May and September—four months. For the rest of the year— one to two months.

The agencies for Venice and the Veneto region are Four Star Living; Hometours International; International Services; Interhome USA; and Villas International.

Central Italy
(Abruzzi, Latium, Marche, Tuscany, Umbria)

This is the area most popular with North Americans (and other foreigners) who want to experience what is correctly perceived to be the heart of Italy, from the tree- and vineyard-covered hills of Tuscany and Umbria and the cities of Rome, Florence, Siena, Perugia, and Pisa, to the ancient, enchanting hill towns such as Arezzo, San Gimignano, Cortona, Todi, Orvieto, Spoleto, and Assisi. Washed by two seas, the Mediterranean and the Adriatic, this is a land with a mild climate and rich vegetation. Many weeks can be spent here profitably, varying one's time between the hills, the mountains, the cities, and the seas. Nonetheless, you'll depart feeling that there remains so much to do and see that a return is essential.

Much has been written about this part of Italy, and it is easy to get an idea of what it is like—its history, foods, people, and lands—from volumes in libraries and bookstores. Nothing, however, is like being there, and it takes time to soak it all in.

ENVIRONS AND ACCOMMODATIONS. The complexity and wealth of things to see and do suggests that central Italy should be divided in two: Rome and its region of Latium and neighboring Abruzzi in the south, and Florence and Siena with surrounding Tuscany and Umbria in the north. Fortunately, the distances within the area are not great (less than 180 miles, or 294 km, between Florence and Rome, with Perugia about halfway, and Siena less than an hour south of Florence). Therefore, your choice of location is a matter of the immediate surroundings you prefer rather than a question of what cities or sites you want to visit during a few weeks' time. Earlier we wrote that if you have two weeks in Italy it is impossible to improve on locating in Tuscany, somewhere within an hour or so by car or rail from Florence or Siena as your central city, or in Umbria near Assisi, Perugia, or Todi. A few days in Rome should be included in your plans, and this is easily accomplished. If you have three weeks, you could book an apartment in Rome for the first or last week.

Although there are hundreds of rentals in central Italy, the preponderance are in Tuscany, most in the hill country, but some also available in the cities. As for being in Florence itself, we again suggest that you not drive a car in the city. An alternative is to tell the agent you want to locate in Fiesole, a pretty hilltop village on the outskirts, or other area in the immediate vicinity of, Florence, and on the city's bus route.

As can be seen from the list of agents at the beginning of this chapter, all have rentals in Tuscany (country and cities), and most in Umbria as well. They all offer a wide variety of locations, sizes, and prices; costs reflect sizes and, to a large extent, standards. Choosing is simply a matter of studying maps and guidebooks to decide on general locale, then poring over catalogs and price lists or evaluating the property profiles sent to you. The competition among owners and among companies in this region is tough, so you can expect to get good accommodations.

ROME AND LATIUM: Fewer agencies offer rentals in Rome and the region of Latium around it, but given hotel and restaurant prices there, it is difficult to rent an apartment that is not lower in price and larger in size than a hotel of comparable standards.

Rome is a complex city, full of the artifacts of dozens of centuries, with modern stores and ancient shops, parks and restaurants, shopping streets and grand boulevards, and cities within cities, so that many rich weeks can be spent there. If, however, your planned stay in Italy is limited to two or three weeks, then a week in Rome and the remainder in another area should be considered.

As for location, the complexity of the city and the changing availability of private rentals make a recommendation of little use, but there are a few that seem constant, available through Vacanza Bella. Another recommendation is a selection of one- and two-bedroom apartments in a venerable building, Residence AldroVandi, in the area of the Villa Borghese park (Rent A Vacation Everywhere is the agent). One of the best approaches is to contact the American director of Rome-based International Services by telephone, or write her with dates, size, standards, and the range of rent you are willing to pay. Take the good advice she or someone on her English-speaking staff offers; they specialize in finding Italian rentals that meet North American standards. (The company has two U.S. contacts if you want to save the cost of an international phone call. Also try Vacanze in Italia, Vacation Home Rentals (VHR) Worldwide, and Villas International. For properties in the beautiful lake country of Latium just north of Rome, contact Cuendet-Posarelli Vacations, Susan T. Pidduck/Cuendet Agent, or, in Canada, DER Tours. These are ideal if you want to be close to, but not in, the city.

See Appendix B for the names and addresses of Italian-based companies that have English-speaking owners or staff and have evidenced a strong interest in North American clientele.

Location and transportation. There is no part of central Italy that cannot be visited easily from any other part. Two *autostrada*'s run north and south, one along the spine of the country and one along the Adriatic coast, and a third connects Florence and the Mediterranean coast north of Livorno. Tolls on these *autostrada*s are high, cumulatively about $15 between Florence and Rome, for example. The primary highways (non-toll) are good and are often divided, such as the one between Florence and Siena and those along much of the west and east coasts. Secondary roads can be slow, usually becoming the main street of each town they come to, and they wind through the hill country (all the better to see it).

Mainline railroads run like the *autostrada*s, along the east and west coasts and along the spine. The trains are good, the prices are modest, and the service is reliable except for occasional work stoppages. There are twenty departures daily, for example, from Rome to Florence, and vice versa; nine daily between Florence and Siena (plus twelve by bus). Where a car is invaluable is in exploring the hills and hill towns that are the essence of Italy.

Unless you have considerable time, you will probably want to spend it all in central Italy, but wanderers can find numerous sailings weekly from Ancona to Yugoslavia and Greece (year-round) and to Egypt (March through October) on big passenger ships with good food and comfortable cabins. Tickets are sold one-way or round trip, like train or bus tickets. These are not cruise ships, and it is possible to take your car, although cars cost as much as a passenger in a class-A cabin. All the sailings out of Rimini are to Yugoslavian ports, and those out of Pescara go only to Split (Yugoslavia). Tickets and information are available in any office of Adriatica Line or at travel agents in east coast cities.

On the west coast, there are many sailings weekly between Livorno and ports on Sardinia and the French island of Corsica; out of Civitavecchia (the port for Rome), there are four sailings daily for the eight-hour voyage to Sardinia. Tickets and information on the Civitavecchia-Sardinia route are available at main railroad stations; the ships are run by the government railroad, FDS, and tickets are the same as those for the trains (cabin extra). For other sailings, see an Italian travel agency or contact Tirrenia Line (see also information on Sardinia in the southern region discussion, below).

Advance booking time. For June, July, and August—six months. For May and September—four months. For the rest of the year—one to two months; Rome—two months.

Southern Italy
(Apulia, Basilicata, Calabria, Lipari Islands, Sardinia, Sicily)

There is a saying in the south of Italy, "The money stops in Rome," because people believe government funds for transportation, roads, streets, and other public works are unfairly and disproportionately committed to Italy from Rome northward, leaving the south in need. To the outsider this may or may not be a valid complaint, but indeed the southern third of the country does seem different from the central and northern regions. Perhaps it is the climate, the soil, the foods, and the traces of Magna Graecia and the Orient as well as those of Rome. Maybe it is the winds of Africa across the Ionian Sea, the weeks on end of sunshine, the hot summers and balmy winters, or the sense that Sicilians and Sardinians are unlike mainland Italians. Whatever it is, a stay in the south is wonderfully different.

ENVIRONS AND ACCOMMODATIONS. There are few rentals in the southern region, relative to the central and northern areas, but enough to make a visit of a week or more possible, and the locations capitalize on the best that the south has to offer.

The region is best explored by car, and most, but not all, of it can be reached by a day trip or an overnighter from a home base anywhere in the area. However, if you want to get very far into Sicily—to Palermo, Trapani, and the west coast—it is best to locate a rental in Sicily for a week rather than try to do it from the area of Naples. Although the *autostrada* runs south from Naples to Reggio at the tip of Calabria, and along much of the north and east coasts of Sicily it is a 460-mile (750 km) trip, between Naples and Palermo, including a ferry crossing from Reggio to the island of Sicily.

THE BAY OF NAPLES AND THE AMALFI COAST: Although scattered rentals are available throughout much of the region, one of the most popular areas to visit and stay is the Costa Amalfinata, the Amalfi Coast, which comprises the south shore of the peninsula between Sorrento and Salerno south of Naples. Here the villas, and apartments in villas, tend toward the deluxe and are priced accordingly, but it is arguably the most ruggedly beautiful coast in Italy. Its location, close to Naples, Pompeii, Herculaneum, Vesuvius, and within easy access to the nearby islands of Capri and Ischia, adds to its virtues—much sunshine, hot summers moderated by the sea breezes, and warm winters. The vegetation is both piney and subtropical, and the main coast towns of Amalfi and Positano are not only beautiful examples of whitewashed southern Mediterranean architecture but are small, manageable, and delightful. Most of the rentals in Amalfi (town) are individual villas, and in Positano both villas and apartments in villas are available. The best times to spend a week or two on this outstanding coast are from mid-March to mid-June, or from mid-September into early November. For swimmers: the sea temperatures are warmer in the fall months.

The rentals on Capri fall into the general category of luxury, but, as is the case with the Amalfi Coast, the setting is idyllic, and most of the properties must be of the luxury type to assure privacy from tourist crowds.

As for Naples itself, it is a strangely dramatic city, and it sometimes seems hard to discern the rubble of antiquity from yesterday's debris. The traffic is mad, and anarchistic drivers have long transformed traffic lights into odd and ignored symbols of a past time; no unsuspecting visitor should actually try to cross a street just because the light has turned green. Yet the tumult of the city, its treasures, the intensity of its citizens, its fine restaurants, its setting, and its climate conspire to draw outsiders to it. Unless you are very urbane, a week at most in Naples is plenty—or, as an excellent alternative, find a rental in the vicinity and take a train or bus (not a car) into the city for daily visits.

The drawback to the Gulf of Naples area, from the city itself south to Salerno and the islands, is the tourist crowds from mid-June through August, when the Italians and northern Europeans join with North Americans and Asians in the streets of Pompeii and on the boats to Capri. The crowds can be avoided by renting a deluxe villa with grounds and by visiting in the low or shoulder seasons.

Transportation in the Naples area is not difficult to find. In addition to the mainline railroads that connect Naples with Rome to the north, Reggio to the south, and Bari and the Adriatic coast to the east, a local called the Circumvesuviana leaves Naples every thirty to forty minutes for Pompeii and Sorrento and points between, and returns from Sorrento with the same frequency. It does not cross over the peninsula to Amalfi on the south coast, but public buses and taxis are available for the short trip. If you have a car (and having one is very convenient in this region) and you want to take trips into Naples from the Amalfi area, we suggest that you drive to Sorrento or Vico Equense, leave the car, and take the train.

The agencies with the best selection of properties in the Amalfi Coast–Naples area are At Home Abroad, Hideaways International, Hometours International, International Services, Rent A Home International, Vacanza Bella, Vacation Home Rentals (VHR) Worldwide, and Villas International. If you are especially interested in Capri, the main agents are International Services and Villas International, and for the privacy offered by more remote islands (Ponza, Panarea), contact International Services.

Advance booking time needed for June, July, and August—six months; for May and September—four months; for the rest of the year—one to two months.

APULIA AND BASILICATA: Except in the cities and larger towns, this southern part of southern Italy seems very far away from the rest. Much of this area is rugged and wild, a serene joining of pine-covered and chestnut-covered hills with olive trees and tended farms. As for the Adriatic coast, aside from fine beaches we do not find much to recommend it, especially between Bari and Brindisi. Neither of these cities is of particular interest for travelers, particularly with so many splendid alternatives in Italy; they are principally ports, and the latter is crowded in summer with young (and not-so-young) North American and European tourists boarding or disembarking from the many passenger ships that sail daily between Italy and Corfu and mainland Greece. Otranto, near the end of the "heel," makes a good central base for exploring Apulia's unusual hill villages and enjoying the good beaches north toward Brindisi. Vacanze in Italia and Villas International are the only agents we find with rentals on the Adriatic coast near Brindisi.

CALABRIA: On the west, Calabria is the "toe" of Italy, separating the Ionian Sea from the Tyrrhenian Sea, which connect only where the mainland

and Sicily almost meet, across the Strait of Messina. In this southern reach of Italy, and especially on Sicily across the strait, Magna Graecia's influence is felt most strongly.

Calabria is a region with a benign climate in which orange and lemon orchards compete with vineyards and olive groves, and flowers and citrus bergamot are grown for the perfumes of Italy and France. The main city of Calabria, Reggio, is a fairly modern town, commanding from its palm-lined promenade a vista across the strait to the city of Messina, on Sicily. A home base in the hills, or in a villa along the Riviera Calabrese between Reggio and Gioia Tauro, makes an excellent center from which to explore all of southern Italy and even Sicily. Two weeks can easily be devoted to this enterprise, especially if a journey to western Sicily is included.

Transportation in the south is by the railroad and the primary highway that circles the "toe" of Italy, mostly following the coastline, connecting Reggio and the Adriatic coast. To get into the hill country of Calabria and into the unique villages of southern Apulia, a car is very helpful, but it is possible to see much of the southland by rail and bus. Travel westward from Reggio is across the strait by boat or ferry to the port of Messina, from which the *autostrada* and the railroads go in two directions to circle Sicily: south to Catania and Syracuse, and west to Palermo and Trapani.

For rentals in Calabria, contact Four Star Living, International Services, and Villas International.

SICILY: The afternoon we walked among Selinunte's great columns—some standing, but more lying tumbled like a devastated forest—we, another couple, and a young boy were the only people in Selinunte, once a city of 100,000, the westernmost outpost of ancient Greek civilization. It was March, and a cool breeze blew off the sea, but we knew it was the right time to be there, long before the crowds from the rest of Europe would arrive in July. North Americans seldom visit western Sicily at any time, although the year-round mild climate makes a visit in the off-seasons not only possible but desirable.

The contrasts in this land are not only between the blue Mediterranean and the scorched summer hills, the green spring fields and the white almond trees in bloom, but between the serenity of the Greek and Roman ruins and the chaos of contemporary Sicilian civilization, especially in the cities. It is much easier to get an idea of the latter than it is of the former, but spending time in Sicily is very worthwhile. And if you go between September and December, or between March and late June, just visiting the ancient sites or walking the narrow, sloping streets of Phoenician Erice on the mountaintop above Trapani is not only worth the journey but restorative of the spirit.

Transportation to and around Sicily is by the railroad that follows the north coast between Messina at the east tip to Trapani at the west, and between Messina and Syracuse along the east coast. The train also cuts diagonally across the island between Catania and Palermo, with a spur to Agrigento on the south coast. However, the length of the south-west coast betwen Trapani and Syracuse, some 225 miles (365 km), has no rail service; bus service is fair. In the low season there is limited bus service from Trapani to Erice, and none to the ruins at Selinunte on the extreme southwest coast.

Much of Sicily is off the main paths, and a car will enhance your visit. One can be rented in any of the main cities, or can be brought by short-run ferry from Reggio on the mainland. We brought ours in by long-run ferry, once from Genoa into Palermo (twenty-three hours) and once from Cagliari, on the south end of Sardinia, to Trapani (ten hours). The ships also connect Trapani and Palermo with Naples, and for a glimpse of yet another culture, book a cabin for the eight-hour one-way voyage out of Trapani to Tunis. You can return on the same ship after a short layover. Contact any Tirrenia Line office in the port cities, or a travel agency.

Rental properties in Palermo, Catania, Messina, or Trapani are not, in our view, the best home bases for visiting Sicily. The cities are hard to cope with, and although there are many treasures to see in them, they are best visited on day trips from a home base elesewhere on the island. At the same time, this area is not well developed in terms of rental villas and apartments, and properties are scattered near such places as Cefalù, Ragusa, and Sambucca. The idea is not necessarily to find the best place to stay in Sicily (because that is debatable), but to find a comfortable, modestly priced villa from which to explore all of Sicily. Contact DER Tours, Four Star Living, International Services, Cuendet-Posarelli Vacations, Susan T. Pidduck/Cuendet Agent, Vacation Home Rentals (VHR) Worldwide, and Villas International. Look over their material, study a map and guide to Sicily, and make a choice. Plan for at least a week.

Advance booking time needed for July and August—six months; for June, May and September—three months; for the rest of the year—one to two months.

SARDINIA: This large island, almost the size of Sicily, differs greatly from Sicily, as well as from the mainland. The people who live there generally see themselves as Sardinians first and Italians second. Its isolation, 155 miles (250 km) off the coast at its closest point, has over the centuries created a society distinct from the rest of Italy, based on agriculture and sheep raising, and only recently moving into some industry. Politically it is an autonomous region, self-governing in its own development, a major part of which has been the rise of tourism.

It is physically beautiful, with a craggy east coast and a central valley of green rolling fields and hills with mountain vistas through which the main highway runs south for 200 miles (330 km) between Porto Torres and Cagliari. The cities are not of special interest, and although Alghero and Arbatax are nice, small, port towns, Cagliari holds little appeal. This is not to say that a week on Sardinia will not be enjoyable, only that it is less unusual than many other parts of Italy. If, however, you are looking for an out-of-the-way, deluxe resort area blessed with sunshine, beaches, shops, and social life, it can be found concentrated on the northeast coast, the famed Costa Smeralda.

There are flights from Italy's major mainland cities and from Nice and Paris into Cagliari, and from the major Italian cities to Alghero, Sassari, and Olbia. By sea, there are large ferryliners from Genoa, Livorno, Civitavecchia (Rome), and Naples to the four Sardinian ports, and between Cagliari and Trapani in Sicily.

There has been very little development of tourist accommodations outside of the Costa Smeralda, but the rentals there tend to be luxury-class villas, making a stay part of the good life. Most visitors are content to spend their week or two in this splendid isolation, but we recommend at least a train trip to Cagliari just to see the countryside. If you have a car, a drive along the east coast is very dramatic, and a visit to Neptune's Grotto on the west coast near Alghero is also worthwhile.

The best contacts for booking a villa on Sardinia are Four Star Living, International Services, Vacation Home Rentals (VHR) Worldwide, and Villas International.

Advance booking time needed for June, July, and August—six months; for May and September—four months; for the rest of the year—one to two months.

THE LIPARI (AEOLIAN) ISLANDS AND PONZA: Off the northeastern tip of Sicily, west of the mainland, lie the six Lipari Islands, among which Stromboli is the best known. They exist as a mix of past and present: some are almost primitive, others are dotted with luxury villas as well as modest homes of the permanent residents, many of whom are fishermen. One island, Panarea, is rich with vegetation and has moved quietly into the world of tourism, but only for those who want to get away, who want tranquillity and privacy, who can deal with the absence of restaurants and hotels, and who can afford rents in the $1,000-per-week range and higher (off-season rents drop substantially).

Ponza is north of the Lipari Islands, almost due west of Naples. Another getaway, it is a more populous and developed island than Panarea, and is more on the tourist paths, but nevertheless it is a pleasant and unusual place to stay. Information on rentals on Ponza and in the Liparis can be obtained from International Services.

10

Portugal

♦

♦ THE AGENCIES

AARP Travel Service (the Algarve; Madeira)
At Home Abroad (the Algarve—Carvoeiro to Salema)
B. & D. de Vogüe Travel Service (north of Lisbon—the Costa da Prato)
Interhome, Inc. USA (the Algarve; Lisbon area)
Rent A Home International (the Algarve; Lisbon, Madeira)
Vacation Home Rentals (VHR) Worldwide (the Algarve; Lisbon area)
Villa Leisure (the Algarve—Carvoeiro, Vale do Lobo)
Villas & Apartments in Portugal (the Algarve—Carvoeiro)
Villas International (Algarve, central coast; Lisbon area)

♦ THE COUNTRY

Portugal, the westernmost country of Europe, is a little smaller than Ohio and slightly more populous (about 10 million), but there the comparison ends. The moderating effect of the Atlantic, the sea itself, the climate, and the relatively low prices join to make Portugal a magnet for tourists. The better the weather, the more the tourists, and the more the tourists, the more expansive the development, especially on the sun-drenched south coast, the Algarve. Much of the resort area development is financed by northern European companies, the rest by Portuguese firms and some international combines.

In the interior, where they have a common boundary, and along the south coast, similarities in climate and topography exist between Spain and Portugal. Spain's Costa del Sol, however, faces the Mediterranean, while the Algarve coast is on the Atlantic. The countries are different in

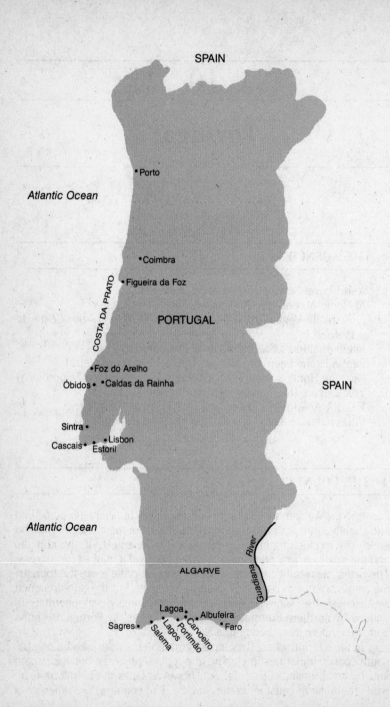

many other ways, from architecture to language and a seemingly slower pace. Fewer visitors are seen off the main tourist trails of Portugal, and some observers have said that Portugal today is like the Spain of twenty years ago. Though that observation is true in some ways, the differences go far deeper, into the Portuguese character itself. This is a rewarding country to visit, not just for the sunshine of the Algarve, but to see the treasure of its luminous past, to visit its castles and cities, and to feel the warmth of its people.

Between the greener north and the sun-bathed beaches of the south, Portugal is a country of contrasts. Equally noteworthy is the contrast between life in the rural areas and life in the cities and resorts. In rural Portugal, little seems to have changed. The entire nation remains relatively poor, but is dotted with cities of industry and commerce, resorts and some of Europe's most captivating and undervisited ancient towns—alive with history, shops, markets, and bustling streets.

We drove into Portugal from Spain, crossing the border near Badajoz, then traveled south toward the Algarve. The olive and almond groves covering the rolling hills were impeccably tended; beneath the miles and miles of rows, the ground was finely tilled. In the village of Entradas, south of Beja, we stopped for coffee and got the feeling that the people in town were not accustomed to foreigners. But their smiles were friendly and the cups of espresso were generous and good. The cost was 25¢ per cup (less than half the price of an espresso in the resorts of the Algarve—a good indication of overall price differences).

Staying for a week on the south coast in an exquisite villa in a resort called Carvoeiro Clube, near the village of Carvoeiro, gave us time to explore the south coast. We then drove northwest to Lisbon, Estoril, and Cascais before moving north to the Costa da Prato, bound for Spain and the Cantabrian coast. Except for the absence of high mountains, this countryside reminded us in more ways of northern California. Cultivated fields of olives and grapes, rolling hills, and forests of pine and cork oak provide many of the nation's principal products. Portugal is physically beautiful, with a benign climate and little or no sense of threat (as is sometimes felt by travelers to foreign countries and big cities).

We were often asked why the number of American visitors had diminished over the past decade. Countries, it seems, go in and out of fashion as tourist destinations, especially with Americans. This is possibly due to the influence of travel agencies, which are, in turn, influenced on a year-to-year basis by everything from world economics to the public relations program of one country or another. Another explanation is that when a political act takes place in one country, Americans do not distinguish that country from the other countries in the area. For example, after the Italy-based *Achille Lauro* was hijacked in the central Mediterranean, Americans stayed away in droves from all of southern Europe.

If these factors indeed influence tourist patterns, Portugal should be very attractive to travelers; the prices are among the very lowest in Western Europe, and there has been no violence or terrorism in recent memory. As for language, there is rarely a problem. For several years English has been a mandatory subject in schools, so it is hard to find a person under the age of twenty-five who doesn't speak some English, often fluently.

Another consideration, which pertains only to the Algarve, is whether or not other equally attractive resort areas are accessible to North Americans with less effort and cheaper transportation. This question is discussed further in the section on the Algarve below. A final factor is that Portugal has not kept pace with most other European countries in developing and promoting its many virtues. There are few places to stay outside of the principal cities, the resort areas of the Algarve, and along the coast west of Lisbon. It is necessary to look a bit harder than in most of Europe for the right two- or three-week rental, but once a place is found, it will be rewarding.

A note on pronunciation. Since many towns and other proper names have an *s* in them, it is useful to know that with few exceptions an *s* after a vowel is pronounced as a soft "sh"; Cascais is pronounced "Cash-caish," Silves is pronounced "Silvesh." The often-seen cedilla, *ç*, is pronounced like a soft *s*, almost a *z:* Açores is pronounced Azores. The *ã* is pronounced "ah," and is usually associated with a final *o*, as in Portemão.

BEST TIMES OF YEAR TO VISIT. In the Algarve, the largest, most developed, and most popular destination area in Portugal, the average daytime temperature in January is 55 degrees and there are five days of rain. In April the temperature rises to 70 degrees or above and rainy days drop to four. By midsummer, clouds are rarely seen, and temperatures in the upper 80s are common; by September, the temperatures have moderated to the low 80s with an average of twenty-eight days without rain. The seasons, which affect prices considerably, are a little complex, but they follow a fairly standard pattern throughout the country, taking into account holiday periods such as Christmas and Easter. Dates given here are approximate.

Low	Shoulder	High	Peak
Nov. 1–Dec. 23	Dec. 24 – Jan. 6	June 1 – June 23	June 24–Aug. 30
Jan. 6–March 14	March 15 – May 30	Sept. 1 – Sept. 30	
	Oct. 1 – Nov. 1		

To those who live there, April, May, September, and October are the finest months. The weather is good, the sea is fine, and, they say, many of the tourists have gone back home. Even November has a large share of sunny days, and the sea is almost warm enough to enjoy.

As for the rest of Portugal, meaning principally the resort towns just west of Lisbon and a few spots along the coast well to the north, May and September are ideal. April and October are also excellent, and March and November are not unpleasant but do have a greater chance of rain and clouds.

GENERAL INFORMATION ABOUT RENTALS. Villas and apartments are the two types of vacation rentals available. A scattering of the villas are private homes, but generally they are individual houses in resort areas, and were especially built for renting. A few of these may be owned by the company responsible for developing the resort, but more often they are the holiday homes of well-to-do Europeans who rent them to, and have them managed by, the development company. These villa clusters dot the Algarve, and many of the companies have U.S. agents (as well as British, German, Swiss, and Scandinavian ones). The houses are predominantly upscale in style, amenities, and price; most are built in the curvilinear, Moorish-influenced architecture for which much of southern Portugal is famous. White is the universal color.

Apartments are also available throughout the Algarve. In the resort settlements and rural areas they are usually in attractive low-rise buildings, with white stucco still prevailing. As land becomes more precious, too many of these settlements are being built like cells in a beehive, but more often they are tastefully designed town houses arranged around a pool, with a nearby restaurant and cluster of shops. In the larger coastal towns of the Algarve, both on and away from the beaches, the apartments are more conventional, often in modern low- and medium-height buildings, some pleasant and some jammed together as builders vie for space.

The villas in the resort area west of Lisbon, and the slowly developing Costa da Prato north of Lisbon, are for the most part individual properties. However, more resorts and purpose-built villas and apartment complexes are surely not far off. In Lisbon proper, and in the towns of Estoril and Cascais, most of the rentals are apartments.

To stay in a villa in an Algarve resort, or in the resort towns near Lisbon, puts one at risk of missing the real Portugal. These resorts, as in any country whose general populace is poor, are set apart from the daily life and real world of the country. Visitors have a tendency to remain in the beautiful isolation of the resort area, buying groceries only at the resort store, eating at the resort restaurants, drinking on the terraces of the resort bars, lying on the resort beaches, and hearing only the English language. Yet inland from the beaches you can see ruins from Roman times and the influence of the Moors in old villages, fortresses, and ancient churches. It is possible to eat in small cafés where good local food is served at very low prices. The answer, then, is to make excursions out from that comfortable villa or apartment to take in all the rest that Portugal has to offer.

TRANSPORTATION. Lisbon is the principal destination city for flights from North America, but there is an international airport in Faro, in the Algarve, that can be flown to, normally with a stop in Lisbon. A car is important in the Algarve and in the Costa da Prato area, but not essential in Lisbon and its vicinity. When renting a car, compare prices. Not just among Hertz, Avis, and National (or between Europcar or Tilden, in Europe), but among these agencies and the large lease/rental brokers such as Auto Europe, Europe by Car, and others (see Chapter 4 for more information). Transportation in each region is briefly described in the following regional sections.

◆ THE REGIONS

Portugal is not so much a kaleidoscope of geographical and topographical regions as it is a consistently beautiful land of rolling hills, with low granite mountains in the north and dry lands along the eastern interior. Lush vegetation and cultivated fields dominate the west, punctuated by hills that rise from the sea, and there is a narrow plain along the south coast.

It is approximately 450 miles (730 highway km) between Portemão at the south and Valença do Minho on the northern border with Spain. The distance from east to west is less than 200 miles (323 km) at the country's widest point.

To explore a large part of the country from a single location in the central west coast near Lisbon is not impossible, especially if you have three weeks or more. A most rewarding approach is to divide your time, devoting a week to the north, including the Lisbon area, and two weeks to the Algarve, or vice versa. You may get some ideas from this chapter on how to apportion your time, but you should also study a good country guidebook. If you have two weeks or less, consider staying in one area and enjoying it in depth.

Most vacation rentals are concentrated in three regions: the Algarve; Lisbon and the nearby Estoril coast; and the Costa da Prato, which is the west coast beginning north of Lisbon. The Algarve is by far the most developed in terms of resort complexes. The seaside towns of Estoril and Cascais and the coast near Lisbon comprise the older, more established resort area, while Costa da Prato's villages are barely touched by tourist development.

Two other areas, which we have yet to visit, are Portuguese but remote from Portugal. The island of Madeira is off the coast of Africa some 500 miles (805 km) southwest of the tip of the mainland, and the twelve islands of the Azores are 790 miles (1,271 km) at sea almost due west of Lisbon. Both are good destinations if you are looking for an island, and rentals are available. Inquire of Rent A Home International and Villas International for property information, and also see the Matur Holiday Club listing in Appendix B.

The Algarve

ENVIRONS AND ACCOMMODATIONS. Highway EN-125 runs for 108 miles (175 km) along the southern coast of Portugal, from the Spanish frontier at the Guadiana River westward to Ponta de Sagres, the south-westernmost point of Europe. The northern border of the province roughly parallels the coast and the highway, some 40 miles (64 km) inland. Thus, the Algarve is a narrow stretch of east-west land influenced by the Atlantic Ocean, which forms its southern and western coasts. An even narrower band actually delineates what visitors and developers alike think of as the Algarve. It is a five-to-ten-mile-wide strip that edges the coast, roughly back to where the EN-125 highway runs. Along its hundred-mile route (160 km) short side roads lead to dozens of beaches, seaside villages, and resort communities. North of the highway are the hills of the Algarve and a scattering of small villages, some of which retain evidence of the Moors, who built cities and fortifications there in the tenth and eleventh centuries. One of these cities, Silves, the Moorish capital of Algarve, was a center of art, culture, and learning rivaling Lisbon—and Granada (Spain). The remains of several crusaders are entombed in Silves's unusual thirteenth-century cathedral.

Much of the strip between the highway and the sea is slightly rolling land, sloping gently toward the coast, where cliffs rise from the sea. The bases of the cliffs are scalloped by beaches of seemingly always clean white-and-yellow sand, all of them named and ranked for beauty and degree of surf in tourist publications and the *Algarve Gazette* (a slick, English-language magazine that vividly portrays foreign life in the province). During the past decade, most of the tourist development has taken place along this narrow strip. It began around Faro and has slowly moved westward. Faro remains the transportation hub, with express train service and buses to and from Lisbon, and has the only international airport in the Algarve.

Driving between Lagos and Portemão, we were only mildly surprised to see a pair of yoked oxen pulling a plow beneath the olive trees. White villas dotted the hillsides, but we knew that the plowman and his family did not live in any of them. These villas are among the thousands in the Algarve owned by sun-starved northern Europeans who have found an almost-year-round holiday paradise. There are even a few houses owned by well-to-do Americans, Spaniards, and Portuguese.

Unless you are seeking only sun, sea, and the comfort and amenities of a resort, it helps to have a car so you can leave the beach and the pool for excursions to the hill country villages. Visits to the ancient walled town of Évora, to Santiago do Cacém near the west coast, or even to Lisbon and its environs are feasible. Because there is nothing exotic about the Algarve resorts themselves, where English is commonly heard, it is important to venture out to enjoy the older Portugal.

The Carvoeiro Clube near the highway town of Lagoa is typical of some of the better rentals in this region. The villa we stayed in was set on about a quarter acre of tended lawns and gardens, separated from other villas by a low white wall. This was one of about seventy individual luxury villas of two bedrooms or more. With terraces, a heated pool, a garage, a fireplace, two full baths, television, telephone, and daily maid service, our rental was spacious, light, comfortable, and stylish. The sea was visible in the near distance, and it was only a two-minute drive to the reception building or to the resort's cluster of shops and restaurants.

Along with the Carvoeiro Clube de Tenis and the less costly villas and town houses of Clube Atlantico and Monte Carvoeiro, Carvoeiro Clube is part of an immense, beautifully laid-out resort area, that stretches ten miles along the palisades of the Atlantic near the village of Carvoeiro. The principal U.S. agents for rentals here are Villas International and Apartments & Villas in Portugal.

The Carvoeiro Clube complex is one of the largest, but there are many resort developments along the coast of the Algarve. Some are less expensive, very few are more expensive. Some feature association with a golf course nearby, and others have their own. Others, known as apart-hotels, are more like fully serviced four- and five-star apartment hotels. A few are quite modest, in style and amenities as well as price, but these are seldom represented by North American agencies. Nevertheless, you should contact all of the agencies shown at the beginning of this chapter to gather information. Some of the properties are budget stretchers, so if you are not looking for a deluxe villa, be sure to make this clear.

The main source of rental property information for travelers willing to book directly is the Portuguese National Tourist Office in New York (see Appendix C for the address). Ask for material on rentals in the Algarve and you will receive descriptive brochures, but rarely any prices. Using this material, decide on and write to companies with rentals that appeal to you. The resort developments are so new, and the competition is so strong, that it is reasonably safe to book a villa or an aparthotel sight unseen *if* you specify that you do not want a place in any of the larger towns (see "A cautionary note," below).

Very few of the moderately priced apartments are represented by North American agencies. Except at peak season, they can best be rented by going there, taking a hotel, and scouting around. The best approach is to go to an office of the Região de Turismo do Algarve (Regional Tourist Agency) in any of the larger towns and inquire.

In addition to the resort areas and the independent country villas, the larger towns of the Algarve, especially Albufeira, have become centers in which young European people gather. They often share the lower-priced apartments, even renting small studios. It is not difficult to find simple places for less than $150 per week. Food and wine are inexpensive, the beaches are great, the sun shines, and the towns' nature changes at night. Remember that some of the young come from other parts of Europe by thumb or bus with very little money, planning to pay for their holidays from someone else's pockets.

A cautionary note. The rush to take advantage of the Algarve's relatively newfound popularity has resulted in some gross overbuilding, especially in the towns along the EN-125 highway. Competition among apartment house owners has meant reduced rates, but we seldom hear about them in the United States, and in any case, a large proportion of these apartments are not in desirable locations. One of the worst offenders is the town of Albufeira, followed by Portemão and Lagos. It was hard to tell whether the rubble in some of the streets of Albufeira and the suburbs of Portemão was from new buildings going up or from old buildings being torn down. The saving features in these towns are the old parts. Once quaint fishing villages, they remain at least partly so despite the rampant construction going on in and around them. Development has moved from east to west, so there are still a few small, isolated, seaside villages that have not yet been hit and have only a few villas or apartments. One we found is Salema, about ten miles (16 km) west of Lagos, which has several very attractive villas for rent through At Home Abroad and a modest apartment building and camping facilities near the beach that have no U.S. agent. (Contact Quinta dos Carriços, Praia da Salema, 8650 Vila do Bispo, Algarve, Portugal; tel: [011-351] 082-65201. The proprietors speak English.)

LOCATION AND TRANSPORTATION. The Faro airport is usually the first, and somewhat disheartening, glimpse visitors get of the Algarve. Rental cars are picked up there, and some of the resorts run shuttle service for booked clients (get the details from the agency you use). Unless you plan to spend all your time in the resort area without exploring the surroundings, we recommend a car rental.

Along the Algarve coast, rail service runs from Vila Real de Sâo António at the Spanish border, through Albufeira and Portemão to Lagos in the west, connecting at Tunes for the mainline run to Lisbon. To the smaller hill towns, and west of the end of the line at Lagos, there is adequate bus service. For example, to get from Lagos to Salema, it is easy to catch the bus, which stops at two points in the little town.

For a visit to Spain, it is only 165 miles (260 km) from Portemão to the great city of Seville, and under 200 miles (325 km) to Cádiz. By rail, the Portuguese line ends at Vila Real de Sâo António, across the Guadiana River from the Spanish rail terminal at Ayamonte, but a through-ticket includes ferry passage across the river (the ferry also takes cars).

PRICES. Rents in the Algarve vary considerably and are affected by size, location, standard, season, services provided, and external amenities (resort shopping center, community pool, tennis courts, etc.). The following approximate rent prices give an idea of what to expect. For low season, shoulder, and peak definitions, refer to the preceding "Best times of year to visit" section. The figures here are in U.S. dollars per week at an exchange rate of 150 escudos per dollar.

	Low	Shoulder	Peak
Simple village studio (Salema)	$175	$220	$275
Simple 1-bdrm (Salema)	250	325	375
3-star city studio (Portemão)	200	280	450
3-star city 1-bdrm (Portemão)	225	300	475
4-star city 1-bdrm (Portemão)	400	500	675
Resort apartment/hotel studio	250	420	675
Resort serviced 1-bdrm town house	335	550	1,200
Resort 3 bdrm. villa, pool, maid	750	1,500	3,000

The marked difference in rates among the seasons is obvious from this table, especially for the period from about June 25 to September 1 (peak season).

As for other prices in the Algarve, despite the fact that they are higher than those in nontourist areas of Portugal, they are low in terms of the low dollar. A good three-course dinner, including a bottle of good wine, will run about $10 per person. Groceries are plentiful and far less expensive than anywhere in Europe or the United States. Rent for a compact car with unlimited mileage is around $120 per week.

ADVANCE BOOKING TIME. For July and August—six months. For shoulder months—two to three months. For the rest of the year—up to one week.

Lisbon Area

ENVIRONS AND ACCOMMODATIONS. The resort area west of Lisbon is smaller in scope and much older and more settled than in Algarve; it centers on the towns of Estoril and Cascais, 10 and 18 miles (16 and 29 km), respectively, from Lisbon proper. Once the playground of the well-to-do, Estoril remains sedately attractive, but despite the few elegant hotels and the famous nineteenth-century casino, it has seen better days. Taking the advice of those who know the area, we stayed in Cascais, a popular, bustling town just ten minutes by train or car along the coast west of Estoril.

This is a relatively small area, but because of its concentration of things to do and see, a week will be full. Two weeks can be enjoyed by exploring as far north as the ancient university city of Coimbra or by tracing the coast west and south of Setúbal, across the Tagus River from Lisbon.

Curiously, North American agencies represent very few rental apartments or villas in the area, although the number of local real estate offices that handle rentals leads us to believe it is not because there is a scarcity (except in peak season).

Lisbon itself is a busy city with a population exceeding 1 million, yet it is quite manageable, except in a car. With seven museums, three noteworthy ancient churches, galleries, excellent restaurants, the opera, and all the other offerings of a large city—at prices much lower than can be found in most other European cities—there is much to do here. Don't miss the Castelo de São Jorge, which has brooded over the city for fifteen centuries. Originally built by Visigoths, expanded and rebuilt by Moors in the ninth century, and itself worth an afternoon, it also affords the best possible view of Lisbon. First-time visitors will be amazed by the similarity between Lisbon's colossal suspension bridge, Ponte Salazar, and San Francisco's Golden Gate Bridge. Built by U.S. Steel, the graceful span across the estuary of the Tagus River was completed in 1966.

Although apartments are available in the city, the Estoril coast area is so close, and the transportation so good, that we see little reason for staying in Lisbon itself. Alternatives are the town of Cascais or its vicinity, Estoril, or more distant—35 miles (57 km)—but beautiful Sintra.

Sintra is a hill town of about 25,000 people. It's magnificent palace and elegant mansions were occupied for generations by royalty and European aristocrats. In a setting lush with vegetation and pine and eucalyptus forests, Sintra captures the imagination with its still-visible opulence. The ruins of a seventh-century Moorish wall and castle rise from a rocky promontory above the town. At even greater heights, the nineteenth-century Palácio da Pena commands a magnificent view of the entire area. Sintra is a romantic and beautiful place in which to stay; it is convenient to Lisbon, to the Estoril coast to the south, and to the fine beaches near Cape Roca, Europe's westernmost point.

Contact Villas & Apartments in Portugal, Rent A Home International, and Villas International for information on Lisbon area rentals. For direct booking, write or telephone: Ultramar Propriedades, LDA, Rua do Regimento Dezanove de Infantaria No. 67 ric, 2750 Cascais, Portugal; tel: 011-351-1-284-4526, fax: 011-351-1-284-4814. This company has an office in England, and the management in Cascais speak English and are very helpful. Give them information on your needs, dates, and price limits. If you do not plan to have a car, request listings that are reasonably close to the Estoril coast rail line; if you will have a car, ask what is available in Sintra.

LOCATION AND TRANSPORTATION. Two-thirds of Portugal is north of Lisbon, but it is nevertheless possible to explore northward to Coimbra and Porto from this area. The outstanding Spanish cities of Santiago de Compostela and, to the northeast, Salamanca, are both a day's drive through interesting country. Locally, trains run every fifteen minutes (every thirty minutes on Sundays and during off-hours) between Lisbon's Cais do Sodré station and Cascais, stopping at Estoril and several other points along the route; travel time is thirty minutes. Suburban trains also run frequently between Lisbon's Rossio station and Sintra, a splendid forty-five-minute trip.

Mainline rail service runs south to the Algarve; north to Porto and on to Vigo (Spain) and beyond; and east to Salamanca and Madrid. Large ferries depart Lisbon for the island of Madeira.

ADVANCE BOOKING TIME. For July and August—six months. For shoulder months—two to three months. For the rest of the year—up to one week.

Costa da Prato

This small area of Portugal is not really defined as a region, but it is included here because a few rentals have been found there and because it is such a delight. The Costa da Prato offers a taste of Portugal usually limited to foreign visitors on day trips or overnighters from Lisbon and its vicinity. To urban Portuguese, however, the villages and beaches of the Costa da Prato have long been a destination for Sunday picnics or weekend excursions.

To stay in this area one must enjoy tranquillity and simplicity; there are no resorts or golf courses as in the Algarve. The beaches of the rugged coast are vast and empty, and big-wheeled carts pulled by donkeys, oxen, and even cows are a common sight along the roads and highways. Excellent regional foods, especially seafoods, are served in unpretentious restaurants and cafés, and the prices are still modest. Although not much English is spoken, we found people friendly and helpful, and language was not a problem.

Neat, clean villages dot the coastal countryside, some of them historically important and scenically beautiful. Óbidos, for example, is a medieval walled town of cobbled streets, whitewashed buildings with gaily colored trim and small restaurants and shops. If you decide on a villa or apartment in the area, plan to arrive early enough in the week to go to Óbidos before your Saturday occupancy date just to stay in the castle, now one of the most beautiful government inns, called *pousadas*, in Portuguese.

The few available rentals are located in the outskirts of Óbidos, Caldas da Rainha, and Foz do Arelho. All are attractive, bright, and comfortable, and it is difficult to choose among them. The attraction of the Óbidos properties is the quality of the village itself; the Caldas da Rainha villas enjoy proximity to a larger town while still being private and in an attractive setting; Foz do Arelho has the advantages of being on the coast. Nothing is very far away from anything else in this region—for example, it is a twenty-five-minute drive from Óbidos to the beach and lagoon at Foz do Arelho, and both Foz do Arelho and Óbidos are within a half hour of Caldas da Rainha.

Some of the rentals are villas and some are apartments in villas; most important, all are oriented toward maximum enjoyment of land and sea. This area is scenically delightful, with much to see and do, peaceful yet in easy reach of Lisbon and the old university city of Coimbra. The rentals we found are available in the United States and Canada through Villas & Apartments in Portugal, Villas International, and B. & D. de Vogüe Travel Services, which, in turn, represents Bowhills Ltd. of England (Swanmore, Southampton, Hants SO3 2QW; tel: 011-44-0489-877-872).

BEST TIMES OF YEAR TO VISIT. Midwinter temperatures in the 60s are not uncommon, indicating a mild year-round climate, but the shoulder seasons—late spring, early summer, and fall—are optimum in terms of rent prices, weather, flowers, and reduced tourist traffic.

LOCATION AND TRANSPORTATION. Caldas da Rainha, the central town of this area, is approximately 65 miles (105 km) from Lisbon. It is the one and only stop for the train between Lisbon and Leiria, 35 miles (56 km) north. A car is very useful in this rather rural area, facilitating trips to remote beach and coastal areas, and drives south to Sintra and Lisbon. There is intertown bus service throughout the area as well as longer distance rail service.

PRICES. A studio apartment in a villa will run about $250 per week in the low season, $350 in the shoulder seasons, and $450 in July and August. A one-bedroom will cost from about $300 to $500, and a three-bedroom villa (in Óbidos) will cost about $400 in low season, $500 in the shoulder seasons, and $900 in peak season. (Prices are based on an exchange rate of 160 escudos per U.S. dollar.) The one-, two-, and three-bedroom villas are excellent for longer-term rentals, a month or more, in the winter or shoulder seasons, when a considerably reduced rent can be negotiated with the agent.

ADVANCE BOOKING TIME. For July and August—six months. For shoulder months—one to two months. For the rest of the year—two to three weeks.

11

Spain

♦

♦ THE AGENCIES

AARP Travel Service (Costa del Sol—Torremolinos; Canary Islands—Tenerife; Puerto de la Cruz)

At Home Abroad (Costa Brava, Costa del Sol)

Four Star Living (Costa del Sol)

Grand Circle Travel (Costa del Sol—Torremolinos, Nerja; Balearic Islands—Majorca, Canary Islands—Tenerife)

Hideaways International (Costa del Sol; Balearic Islands—Ibiza)

Hometours International (Costa Blanca—Villajoyosa, Costa del Sol—Fuengirola; Madrid)

Interhome, Inc. USA (Costa del Sol)

International Lodging Corp. (Costa Brava, Costa del Sol–Marbella, Nerja; Balearic Islands—Ibiza, Majorca, Minorca; Madrid)

Overseas Connection (Costa del Sol—Marbella, Puerto Vanuse; Balearic Islands—Ibiza, Majorca)

Rent A Home International (Costa Brava, Costa del Sol; Balearic Islands—Majorca; Madrid)

Rent A Vacation Everywhere (RAVE) (Costa del Sol)

Tour-Host International (Costa del Sol; Balearic Islands—Majorca)

Vacances en Campagne, Islands Unlimited Divison (Balearic Islands—Majorca)

Vacation Home Rentals (VHR) Worldwide (Costa del Sol—Estepona, Marbella; Balearic Islands—Ibiza, Majorca, Minorca)

Villa Leisure (Costa del Sol)

Villas International (Costa Blanca—Alicante; Costa Brava; Costa del Sol—Almería to Marbella, Nerja; Costa Dorada; Valencia; Balearic Islands—Ibiza, Majorca, Minorca; Canary Islands—Grand Canary, Lanzarote, Tenerife)

♦ THE COUNTRY

The second largest country in Western Europe after France, Spain has an area larger than California and almost double the population. Twenty percent of this is concentrated in the four largest cities: Madrid, Barcelone, Valencia, and Seville. The north-south and east-west highway distances of almost 600 miles (968 km) make it difficult to explore Spain from a single home base location. This is complicated by the fact that, except for Madrid, there are very few short-term rentals that are not on one of Spain's famous coasts.

Roughly half of the country's 1,900-mile (3,260 km) mainland coastline is washed by the Atlantic, and half by the Mediterranean. Of this total, two-thirds is rugged, spectacularly beautiful, and beachless. The remaining 600 miles (980 km) or so contain some of the most desirable beaches in Europe. As for the seas, it is the Atlantic, especially along Spain's southern coast, that is the warmest on a year-round basis. But swimming is possible in either body of water from late April through most of October, and is excellent from mid-May through September.

For foreigners, especially other Europeans, the popular destinations in Spain are the mainland coastal areas and the Balearic and Canary islands, so the majority of vacation rentals are there. Relatively few apartments in Barcelona, Madrid, Valencia, and other cities are represented by U.S. and Canadian agencies, but this poses no great problerm. A villa or apartment may be booked in an area close to the city or cities of your special interest and you can commute by train or rented car. In this way, the home base can be away from the crowded, more expensive city centers, yet have access to the cities' resources. Fortunately, as is described in the section on Spain's regions, below, each of the principal coastal areas has its nearby city or cities. Clockwise around the peninsula from the north: Barcelona is on the Costa Brava, Tarragona is on the Costa Dorada, and Valencia dominates the Costa del Alhazar, Alicante and Cartagena share the Costa Blanca, and the Costa del Sol runs from Almería to Algeciras.

In terms of new toruism, the two other coasts of mainland Spain are still barely developed. These are the Atlantic coast between the Strait of Gibraltar and the Portuguese border (Costa de la Luz), and the north coast along the Cantabrian Sea. Perhaps it is a matter of time before they, too, become dotted with resorts and villas, but except in the vicinity of cities, these coasts are not heavily populated. Two cities in the north, San Sebastián and Santander, are resorts of the old type. They were developed in the last century and are still enjoyed by travelers who prefer elegant ninteenth-century surroundings to those of the late twentieth century. We could find no U.S. agent with rentals in or near these cities.

Of the coastal areas of Spain, Europeans favor the south, particularly the resorts clustered along the Costa del Sol. Along a 30-mile (48 km) section of its 230-mile (370 km) length, the area is heavily congested. For many who drive south to the Costa del Sol, or who fly into Málaga, it looks as if the only way to turn is westward to Torremolinos, Marbella, and points in between. To North Americans who have never visited Spain, these towns on the Costa del Sol are the most recognizable. However, as high rises and villa clusters fill the space, developers are moving eastward. But despite the rampant development that has taken place along this beautiful coast, there remain many excellent places in which to spend several weeks. It just takes some work, selecting and studying agency catalogs, brochures, and prices. The wide choice of areas, not only along a single coast, but from among the coasts themselves, means that there is a place for every preference. "Where to Stay," below, outlines these choices.

BEST TIMES OF YEAR TO VISIT. Spain's coasts enjoy a benign climate, but the dead of winter can mean many uncomfortable days, even in the south. In fact, some of the apartment hotels and condominiums close during late November and December. Typically, however, March brings sunny, warm days to the south, and by April the weather in the northern Mediterranean coast and Balearic Islands is delightful—and it remains so into October. As elsewhere in Europe, the high season for prices has less to do with weather patterns than with habits of European vacationers. Therefore, rental and other prices during the hot days of July and August are the highest, and in spring and fall they are in either the low or shoulder range.

Given the nature of the weather, the seasonal prices, and the patterns of European tourist travel, the best months for visiting the Costa del Sol are April, May, and early October. For visiting the Costa Brava the best months are April, May, and September. For the northeast coasts (Costa Brava and Costa Dorada) May and September are optimum, and although April and October are usually delightful, the weather is more unsettled. The effect of the seasons on rent prices can be seen in the table in the "Prices" section, below.

As for Madrid and the interior, the winter months can be cold and unpleasant, while summer is hot and dry. "Nine months of winter and three months of hell" is how some describe the weather in Spain's high interior plateau. Because apartment rates here seldom change with the seasons, the decision about when to go is less affected by rental prices than by the weather and the tourist crowds. From mid-April to the end of May, and again from late September to mid-October, are the best months.

PRICES. Although some schedules show four or five seasonal prices, in general there are three, plus the Easter season (which, of course, changes from year to year). Easter week, called *Semana Santa* (Holy week), actually begins to have its effect two weeks before Easter Sunday, and takes another week to dwindle off. Much of Europe is on the move at this time, especially in predominantly Catholic countries such as Spain. On the one hand, the experience of spending Easter in a Spanish city is profound, but on the other hand, crowded restaurants, hotels, trains, and ferryliners are to be expected. Aside from Easter week, the following is a typical seasonal price schedule; the prices are in dollars per week, and the amounts indicate the order of seasonal change as well as *average* prices for a range of property types. (The exchange rate for the figures in the table is 120 pesetas per U.S. dollar.)

	Low (Nov. 1–Apr. 30)*	Shoulder (May 1–June 15) (Oct. 1–Oct. 30)	Peak (June 16–Sept. 30)
1-bdrm basic apt.	$300	$375	$ 550
1-bdrm deluxe apt.	400	550	800
2-bdrm resort villa	650	800	1,050
2-bdrm private villa	700	850	1,200
3-bdrm deluxe villa	800	1,300	2,000+

*Prices for the roughly three weeks of Easter are usually at, or above, the peak season rates. To these prices, add 6% Spanish tax and, often, a cleaning fee in the $30-per-week range. Some luxury villas can exceed $5,000 per week.

All else being equal, the prices in the resort areas of the Costa del Sol and the Balearic Islands are somewhat higher than those on the other coasts. Also, rents are lower if you are willing to take a place away from the sea—in the hills above the Costa del Sol or tucked a few kilometers back from the Costa Brava. If you want to spend less of your travel budget on your villa, *finca*, or apartment, tell the agency you are willing to locate back from the coast. (A *finca* is a Spanish country house; it may be a farmhouse or a converted outbuilding of some sort. The property description matters more than what it is called.)

If you are planning a week in Madrid or its vicinity, you will find few apartments available through U.S. agents, but with the price of hotels there, renting for a week makes economic sense. A room in the five-star Ritz runs about $470 per night, and a small room in a modest hotel is about $85. By contrast, a large, luxury one-bedroom apartment in the fully serviced, centrally located Eurobuilding is about $140 per night ($900 per week). In the more basic, modern Centro Norte, rates run from $300 to $450 per week. (Both these aparthotels can be booked through Hometours International; others are available through Rent A Home International. See listings in Chapter 3.)

WHERE TO STAY. Where you locate your home base depends on the main purpose of your visit. Do you want to explore as much of Spain as possible? Or would you rather remain within a single area and enjoy the beaches, sea, sunshine, and regional towns and cities? To see such widespread cities as Barcelona, Tarragona, Valencia, Granada, Córdoba, and Seville, for example, you should select two locations. Three weeks could be divided reasonably by spending one on the Costa Brava or Costa Dorada—with easy access to eastern Spain, and two weeks on the Costa del Sol or the less developed Costa Blanca. If Madrid fits into your plans, the best approach might be to take a hotel there for a few days. If so, visits to Toledo and Avila should be scheduled.

Personal inclinations are also important. If you prefer resort life, then the area between Málaga and Marbella offers good choices from condos to villas. For a less-developed area, ask the agents about resorts east of Málaga, in or near the villages of Torre del Mar, Nerja, Almuñécar, and as far east as Almería. If you desire more privacy than a high-rise resort area affords, make clear to the agencies you contact that you want something in a villa village, not a large apartment building. Finally, if you are seeking tranquillity, private villas are available through many of the agencies—just make clear this is what you are looking for.

Two other inviting destinations are the Balearic Islands, in the Mediterranean off Spain's east coast, and the Canary Islands, off the Moroccan coast some 500 miles south of the Spanish mainland. More information on rentals in the islands is included in the "Regions" section.

Competition among the companies that have properties and resort developments is pretty fierce. At last count there were eighteen agencies in England alone representing properties on the Spanish "costas," mostly on the Costa del Sol. Another fifteen in the United States, plus many in other European countries, indicates the scope of the rental offerings here, suggesting that it is important to choose carefully and compare prices.

For Europeans, who are accustomed to seeing great cathedrals, museums, ancient buildings, and monuments in their daily lives, but who have relatively little access to sun-warmed sandy beaches, the resorts have a great appeal. Fortunately for North Americans, there are numerous cities and towns on the coasts and nearby, behind the Sierra Nevada range, that are rich in the culture, history, and ambience of Spain. Thus, a home base on the Costa del Sol—or on the less-crowded Costa Blanca, which stretches to the northeast beyond Alicante—is ideal for exploring southern Spain as well as for basking in the sun.

◆ THE REGIONS

Spain's forty-eight provinces are divided among ten formal regions including the Balearic Islands and the distant Canary Islands. Unlike most other Western European countries, which have hundreds of vacation rental properties widely scattered throughout, such rentals in Spain are concentrated in the coastal areas and the island groups. With the exception of those in Madrid, few rentals are available in the interior rural areas and cities. In order to be useful to readers, this guidebook is divided into two regions on the mainland, with short sections on the Balearic Islands and the Canary Islands.

The Southern Coasts
(Costa del Sol, Costa de la Luz)

ENVIRONS AND ACCOMMODATIONS. The Costa del Sol is the Mediterranean coast of Andalusia, Spain's largest and most diverse region, which occupies the entire southern area of the Iberian Peninsula from the Portuguese border east beyond the point where the coastline turns northward. The Costa de la Luz is the Atlantic third of this coast, between the Strait of Gibraltar and the Portuguese border.

COSTA DEL SOL, WESTERN PORTION: Earlier in the chapter we noted that the Costa del Sol is Spain's best-known and most popular tourist area and therefore the most developed in terms of resort communities. Some of these communities are purpose-built rental villas clustered around swimming pools and resort shops. Others are apartment buildings set on grounds complete with pools and tennis courts. Then there are combinations, with resort-type shopping centers to serve vacationers staying in the high-rise condominiums and aparthotels. These resorts can be found here and there along most of the Costa del Sol, but are mainly concentrated along the forty miles between Málaga and Marbella. Beyond Marbella the resorts thin out a bit, but they extend as far as Gibraltar, across the small bay from Algeciras.

The most popular area in the western reaches of the Costa del Sol is in the vicinity of Sotogrande, where one of Europe's best golf courses shares the space with tennis courts and riding paths. The resorts in this area are largely British enclaves, partly because of British investment in the area and partly because inexpensive flights are available between Great Britain and British Gibraltar, half an hour's drive away. (Contact Villas International regarding Fincasol's Sotogrande and the Puerto Sotogrande Apartments; for direct inquiry, write Fincasol Holidays, 4 Bridge Street, Salisbury, Wiltshire, England for a brochure. Tel. 011-44-072-226-444.)

Away from the coast lies what Andalusians regard as the "true Spain." Here is the land whose ancient history is still evident. Moorish influence is seen not only in such marvels as the thirteenth-century Alhambra at Granada and the mosque at Córdoba but also in the white villages that seem to spill from the hilltops. It is an area so rich with places to go and important things to see that a few weeks will not seem like enough time.

The decision of where to stay along the 85 miles (140 km) west of Málaga is somewhat perplexing. An effective solution is to contact the agencies listed in this chapter and ask for brochures and prices, then study them to find what appeals to you within the price you want to pay. Some agencies specialize in apartments (Hometours International and Interhome, Inc. USA, for example), others in deluxe villas (Overseas Connection and Villa Leisure), and still others in a variety, from modest to luxury apartments and small-to-elegant villas (Vacation Home Rentals [VHR] Worldwide and Villas International). Hideaways International offers a few elegant private villas, and both AARP Travel Service and Grand Circle Travel include apartments in modern complexes in their extended-stay packages.

If you are looking for a resort in a less-populated area, remember that the farther west you go from Málaga the thinner the concentration of resorts—or look east of Málaga, or go all the way to the Costa Blanca.

COSTA DEL SOL, EASTERN PORTION: The coastal zone east from Málaga becomes less populated and is punctuated by fewer towns and resorts than the western half; toward its eastern extremities, the landscape is dryer and the summer days are hotter. Development, of course, takes time, so the concentration of building in the Torremolinos–Marbella area west of Málaga during the past ten or fifteen years has meant less attention to the east. Nevertheless, changes are taking place. Thirty miles (50 km) east of Málaga, the once-quiet fishing village of Nerja has become the site of large-scale development, including villa villages and the Aparthotel Marinas, whose architecture vaguely resembles Caesar's Palace (or perhaps the Dunes) in Las Vegas. Although Nerja's city fathers recently placed a three-story limitation on buildings, the height and scope of many of these white apartment buildings, which appear elsewhere along the Costa del Sol, seem incongruous. Still, relative to the western part of the Costa del Sol, the area around Nerja and east to pretty little Almuñécar is uncrowded and peaceful. Nightlife in the nearby resorts and towns makes the area interesting for those who like to play round the clock. East of Almuñécar is Motril, not an enticing town, and beyond that is Almería, the interesting main city of eastern Andalusia, developing into a tourist destination.

If you are inclined toward a less resortlike atmosphere than exists in the Torremolinos–Marbella area, then seek out a villa or apartment along this eastern stretch. A home base even as far east as Almería does not rule out visiting the cities of Cádiz, Seville, and Córdoba, although it adds a few hours to the journey—it is approximately 140 miles (230 km) between Almería and Málaga. The stretch between Nerja and Almuñécar provides the best of both worlds, and both towns are good centers to be near.

An example of a restrained resort for this area is El Capistrano in Nerja. With some 500 units in three "villages," it is one of the more pleasing complexes in the area, offering separate villas, apartments, and so-called pueblo villas (consisting of an upper and lower apartment in each villa). The pueblo villas cascade down the hill, so there is a bit of walking involved. As for top or bottom, the lower units open onto small gardens, and most of the upper ones have a view. The individual villas are arranged like a compact Mediterranean neighborhood, and the apartments are in low-rise buildings. Most of the units are privately owned (predominantly by British nationals) and are managed by the resort. Maid service is provided three times weekly. With so many types and sizes of accommodations there is a wide variety of rental prices, but the range is from about $300 to $650 per week for a one-bedroom individual villa, $280 to $550 for a one-bedroom pueblo villa, and from $220 to $350 for the least expensive apartment. The first figure is for low season (November 1, to April 1), and the higher firgure is for peak season (July 1 to September 1). For information on El Capistrano, contact International Lodging and Travel Corp. For other rentals, inquire of Interhome, Rent A Home International, and Villas International.

As for the best times to go to the Costa del Sol, the weather in the shoulder months—from mid-April through May and again in October—is usually warm and sunny, large crowds have not yet arrived, and rents have risen slightly but are still far below peak. Although mild, March weather can be chancy.

COSTA DE LA LUZ: The Atlantic coast from the Strait of Gibraltar west to the town of Ayamonte on the Portuguese border is strangely devoid of development for foreign tourists. Yet it is a beautiful coastline with long stretches of sandy beach, much of it bordered by pine-covered hills; the climate is even better and the sea warmer than on the popular Costa del Sol to the east.

Sometimes the pattern of development is inexplicable, but we have not yet found a U.S., Canadian, or British agency that offers rental properties on the Costa de la Luz. This suggests, of course, that it is relatively free of foreign tourist impact, an intriguing feature for many travelers. The beach resorts at Punta Umbria, Ayamonte, Sanlúcar de Barrameda, and elsewhere are not only good locations for enjoying the sea, they are also good places from which to visit the essential cities of Seville and Córdoba. If you are interested in exploring the western provinces of Andalusia for a week, go in spring if you can, or in early summer or fall. Take a hotel in Huelva, Sanclúcar, or Cádiz, and drive to the smaller coast towns looking for apartments or villas to rent. Except in high season, you will see signs reading ALQUILAR—"To Rent." We found Cádiz easy to manage, and its restaurants very good. The country is strikingly beautiful, especially between Algeciras and Cádiz, with white villages spilling from the hilltops. A fruitful week can easily be spent in this area; before long it will surely become famed as a sunshine mecca for northern Europeans.

Location and transportation. Rich in resources, Andalusia will give you a good feeling for Spain. Do not short it for time. Unless you know you will return, you are likely to feel some regret at leaving after two or three weeks. Except for Cádiz, the main cities of interest in the region are away from the coast, so although a Costa del Sol home base is great for sunshine, beaches, shops, and nightlife, it is the interior of the region that is truly important for experiencing the real Spain.

Flights from North America usually land in Madrid, from which they extend to Seville or Málaga. There is mainline rail service between Madrid and Cádiz via Linares, Córdoba, and Seville, and between Málaga and Madrid via Córdoba. There is also service between Málaga and Algeciras, Granada, and Almería. Trains run every thirty minutes on the twenty-five-minute trip between Málaga and the resort towns just west of it as far as Fuengirola via Torremolinos. There is no rail service along the Costa del Sol west of Fuengirola or east of Málaga; that is, Marbella, Nerja, Almuñécar, Motril, and the stretch beyond Motril to Almería are not served. The bus service is good, however, so much of Andalusia, and all its principal cities, can be seen by train, bus, or a combination of both. For convenience, however, and for getting into the smaller towns and exploring the stimulating scenery of the snow-clad Sierra Nevada, a car is very useful. It is usually much less expensive to arrange for a car rental before leaving the United States or Canada, especially by renting through one of the rent/lease broker companies discussed in Chapter 4.

This region is so large, complex, and fulfilling that many weeks can be spent within its boundaries, but for a glimpse of North Africa, it is a simple matter to visit Tangier in Morocco. A day trip is feasible, but a stay of a night or two makes the visit more worthwhile. Passenger ships leave several times daily from the commercial dock at Algeciras for the two-and-a-half-hour trip to Tangier. The easiest approach is simply to drive or take a taxi to the Trasmediterranea/Limadet terminal, buy a round-trip ticket, and board. Before boarding, however, your passport must be stamped for exit by the Spanish authorities. There is a bank on board for currency exchange. For another interesting experience, take a day trip on one of the numerous daily sailings out of Algeciras for Ceuta, a Spanish enclave and free port on the coast of Morocco. The shipline is the government-owned Trasmediterranea, which also operates on routes out of Málaga and Almería across to Spanish Melilla in Africa. Other routes are the long (600+ miles) one between Cádiz and the Canary Islands and those that connect both Barcelona and Valencia with the Balearic Islands. If you want to visit Melilla, check the sailings carefully so you won't be stuck there longer than you want to be. (See the sections on the Balearic Islands and the Canary Islands below for more information on ocean travel to and from the mainland.)

Advance booking time. For July and August—six months. For June and September—four to five months. For the rest of the year—up to six weeks.

From October through May it is possible to find a place on arrival without advance booking.

The Eastern Coasts
(Costa Blanca, Costa Brava, Costa de Alhazar, Costa Dorada)

ENVIRONS AND ACCOMMODATIONS. The Costa Blanca is the southern section of the eastern coast, connecting with the Costa del Sol as the peninsula turns southward. It runs some 230 miles, comprising the east coasts of Andalusia, the region of Murcia, and the southern half of the Valencia region. Cabo San Martin and Cabo San Antonio northeast of the city of Alicante delineate the line between the Costa Blanca and the Costa de Alhazar, which runs northward along the sweep of the Golfo de Valencia. The next segment is the Costa Dorada, which begins just south of

Tarragona and runs just past Barcelona, where it becomes the more rugged Costa Brava and goes on north to the French border.

There are many miles of beaches, a half-dozen important cities, and dozens of resort towns along this sun-bathed Mediterranean coast. Again, however, development for foreign tourists has been selective and is concentrated in the most attractive areas.

COSTA BLANCA AND COSTA DEL ALHAZAR. Many meterologists have declared this coastal region to have the best climate in the world. The Costa Blanca stretch of the Mediterranean coast is second only to the Costa del Sol in popularity among travelers and vacationers who come to Spain. Whether to stay in this area or on the Costa del Sol is a difficult decision; both have similar resort styles, good climate, and much to see and do. The answer is to divide your time evenly if you have two weeks. But if you have three, the importance of visiting Seville, Córdoba, and Granada tips the scales in favor of the Costa del Sol or Costa de la Luz. Nevertheless, the sense of a less-concentrated tourist population than in the Málaga–Marbella area is certainly a plus, and it is not hard to find isolation in the dry country south of Alicante. Alicante itself is a splendid small city, the heart of the Costa Blanca, with much that is ancient and much that is new and sophisticated.

To the north of the Costa Blanca, along the Gulf of Valencia, is the Costa del Alhazar. The northern half of this area is a mixture of ports, resorts, industrial towns, rice paddies, and the vast citrus groves that produce 25 million tons of oranges and lemons for Europe's markets. The main city of the Costa del Alhazar ("Orange Blossom Coast") is Valencia, the colorful river city of oranges and flowers. In the hinterlands, Albacete and Murcia are both within day trip distance, but allow more time if you can.

Regrettably, most of the North American agencies have concentrated their efforts in the Costa del Sol, the assumption being that the most well known and popular areas must be the best (or the most marketable). This leaves Costa Blanca properties underrepresented, but there is nevertheless a fair selection of them. The majority of rental properties available through U.S. agencies are along the scenic northern end of the Costa Blanca, between Alicante and the point of land that noses into the sea at Cabo San Martín. Some of the coastline is dominated by hotels and apparent complexes, but there are scattered, often privately owned, villas available in the hills overlooking the coast.

Typical of the more modest accommodations along the Costa Blanca is the Eurotennis apartment hotel in the little town of Villajoyosa. About 25 miles (41 km) up the coast from Alicante, it boasts tennis courts, a pool, and other resort amenities. All apartments face the sea and have private balconies and small kitchens. At prices from about $320 per week (for two persons) in low season to $450 in shoulder months and $650 in July and August, it makes a good base from which to explore the region (Hometours International is the U.S. agent). A wider variety of rentals is available from Villas International, including apartments in Valencia and Alicante. This agency asks where you want to be and how much you want to pay, then sends an assortment of property profiles. Specify the coast or hills on the north end of the Costa Blanca, between Alicante and Denia; mention Jávea or, of course, Valencia or Alicante if you want to be in a city. If you have a car, the smaller city of Alicante is the easiest to manage.

If you cannot find what you are seeking from the U.S. companies and wish to widen your options for villa rentals, contact VillaSeekers (Romeland House, Romeland Hills, St. Albans, Hertfordshire AL3 4ET, England; tel: 011-44-727-662-00) or Paloma Holidays (6 Farncombe Road, Worthing, West Sussex BN11 2BE, England; tel: 011-44-903-820-898).

If your visit is planned for summer, especially in July or August, you must book well in advance, but in the low season, and even in May to mid-June and in October, it is possible to find a rental after your arrival. Check the local tourist office, real estate agents (*immobilières*) or look for signs reading ALQUILAR. One approach is to book a hotel in Alicante or Valencia for a day or two and look for a place on the coast. Many of the renting agents, especially around Jávea and Denia on the "nose," have links with British companies, so English is widely spoken.

An international airport serves Valencia, but often the best arrangement for transatlantic flights is via Madrid. Mainline rail service runs between Valencia and Madrid, between Alicante and Madrid, and along the coast between Valencia and Alicante except for a section between Gandía and Denia. Unless a rail spur is completed before you arrive, the only way of going by train between the resort towns of Denia and Jávea and Valencia is to go through Alicante and change there to a local. Good bus service is also available, but a car is very convenient.

When you aren't traveling to the inland cities and up and down the coast, a voyage to the Balearic Islands for two or three days is interesting and fun. Passenger ships depart six days a week in both directions between Valencia and Palma (Palma de Mallorca), on a seven-hour voyage each way. It is easy to depart one day, stay overnight, and return the following day. Sailings between Valencia and Ibiza are only four times a week (two in winter), so plan more carefully, because you will need to stay on Ibiza longer. The fares are modest, the ships are pleasant, the food is good, and it is an enjoyable, easy adventure. Unless you want a cabin, just take a taxi to the terminal at the dock, buy your ticket, and board. If the taxi driver doesn't speak English, say *"Trasmediterranea, al*

Grao de Valencia." (It is pronounced "TRAS-mediterranea"—no "N" in the first syllable.) Every driver knows the terminal to the Balearics. For an extended adventure, many travelers book a trip from Valencia to Ibiza, on to Majorca, and the return; or they continue from Majorca to Barcelona and return to Valencia by rail. If you want a cabin, or if you plan the longer itinerary, it is best to book in advance through a travel agency in Valencia, Alicante, or another major town.

Advanced booking time needed for July and August—6 months. For June and September—four to five months. For the rest of the year—up to six weeks. From October through May it is possible to find a rental on arrival without advance booking.

COSTA BRAVA AND COSTA DORADA: The region of Catalonia, comprising the provinces of Tarragona, Lérida, Gerona, and Barcelona, is a complex area of cosmopolitan cities and simple villages. The mix of languages (Spanish and Catalan), seaside resorts, snow-capped Pyrenees, monasteries, cathedrals, and vineyards provides variety and interest for any visitor.

Most rental properties in this region are along the coasts, but even there they are not concentrated in newer tourist resorts to the extent that they are on the Costa del Sol. Although the climate is mild and there is much sunshine, this area does not have the reputation of the southern coasts. Nevertheless, summertime means crowded beaches and full accommodations, especially along the southern end of the Costa Brava, an area popular with European tourists. Considering the crowds and the weather, by far the best times of year to visit Catalonia are from mid-April to mid-June, and again in September (except for the two weeks around Easter).

The Catalonian coast is about 250 miles long, with the southern two-thirds designated as the Costa Dorada and the northern third as the Costa Brava. In the center is the busy port of Barcelona.

Costa Dorada: Valencia's Costa del Alhazar adjoins, and is hardly distinguishable from, the Costa Dorada ("coast of gold"). Commencing just south of Tarragona, it becomes the Costa Brava north of Barcelona. The resort towns along the southern two-thirds of this coast, and the land that borders it, are not impressive, which may explain why this is not an area particularly favored by British and American tourists (or rental agencies). However, Tarragona, the peaceful beauty of the monasteries of Santes Creus and Poblet, the wine country of Penedés (Torres, Freixenet, Codorniu and others), and the compelling trip to Montserrat are richly rewarding to travelers.

It is difficult to book ahead for a rental to serve as a home base in southern Catalonia. The best approaches are either to take an apartment in Barcelona or to visit the area during spring or fall and drive into the coastal towns looking for a place to rent on the spot. As is noted in Chapter 1, in 1984 we drove into the town of Sitges (pronounced "SEE-jus"), 20 miles (32 km) south of Barcelona, and rented a modest apartment on the beach where we lived for four months. Because there are numerous small apartment buildings in Sitges, it is possible to drive or walk around checking out apartments with ALQUILAR signs on them. Do not try this during the high season from early June to September 1, or during the two weeks before and the week after Easter. The best months are September and May. Our apartment address was: Apartamentos Can Negret, Balmins 1, Sitges (Barcelona), Spain. You can write in English, addressed: Attn. Sra. Maria Viñola.

North of Barcelona, the Costa Dorada extends another 40 miles (64.5 km) or so, distinguished by the impact of Barcelona's population on formerly quiet little fishing towns such as Premiá de Mar, Mataró, Arenys de Mar, and Canet de Mar. There is little point in trying to find a home base there, especially when there are more favorable areas just up the coast.

As for Barcelona itself, like most large cities it is a mix of the good and the bad; and like cities everywhere, it is expensive. It is vital and busy, full of great restaurants, stores, museums, parks, theaters, and churches. A week spent there would be stimulating and full. It is also a fairly good home base from which to explore surrounding Catalonia. The railroad runs along the coast and into the interior, so it is easy to visit the main cities and towns of the region. If you have two weeks or more for this region, a week in the city and one somewhere on the Costa Dorada would be an excellent combination. The bus and subway systems are very good, so a car is not necessary. Contact Rent A Home International and Villas International for apartments here.

Costa Brava: Forty miles (64.5 km) northeast of Barcelona the main coast highway turns inland toward Gerona, and a branch highway continues along the Costa Brava. It is an exciting coastline: craggy mountains rise from the sea, with the road following the contours for a few miles, rising to the heights then dropping back to the level of the sea, where the towns settle along the coves and sandy beaches.

The largest of the resort towns of the Costa Brava is the southernmost, Blanes (pronounced "BLAH-ness," pop. 20,000), with three miles of sandy beaches. Other popular towns, strung along the coast, are Lloret de Mar, Tossa de Mar, San Feliu de Gixols (pronounced "gwee-SHOL"), and Platja d'Aro, pleasant places but crowded in peak summer. Continuing northward, other small towns dot the coast: Palamós (which is not particularly enticing), Estartit, Playa de Pals, and, across the Golfo de Roses, the villages of Roses and Cadaqués, both of which are less affected by tourist development than the resorts farther south. Overall, the farther north of Barcelona the better in terms of simplicity and reduced tourist impact.

Part of the problem in finding a villa in Catalonia seems to stem from a tendency for the region's well-to-do not to rent their unused vacation homes (Catalonia is a prosperous part of Spain). During the months we lived in Sitges, for example, we were surprised to see that many of the large, attractive, summer homes stood vacant and closed all week, sometimes for many weeks, then were opened for a weekend or a few days when the owners came to town. The consequence is that, although villas can be found, the majority of rentals are apartments. If you are careful in reading property profiles, or if you tell the agency that you are not interested in a high-rise apartment building, apartments in smaller buildings can be just right.

For villas and apartments on the Costa Brava, contact At Home Abroad, International Lodging Corp., Rent A Home International, and Villas International.

Catalonia is not so large that it cannot be explored from any home base in the region. For example, using Barcelona as a central coastal location, it is a four-hour drive up the Costa Brava to the French border (two hours by *autopista*), two hours to Tarragona, and another two south to Valencia by car or train. Overnight visits to the French cities of Narbonne and Carcassonne are possible, and a four-hour drive northwest from Barcelona will get you high in the Pyrenees, into the Principality of Andorra.

The railroad south follows the coast all the way to Valencia, but the northward coastal route from Barcelona goes only as far as Blanes. Although there is bus service between all the towns of the Costa Brava, a car facilitates independence.

Port-to-port passenger ships sail daily between Barcelona and the ports of the Balearic Islands: Palma on Majorca, Ibiza on Ibiza, and Mahon on Minorca. Voyage durations vary from eight to ten hours, and it is possible to take an itinerary through the Balearics, stopping for an hour or so at each port, or staying over and catching a ship the next day. The shipline also offers inexpensive weekend cruises called *Cruceros-Fin de Semana* through the Balearics, returning to Barcelona. Contact any travel agent in Barcelona, or go to the Trasmediterranea terminal at the harbor at the foot of The Ramblas.

Advance booking time needed for July and August—six months. For June and September—one to two months. For the rest of the year—up to six weeks.

From September through May it is possible to find a place on arrival without advance booking.

The Balearic Islands (Islas Baleares)
(Formentera, Ibiza, Majorca, Minorca)

ENVIRONS AND ACCOMMODATIONS. Clustered between 70 and 210 miles (112.6 and 338 km) off the east coast of the mainland (or "peninsula," as it is often referred to) lie the Balearic Islands (Islas Baleares). There are three major islands, one smaller inhabited one, and a scattering of islets. The distance by highway across the largest island, Majorca, is roughly 60 miles (100 km), while Minorca is about 30 miles (50 km) at its widest and Ibiza from the south to the north tip is under 22 miles (35 km). Much is packed into the relatively small area of these islands, from beautiful isolated beaches to the international sophistication of Palma, the largest city of the Balearics, with a population of more than a quarter million. Formentera, although inhabited, has few rentals available. It can be visited as a day trip from Ibiza.

The islands have an ancient history that dates from the Bronze Age and before. A more recent chronology begins with the Moors and advances through the Catalans, intermittent occupations by the British and the French, and finally to Spanish rule. For years a playground for Spanish and other European aristocrats, the Balearics became increasingly popular with vacationers in the 1920s, and now are the destination of hundreds of thousands of tourists each year, about half of whom go during July and August.

Majorca is, on the whole, the most settled of the islands, with the greatest permanent and summer tourist populations. It has the grandest of the hotel and apartment complexes, and has the city of Palma, with its smart stores, shops, and restaurants. Ibiza is equally popular, providing an unusual mixture of luxury *fincas* and private villas. Ibiza town is known not only for its old quarter cascading down the slopes of a hill but for its mod shops, discotheques, tourist cafés, and semipermanent population of international young people, some of whom are involved in the dozens of tourists enterprises.

Minorca is the most rural overall, with the least flamboyant tourist developments. The towns of Mahón and Ciudadela, although full of shops and places to eat, are quieter, simpler towns than Ibiza and Palma.

To decide which island to visit, one solution is a week on each or, if your time is short, a week on two. If you have to choose one, read the island profiles in this chapter, peruse a guidebook to Spain and decide which one best suits you.

BEST TIMES OF YEAR TO VISIT. During the two weeks before Easter and the week after, the islands—especially Majorca and Ibiza—are crowded. This is followed by a period until early June when the weather is generally excellent, the tourist crowds are thinner, and the prices are lower. Peak summer season here, as elsewhere in Europe, is July and August, plus most of September. Shoulder seasons are between the end of the Easter holidays and July 1, and again in October. April, except for Easter weeks, is sometimes a fourth season for prices (just a notch above low). Low season is November through March, with a possible peak for the Christmas holidays. Winter is mild, but can be depressingly gray and rainy, as Chopin discovered during the winter of 1839–40. The sad music he wrote there presumably reflects the mood prompted by the weather. The optimum periods, then, are from a week after Easter to mid-June, and again in October.

MAJORCA: Unlike the newer complexes on Ibiza, Palma is a settled resort city, the sweep of the Paseo Marítima along the harbor conveying a sense of permanence. Elsewhere on Majorca, the small coastal towns have developed resort areas around the older villages; many are in beautiful settings with good beaches, restaurants, and shops. In addition to the apartments available in or near Palma and villages such as Valldemossa and Sóller, and in large new developments such as Magaluf and Playa de Palma, private villas and *fincas* are available for rent. They are scattered throughout the island; some are fairly basic, but most are deluxe, and many have pools and gardens. Deciding on a place to stay for one or two weeks on Majorca naturally depends to a large extent on your budget. The privacy of a *finca* will cost more than an apartment in a resort development or in Palma, and the island is small enough that all of it can be explored from any location. Majorca is the only island with a small, low range of hills, making its northwest coast especially pleasant.

The U.S. agencies to contact for specific information and prices for Majorca properties are AARP Travel Service, Grand Circle Travel, International Lodging Corp., The Islands Unlimited division of Vacances en Champagne, Overseas Connection, Tour-Host International, Vacation Home Rentals (VHR) Worldwide, and Villas International.

IBIZA: Ibiza town surrounds a harbor on the southern coast of the island and is dominated by D'Alt Vila ("the old city"), built in the seventeenth century on a hill over the foundations of an eighth or ninth century Moorish settlement. Outside the walls of D'Alt Vila, the town can hardly be called up-to-date, although many of the old buildings house a great variety of the most modern—or at least mod and upbeat—boutiques and other shops in the Balearics. Three cultures co-exist on the island: the culture of the past, as manifested in the rural people and their ways and language; the culture of neon and the young; and the culture of the mix between Ibizans of Ibiza town and the resort enclaves.

Ibiza is different things to different people. The town's nightlife and its sidewalk cafés and discotheques draw some, while the tranquillity afforded by an exclusive villa in an isolated part of the island lures others. The appeal is heightened by the sea, the beaches, and the laid-back life. The entire permanent population of the island is only about 18,000, with the unusual character of Ibiza town dominating the urban aspects of staying there. A getaway for well-to-do mainland Spaniards and other Europeans, Ibiza has numerous lovely properties for rent.

The U.S. agencies to contact for specific information and prices for Ibiza rentals are Hideaways International, International Lodging Corp., Overseas Connection, Vacation Home Rentals (VHR) Worldwide, and Villas International.

MINORCA: Second largest of the Balearics, Minorca seems to be the one off the beaten track, although that is a comparative matter. There are indeed tourist developments, a golf club or two, delightful small towns, and restaurants, but overall this is less directed toward the tourist economy than on the other two destination islands. Minorca's 125 miles of coastline is scalloped with coves and sandy beaches, far less crowded than the more popular beaches of Majorca and Ibiza. Life is slower paced there, and it is easier to get away from the developed areas and find isolation. At the same time, there is no lack of shops and good places to eat. Both the capital, Mahón (pop. 18,000), and Ciudadela, across the island, are very nice towns; the latter is one of the most attractive on the islands.

There are apartments and villas available for rent on Minorca; some are independent and some are in villa communities. A look at price lists indicates that rentals cost perhaps a little less on Minorca than on the other islands, but this will not last. In addition, the properties tend to be in the upper-middle to luxury categories, with only a scattering of more modest rentals. There are not the hundreds of rentals to choose from on Minorca as there are on the Costa del Sol and other mainland destinations, but certainly there are enough to offer a good choice.

The U.S. agencies to contact for specific information and prices are International Lodging Corp., Vacation Home Rentals (VHR) Worldwide, and Villas International.

If you cannot find exactly what you want, or need more information, you might want to make a direct contact—or write to one of the British companies that have been involved in the villa rental business on Minorca for years: San Clemente Villas, Sa Vinya (29 Avenida del Dr Guardia, Mahón, Menorca, Baleares, Spain; tel: 011-34-71-360434) or Patricia Wildblood, Ltd. (Calne, Wiltshire SN11 OLP, England; tel: 011-44-249-817023).

TRANSPORTATION. There are several flights daily between Barcelona, Valencia, Madrid, and other mainland cities and the Balearics, as well as direct flights into Palma from other major European cities. The bus system on all the islands is adequate, but there are no trains. A car is a must if you rent a place outside of the main towns or resort areas. If you have a car on the mainland, it can be ferried with you from Barcelona or Valencia and, once there, between the islands. However, rental cars are available in Palma, Ibiza, and Mahón, and the cost of ferrying one is fairly high.

One of the most pleasant, leisurely, and inexpensive ways to travel to and from the mainland, and between the islands, is via the government's Trasmediterranea Line. These big vessels dominate the harbors on Mahón, Palma, and Ibiza as they come and go between these island ports and the mainland cities of Barcelona and Valencia. The ships sail port-to-port routes, which means that you buy a ticket for passage just as you do for a bus or a train: one way, round-trip, or from one port to the next. Unless you want a cabin for one of the longer night voyages to or from the mainland, traveling by sea can be arranged just by going to the terminal at the harbor, buying the tickets to the destination you want, and boarding. For a cabin, it is best to book in advance through a travel agency in any main town in Spain. Feel free to take a picnic lunch, or you may dine or snack on board. Most of the ships have swimming pools, lounges, discos, and casinos. Ticket prices are modest, and the sea journey is informal and enjoyable.

PRICES. There is, of course, enormous variation in rental prices, depending on season, size, and standards, but the following will give you an idea of what you can expect. Prices are in U.S. dollars per week, at an exchange of 120 pesetas per dollar.

ADVANCE BOOKING TIME. For July and August—six months. For June and September—two to three months. For the rest of the year—up to six weeks.

	Low	Shoulder	Peak
Simple studio apt.; Minorca	$160	$322	$433
Modest 2-bdrm apt. in villa; Minorca	230	368	598
3-star, studio, seaside; Majorca	230	437	575
3-star, 1 bdrm, seaside; Majorca	335	550	900
Simple 3-bdrm *finca;* Ibiza, Minorca	440	550	650
Modest 3-bdrm villa; Ibiza	600	700	1,000
Lux. 3-bdrm villa; Ibiza, Mallorca	900	1,600	2,500 +

The Canary Islands (Islas Canarias)
(Gran Canaria [Grand Canary], Lanzarote, Tenerife)

This archipelago of seven main islands plus smaller islets lies off the coast of southwestern Morocco, some 600 miles south of mainland Spain. Known as the Land of Eternal Spring, the climate is dominated by Africa, not Europe, and upflowing currents make the sea inviting to swimmers in all but the winter months, and very pleasant from mid-April through October. Although rentals are available on all the major islands, they are hard to find, especially from this side of the Atlantic, so we describe only the three main islands where properties are available through North American or British agencies.

Each island differs from the others, and a visit to one does not represent a visit to all the Canaries. For a two-week stay, a week each on two of them is the most rewarding. Which two depends on your personal interests. Before you decide, studying a good guide to Spain and the Canaries is a necessary first step.

TENERIFE: The most popular (Canary Island) among travelers, Tenerife is the largest and most diverse, with the most beautiful scenery. El Teide, the island's dormant, snow-capped, 12,100-foot volcano, influences everything from the weather to the vegetation. At the massive mountain's low peripheral zone, from sea level to a thousand feet or so, the vegetation is subtropical, making this part of the island a land of bananas and coffee, camelias and bougainvillea. The west coast produces tomatoes for the markets of Europe, and the south and east coasts, shielded by the mountain from rain, are desertlike. On the slopes above two thousand feet the climate is southern temperate and the vegetation is conifer and deciduous trees; numerous farms take advantage of the rich soil of this area. Here people of pretty little villages such as Orotava and Cien Fuegos look out on the slopes below and toward El Teide above.

The principal town is Santa Cruz de Tenerife, which we found much more pleasant and manageable than larger Las Palmas on neighboring Grand Canary Island (Gran Canaria). Most visitors who plan to stay more than a day or so pass up Santa Cruz to rent apartments in the resort city of Puerto de la Cruz, on the north coast 25 miles (40.2 km) away. This is a Euopean-style resort town, not typically Canarian: it is modern and upscale, created to provide a comfortable-to-luxurious stay for Britons, Germans, Scandinavians, Swiss, and other Europeans. The British, especially, fly down to Tenerife much as New Yorkers take a sun break in Florida. If you prefer to be outside the Puerto de la Cruz area, inquire of Villas International about rentals on the south of Tenerife, near Playa de las Americas, and also in Los Christianos.

For information on specific rental properties on Tenerife, contact AARP Travel Service (packages), Grand Circle Travel (packages), and Villas International.

There is a major international airport on Tenerife. Both public buses and tour buses go almost everywhere, including the top of El Teide, but a rental car opens up other areas, such as private spots on the isolated south coast.

GRAND CANARY: The capital city of Las Palmas, at more than a quarter million people, is the largest city on the Canaries. Its main virtues are the balmy climate and the long, curving beach dotted with good restaurants and hotels. The island itself has many good beaches, a few pleasant villages, and beautiful scenery. As on Tenerife, the southern and eastern coasts are dry, and the weather is influenced by the island's mountain, Pico de Nieves (elevation 6,500 feet). Although rentals are available on Grand Canary (from Villas International), we can only recommend a week there if you have plenty of time to explore the other islands. However, because it is the terminal for ships sailing between mainland Cádiz and the islands of Tenerife and Lanzarote, you might stop for a day or two to visit some of the high points of the city and to travel around the island.

LANZAROTE: The easternmost of the Canary group, this island is for travelers who enjoy the unusual. Little has changed since Lanzarote was formed by volcanic upheaval a few million years ago. Unlike the other islands, Lanzarote lacks a single high mountain peak to catch or create the clouds needed for rain. Except in the oases, scant vegetation leaves bare the tortured geologic formations of past aeons. The dark lava deposits along the coast contrast with the crystal blue sea and the yellow sand, much of which has blown across the fifty or so miles form the deserts of southern Morocco. This combination makes for interesting, strikingly beautiful beaches, excellent for swimming and snorkeling, often in total isolation.

Lanzarote's main city, Arrecife, is different from other Canary Island cities; more a town of the desert than a town of the subtropics, with low white buildings, narrow streets, palm trees and colorful plants, and, of course, the city's center for restaurants, nightlife, and shopping. Although you can drive all the main roads of the island in a day—there are only about 120 miles (200 km) of them—it is impossible not to stop in pleasant villages such as Teguise, or elsewhere along the route, to swim or to photograph this remarkable land. It is not an easy place to forget.

Lanzarote is not touristy, and although there are certainly enough resources to provide all the things that visitors need (car rentals, restaurants, shops, supermarkets, and so on), it is easy to find privacy—and even isolation. The air and beaches are clean, there seems to be no violence, and the people are friendly and often shy. Next to the larger island of Fuerteventura, just to the south, Lanzarote is the least developed of the islands to which tourists come. Until recently, in fact, it was a place known mostly to well-to-so-do mainland Spaniards and a handful of other Europeans who sought privacy in one or two isolated but elegant apartment hotels tucked along the coast, where ocher cliffs meet the sea. Now, however, the virtues of the island and these apartments, and several newer clusters of rental villas, have become better known, first to the British, and now to at least one U.S. agency. They are enclaves of modernity in an unusual and fascinating land.

To help you decide, read about Lanzarote in a guidebook to Spain and the Canary Islands, or contact the National Tourist Office of Spain in New York for information. Prices are, as they are in other areas where almost everything must be imported, on the high side.

There is an airport at Arrecife, connecting it with Tenerife and Grand Canary. For travel on the island, a car is important and can be rented at Arrecife airport.

Contact Villas International for information on their rental properties on Lanzarote. You might also want to contact one or more of the following: Lanzaway Holidays (6 Lombard Street, Abingdon, Oxon OX14 5SD, England; tel: 011-44-235-3588) or Mundialanza, Ltd. (2 Halstead Chambers, Market Hill, Royston, Hertfordshire SGB 9JS, England; tel: 011-44-763-47456). There is also a remote settlement of cottages, for very independent travelers, which can be contacted directly: Playa Famara Bungalows, La Caleta, Lanzarote, Islas Canarias, Spain; tel: 011-34-28-845-132.

The best times of year to visit Lanzarote are from April to mid-June and from mid-September through October.

TRANSPORTATION. The principal international airport is on Tenerife, but there are also flights between major cities in mainland Spain and Grand Canary and La Palma and Lanzarote. There are also regular flights among the other islands, except Gomera and Hierro.

Large ferryliners of the government's Trasmediterranea Line sail on port-to-port routes between Cádiz on the mainland and Tenerife and Grand Canary. In summer there are departures every other day in both directions; the winter schedule from September 15 to June 15 is one sailing per week. The voyage takes about three days, and if you have the time it adds much to the adventure. A dining room and snack bars are on board, as well as lounges, a casino, an outdoor bar, and a swimming pool (empty between October and June). It is very inexpensive to travel deck class (no cabin), but because you'll spend two nights on board, having a cabin is important. They are priced about the same as rooms in a modest hotel.

If you are traveling between October and June (except for the three weeks around Easter), passage and a cabin can usually be booked the day before sailing. Between mid-June and mid-September, however, it's usually necessary to made reservations two weeks in advance. Unfortunately, there is no Trasmediterranea agent in the United States or Canada, so the best approach to booking a cabin in summer high season is to telephone the office in Cádiz (tel: 011-34-56-284-350) before departing for Europe. For booking during the low months, contact any travel agency or Trasmediterranea office in Spain, or any Melia Travel Agency in Continental Europe.

The Trasmediterranea ships also provide the best means of transportation among the Canary Islands. Ferries run between Tenerife (port of Christianos) and the island of Gomera, and between Santa Cruz de Tenerife and Santa Cruz de la Palma, both worthwhile day trips. Ferryliners and hydrofoils also operate between Santa Cruz de Tenerife and Las Palmas on Grand Canary (three and a half hours by ship, one and a half hours by hydrofoil), and routes extend on to Fuertaventura and Lanzarote.

12

Switzerland

◆ THE AGENCIES

Coast to Coast Resorts (Lake Lucerne—Seelisberg)
Eastone Overseas Accommodations (throughout Switzerland—through Interhome, Inc. USA)
Four Star Living, Inc. (throughout Switzerland)
Grand Circle Travel, Inc. (Bernese Oberland—Gstaad, Interlaken; Grisons—Davos; Lucerne Canton—Lucerne; Ticino—Locarno)
Hometours International (Bernese Oberland—Gstaad, Interlaken; Grisons—Laax; Ticino—San Benardino; Valais—Albarela, Champéry; Vaud—Villars)
Idyll, Ltd. (Bernese Oberland—Thuner See/Interlaken)
Interhome, Inc. USA (many properties throughout Switzerland)
Overseas Connection (Bernese Oberland—Gstaad; Grisons—St. Moritz)
Rent A Home International (northeastern Switzerland/Lake Zurich; Ticino—Lugano; Valais—Zermatt; Vaud—Château d'Œx; others)
Rent A Vacation Everywhere (RAVE) (throughout Switzerland)
Swiss Touring U.S.A. (Bernese Oberland—Beatenberg, Kandersteg, Wengen; Ticino—Lugano; Valais—Montana-Vermala, Zermatt)
Vacation Home Rentals (VHR) Worldwide (throughout Switzerland)
Villas International (Bernese Oberland—Brienz, Grindelwald, Gstaad, Interlaken; Geneva Canton—Geneva; Grisons—Davos, Klosters; Jura; Lucerne Canton—Lucerne; Ticino—Locarno, Lugano; Valais—Montana-Vermala, Verbier, Zermatt; Vaud—Lausanne Villars)

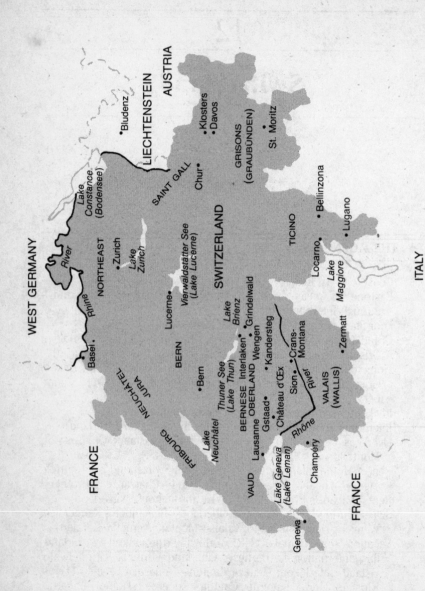

◆ THE COUNTRY

This little country, less than a third the area of England, presents four faces to foreigners: the winter Switzerland of resorts and cold weather sports; the summer Switzerland of Alpine lakes, meadows, and villages; the Switzerland of great lakes and steamers; and the urban Switzerland of Zurich, Bern, Geneva, Basel, Lausanne, and Lucerne.

A trip from Geneva at the eastern border with France to the Austrian border near Bregenz takes five hours by car or train. But despite Switzerland's small size, its diversity, beauty, and facilities for travelers are legendary. The country's virtues attract tourists in numbers disproportionate to its size, and as can be seen from the long list of agents offering properties there, the most popular way of staying is in vacation rentals. With its U.S. agent, the Zurich-based company Interhome alone lists more than 3,000 rentals, and although it is the largest in Switzerland (and in Europe), there are others with excellent selections.

BEST TIMES OF YEAR TO VISIT

WINTER: In Europe only Austria, the Trentino–Alto Adige of Italy, and the Savoy region of France rival Switzerland for the number and style of ski resorts, ski runs and lifts, and the shops, restaurants, and nightlife that draw skiers and snow-bunnies. The names Gstaad, St. Mortiz, Davos, Wengen, and Zermatt conjure up accurate images of the young, the rich, and the stylish. Among them, serious skiers (*"piste bashers"*) stick together on the slopes, on the decks of fashionable Alpine hotels, and in the restaurants and jet-set nightclubs of towns nearly buried in snow.

The best skiing depends on the altitude of the resort area and its mountains, and judging this entails some serious study of a good guidebook. Gstaad, for example, is a popular and glamorous ski resort, but is among the lowest in altitude, so good snow conditions early (December) and late (Easter) cannot be counted upon. On the other hand, Zermatt, which has the highest runs in the country, and the less-glitzy Wengen, whose runs are in the shadow of the Jungfrau, tend to have better snow conditions both early and late. Thus, winter visit plans depend on complex elements. One factor, however, is constant: In the ski resorts, December is the peak season for prices and crowds, followed by a relatively low period in Janaury, then picking up in February and March. If snow conditions are more important to you than nightlife and people-watching, go early or late in the season to one of the higher altitude resorts.

SPRING, SUMMER, AND FALL: Most of Switzerland's winter resort towns are reborn each year with the coming of summer. When the snow disappears, the nature of the tourists changes, and the character of the towns changes also. Many summer visitors come on tours, and for these people, skiing may never have been an attraction. Flames have ceased roaring in the fireplaces of cozy après-ski lodges. The decks and terraces of restaurants are filled with a clientele generally older than the skiers. They hike or walk the Alpine meadows; wander the narrow, sunny, village streets; ride horseback or play tennis; and sail or take steamer cruises that stop at towns that dot the shores of Switzerland's large lakes.

Just before and after the winter sports seasons Switzerland seems to close up for a month or so. During the first week of a recent November, for example, we drove the few miles from Interlaken to Lauterbrunnen, where we boarded the little electric cog train up to Wengen (where cars are restricted). The sun was warm, the Jungfrau and the Eiger stood clear against the blue sky, and we ate lunch and enjoyed a beer on the deck of a pleasant café—the only one open in town. Perhaps ten foreigners were in Wengen, including us. There was no snow and no skiing; none of the clubs, few of the shops, and only one hotel were open. The time, of course, was low season. To us, it was a trade-off; the tranquillity and natural beauty of the area, the sense of solitude, and the absence of lines for the train made for a perfect day. (Chalet rentals in Wengen are available through Swiss Touring, USA.)

From late October until the beginning of ski season, and again from the end of the ski season until the beginning of the late-spring tourist season, many of the Alpine resort towns and nearby valley cities such as Interlaken are quiet, and some of the hotels, rental properties, and tourist attractions are closed. Because fewer rentals are available during these periods, you might have to look a bit harder to find one, but there are still many to choose from in these off-seasons.

Summer is a delight, although the crowds from mid-June through August, as in most popular European destinations, can be frustrating. Avoid these months unless you don't mind large numbers of fellow tourists, or are interested in getting off the beaten track into the high country.

Taking into account seasonal prices, weather, crowds, and operative tourist activities (lake steamers, gondolas, cog railways, shops, and restaurants), the optimum nonski-season periods in which to visit are from mid-April to June and again from mid-September through October. In early spring there may still be some snow around the higher towns; in late fall the fog often lays in the valleys, but the towns at higher elevations remain in sunshine.

GENERAL INFORMATION ABOUT RENTALS. The term *chalet* is commonly used for rental properties in the villages and smaller towns of Switzerland. It can mean either a separate, individual house or a larger building constructed in the "chalet" style but containing two or more apartments. Larger buildings may simply be called *apartments* or *aparthotels*, even if they are constructed in chalet style. *Chalet style* generally means a cube-shaped building with a peaked gently sloping roof, balconies, real or decorative window shutters, wood construction or wood trim, and often gaily painted walls. The summer image includes windowboxes full of colorful flowers; in winter they are buried in snow. These images are very close to the truth in the Alpine towns throughout the northern, eastern, and western regions of the country.

In the southeast, especially in the Italian-speaking region of Ticino, the Italian/Mediterranean influence is manifested not only in the mild climate, vegetation, and life-style, but in the architecture as well. Rental properties in the area of Lake Maggiore and Lugano are either villas, apartments in villas, or in more modern apartment buildings.

In the country's larger cities, the rentals are in apartment buildings, as varied in type and style as they are in North America. And large, modern apartment complexes have been built even in some of the valley towns, so do not assume that anything you rent will be in a quaint chalet. Select carefully if you are interested in a specific style.

Swiss rentals are invariably immaculate, even the simpler country houses and Alpine chalets. There is a certain Swiss reputation to live up to, and most owners do so, maintaining comfortable and attractive properties. They are cozy in winter and light and airy in summer, usually situated to take advantage of their surroundings. Utilities are generally included in the rent, and linens and towels are normally supplied (but verify this with the agent).

The superior quality of most of the rentals, combined with the mountians, lakes, scenery, and the orderly towns and villages, places these properties near the top of the European list in terms of desirability and price. The extensive use of wood in Swiss resorts and mountain towns gives even the largest and most expensive rentals a rustic charm. Perhaps rustic luxury is the most apt term, because these properties offer every comfort and modern convenience.

PRICES. Prices vary immensely, influenced not only by the size and standards of the rental but by the village or town in which it is located. For example, placement in the community (close to the ski lifts, adjacent to the lake, with a view of the Matterhorn) and the season are significant. Zermatt, for example, is principally a winter resort, and seasonal prices vary accordingly. To illustrate, the following schedule shows the varying prices for a typical studio apartment in a well-located, large, chalet-style building in Zermatt. It is also a good example of the complexity of the seasonal changes. The dates and prices are approximate, and are per week per apartment, including utilities and laundry based on an exchange rate of 1.5 Swiss francs per U.S. dollar.

December 15 to January 7 and February 1 to March 15	$500
January 8 to February 1	$395
March 15 to March 31	$500
April 1 to April 15	$450
April 16 to June 30 and August 26 to December 15	$375
July 1 to August 25	$385

In Lucerne, Interlaken, and other cities at lower altitude, and in the villages along the large lower lakes, the reverse dates apply; July and August are the costly months, and the shoulder periods remain the same. An illustration is a chalet apartment hotel in Interlaken. The prices are per week, for a studio apartment, everything included; dates are approximate.

November through April	$400
May through June, and October	$510
July through September and December 20 to 30	$620

For more spacious, four- and five-star-class private chalets and apartments in the most popular resorts, rents of $1,500 to $3,500 per week and more can be expected in winter and summer peak seasons, dropping by about one-third in the off-seasons. These rentals, however, are not only of exceptional standards but are usually large enough to accommodate four to six or more persons.

A double room in a modest, three-star hotel in Interlaken, including Continental breakfast, runs about $70 per night ($490 per week) in winter, $80 per night ($560 per week) in the shoulder months, and $95 per night ($665 per week) in June through September. A four-star accommodation will cost about $95 per night ($665 per week) in winter to about $115 per night ($805 per week) in the high months. A double room in a five-star hotel in Zurich (the Savoy) is about $300 per night, similar to a room in the top hotels in the ski resorts.

Overall, Switzerland is not among Europe's less expensive countries, but rental prices can be quite reasonable in the off-seasons and slightly-off-seasons. And, standard for standard, they are always cheaper than hotels.

WHERE TO STAY. Switzerland's small size makes all of its parts accessible from any of the others, given a stay of two or three weeks. The country also has a large number of vacation rentals, principally located in the most popular Alpine resorts, but with a good selection scattered elsewhere. Thus, a decision on where to stay need not be based on where the rentals are, but on what you are looking for. Nearly all of the country is delightful.

To a large degree, our advice to anyone planning a spring, summer, or autumn trip is the same advice we give to winter sports enthusiasts: Go into the Alps. But during the nonwinter months, it is also important to devote time to the larger lakes—Lucerne, Thun, Brienz, Constance, Geneva—and to the towns and villages along their shores. The ideal approach is to plan a week or more in each of two home-base locations.

First-time winter visitors, especially skiers, should study a good guide to Switzerland and check out magazines on the subject of the ski resorts and their runs. Among the major resorts, Gstaad and St. Moritz are generally rated the glamorous resorts, the most fun if your budget is unlimited; the rentals there are generally in the deluxe category. Zermatt usually gets good scores all around for scenery, character, the highest-altitude runs (and longest ski season), varied slopes, good town and mountain restaurants. St. Moritz is great not only for downhill skiing but has miles of Nordic trails, as well as facilities for bobsledding, skating, watching (or playing) polo on the frozen lake, and even curling; in short, it is a winter playground with something for everyone. Davos and Klosters, in the eastern canton of Grisons (Graubünden), north of St. Moritz, provide excellent skiing and a good selection of rentals, with Klosters offering a more staid atmosphere than many of the more recently developed resorts.

◆ THE REGIONS

Topographically, Switzerland can be divided into three horizontal bands. The top one, bordering West Germany and comprising about one-sixth of the country's area, is the Jura, a range of wooded hills and relatively low mountains. The next band, also about one-sixth of the country, is the Plateau, the long sweep from Geneva in the southwest to the east end of Lake Constance (Bodensee). This region is the most industrially developed, containing roughly 70 percent of the population and all the principal cities except Basel. The southern band, comprising two-thirds of the country, is the area most people think of when they envision Switzerland: the Alps.

The other parameters that define the different natures of Switzerland's regions are the languages and culture of the country adjacent to each region. Seventy-five percent of the populace speak German, 20 percent speak French, 4 percent speak Italian, and 1 percent speak Romansh. The dominant language is a clue to the cultural characteristics of a canton. Geneva, Lausanne, and Neuchâtel, for example, have a decidedly French atmosphere; Zurich, Lucerne, and Interlaken are Germanic in character; and Lugano, Locarno, and Bellinzona have an Italian nature.

The language distribution is rather clear-cut, often more so than the boundaries, of the three topographical regions. The canton of Valais, for instance, is linguistically split. The people of two villages just a few kilometers apart may speak different languages. Thus, the character of any single part of Switzerland can only be described after complex research. The towns, foods, architecture, language, and dress of the Alpine region of the east (Grisons) are different from those of the Alpine areas of French-influenced Valais in the southwest, and both are different from the German-influenced regions that compose the central area from the north border down to Italy. Even many of the same cantons have different names, depending on the language. Valais is the French name for the German Wallis; Grisons is the Romansh name for the Swiss-German Graubünden. Before deciding on the most compatible location for a home base, consider the nature of these different surroundings. Study a guidebook, a good one should show both the topographic and linguistic characteristics of the country. Also, contact the agencies that offer properties in the regions you are interested in, or throughout Switzerland, for information.

The following sections describe Switzerland's regions broken down by language.

The West
(French-Speaking Cantons—
Jura, Neuchâtel, Vaud, western Fribourg,
western Valais)

ENVIRONS AND ACCOMMODATIONS. This region encompasses the low hills and pasturelands of the sparsely settled north and the rugged Alps of the south. Lake of Neuchâtel, the largest lake totally within Swiss borders, lies in generally flat land and is ringed with towns and resort villages, some of which are among the most traditional and picturesque in the country. To the south lies Lake Geneva (Lake Leman), with its south shore in France and its north shore in Switzerland. At its western tip is Geneva, and near the center of the north shore is Lausanne, both high on the list of cities to visit. Steamer voyages on these two great lakes, either touring nonstop or docking at villages along the route, make for delightful days.

The Rhône flows from east to west through Valais, emptying into Lake Geneva at the east end, and from the west end at Geneva resumes its route toward the Mediterranean. Much of its route is bordered by high mountains. The towns and villages here are ideal for visiting in summer; in winter they become major destination ski resorts. Among these is Montana-Vermala, in an area better known as Crans/Montana, a five-town area that supports Switzerland's largest winter sports complex. A ski resort especially popular with the young of Europe is Verbier. Château d'Œx (pronounced "Château Day"), Villars, and Champéry are more family oriented, and in summer are excellent Alpine getaways.

Two weeks of spring, summer, or fall could be pleasantly spent in this region alone, perhaps one in an apartment in Geneva (expensive) or the easier-to-manage cities of Fribourg or Lausanne, and one week in an Alpine village or on Lake Geneva. In winter, the time would most likely be spent in one of the ski resorts, perhaps with one week devoted to a resort in Valais or Vaud and a second week spent in an eastern base such as Davos, Klosters, or St. Moritz.

No fewer than eight agencies in the United States represent properties in this Swiss region (look for names followed by one of the cantons of this region).

LOCATION AND TRANSPORTATION. The distance from Geneva to Zurich is only 170 miles (275 km), and from there it is another 75 miles (124 km) to Bregenz (Austria), at the east end of Lake Constance. For a taste of Italy, it is about three hours by highway or rail from Geneva southeast to Turin and two hours on to Milan. To the west, it is 95 miles (155 km) from Geneva to Lyon (France), and 125 miles (210 km) to Dijon.

Mainline railroads border Lake Geneva and Lake of Neuchâtel, and connect the major cities of the region with Bern, Zurich, Basel, and beyond—and to the major cities of France. Secondary lines serve a large number of smaller towns, despite the rugged terrain of the south. Where regular trains cannot run, cog railways take over.

If you are planning to spend most of your visit in an Alpine village, be sure to determine from the agent whether vehicles are allowed. Although driving is an excellent way to explore Switzerland, if the village you plan to stay in does not allow cars you might perfer to travel by train and cog railway from Geneva, Lausanne, or other main city instead of parking your car at the cog station below your destination village. Be sure to get the specifics from the agent.

Central Switzerland, North to South
(German-Speaking Cantons—Basel, Bern, eastern
Fribourg, Lucerne, eastern Wallis (Valais), Zurich)

These six cantons, or parts of cantons, are only some of the nineteen in which German is the predominant language. These are the principal regions in which rentals can be booked through agents in the United States or Canada, and they represent the areas of most interest to foreign visitors. If you want to stay in a specific area not covered in this section, contact one of the agencies that represent properties throughout Switzerland, or see Appendix B for the names and addresses of rental companies in Switzerland.

ENVIRONS AND ACCOMMODATIONS. West Germany on the north, Austria on the east, and Italy on the south border the French-speaking areas of the cantons of Fribourg and Valais. This greatly varied area comprises the rolling hills and broad valleys of the Plateau in the north, range after range of mid-height mountains toward the center, and the high Alps in the south. Lake Zurich (Zürichsee), Lake Constance (Bodensee), and Lake Lucerne (Vierwaldstätter See) are in this area, along with the lesser-known and smaller Lake Thun (Thuner See) and Lake Brienz (Brienzersee). Together they lie along the northern base of the Jungfrau/Eiger massif.

Zurich, the area's principal city, is the largest in Switzerland (pop. about 1 million). It has its own attractions for tourists, and there are apartments available, if you are inclined toward a city stay.

In an area as scenically beautiful, even astounding, as this, it is difficult to suggest one part in which to establish a home base. But despite the lure of the big lakes of the north, and that of the steamers and the villages and cities on their shores, it is the Alps and lakes of central Switzerland (Lucerne canton), the Bernese Oberland (southern Bern canton), and the canton of Valais that draw travelers from all over the world. In fact, because so many come in the summer, we again emphasize that if you can visit in April, May, September, or even early October, your stay will be much more rewarding (and less expensive).

CANTON OF LUCERNE: The Lucerne area is a special delight for persons who love mountains but are not climbers or hikers. The surrounding Alps are amazingly accessible, and with no more effort than it takes to walk a city block or two you can take a cable car to the top of Mount Pilatus. Or take an elevator to the resort village of Bürgenstock on a nearby hill, or the cog railway or cable car to the top of 6,000-foot Mount Rigi for a view that's hard to rival. Lake Lucerne itself, like most of the Swiss lakes, is also easily accessible, affording great views of the mountain country from the decks or dining rooms of the lake steamers that call on the waterfront villages. For winter visitors, Lucerne canton does not offer the number or quality of ski runs found in the canton of Valais (Wallis) or the Bernese Oberland, but cross-country skiing is very popular.

BERNESE OBERLAND: Surrounding Lucerne to the west and south is the canton of Bern, divided into the Bernese Mittelland and the Bernese Oberland. It is the Oberland and the Valais canton to the south that draw the majority of visitors. The preponderance of Alpine villages and resorts, and in them the majority of Swiss vacation rentals, are located in the Oberland and in Valais.

The lakes Thun and Brienz, long and slender, lie end-to-end, with the town of Interlaken in the center where they almost touch. The city of Thun at the west end and the pretty village of Brienz bracket the lakes. From much of Interlaken there are unobstructed views south to where the peaks of the Jungfrau, Mönch, and Eiger stand together, forming only a part of the great range that separates this valley from that of the Rhône beyond.

Interlaken itself is an old-fashioned resort town that serves as a popular base from which to enjoy everything from boating and steamship cruises on the lakes to exploration of the Bernese Alps. Its population of 13,000 almost doubles in the summer months, and also increases during ski season. Many skiers stay closer to the slopes at village resorts, but it is certainly possible to commute daily from Interlaken to any of several ski villages in the vicinity. From late spring to late fall these mountain villages are perfect centers from which to climb, hike, take cog railways or gondolas to the heights, or descend to the large lakes below. This is a wonderfully complex world of mountains, valleys, villages, lakes, and waterfalls, made even more amazing by its accessibility. A tunnel, for example, spirals for 4.3 miles (7 km) inside the Eiger, to the Jungfraujoch, the highest railroad station in the world at 11,360 feet (3,500 m).

Deciding which village to settle in for one or two weeks is a little complex, but it is also hard to go wrong. Look over the small list of towns below, and contact the agencies with properties in the Bernese Oberland and those that offer properties throughout Switzerland. If particular towns from the list or a guidebook to Switzerland sound appealing, specify that you want information on rentals there. Interlaken, of course, is one good possibility.

> *Wengen:* Mountain village. No cars, accessible by train from Interlaken or cog railway from car park at Lauterbrunnen. Busy but not glitzy in winter; peaceful base for summer hiking. Great views, high meadowland at base of Jungfrau massif; excellent ski runs.

Restaurants, grocery stores, shops; access to the railway to the Jungfraujoch; 9 miles (15 km) south of Interlaken.

Grindelwald: Mountain village. Accessible by car or train, 12 miles (20 km) from Interlaken; access also by cog railway from Lauterbrunnen. Busier than Wengen because of car accessibility. Great views, high valley at base of Eiger and Schreckhorn; popular ski area. Restaurants, grocery stores, shops; access to the railway to the Jungfraujoch.

Brienz: Small town on shore of Lake Brienz 12 miles (20 km) by highway east of Interlaken. Woodcarving center; many tourists in summer, but pretty and peaceful at other times. Restaurants, shops, boating.

Mürren and Gimmelwald: Relatively high-altitude villages (5,345 feet; 1,645 m). No cars; accessible by cog railway from Lauterbrunnen. Principally a ski area, but good base for hiking; 9 miles (15 km) south of Interlaken.

Gstaad: Major international summer and winter resort in area of many smaller resort villages. Forty-seven miles (75 km) southwest of Interlaken by highway or rail. Swimming, tennis, horseback riding; good skiing and high social life; fine restaurants. Expensive.

Kandersteg: A pretty, traditional summer and winter resort village at foot of Blüemlisalphorn. Thirty-seven miles (60 km) southwest of Interlaken via Spiez by highway or rail. Hiking, swimming, tennis, riding; relatively unaffected. Restaurants, grocery stores, shops.

Beatenberg: Small village a ten-minute ride on the funicular—a mountain railway—above the north shore of Thuner See. Convenient to Interlaken and the lakes. Good choice for those who would avoid larger towns.

CANTON OF VALAIS (WALLIS): In the preceding section on the French-speaking region of Switzerland, the western half of the Valais canton was profiled. Called Wallis by the German-speaking populace of the eastern half, this is a topographical continuation of the canton, still dominated by the valley of the Rhône River (German: "Rotten"), which cuts an east-west swath through the Alps on either side. More than fifty peaks rise above 13,000 feet (4,000 meters), and in lower Valais fertile farms grow strawberries, tomatoes, and apricots. In addition to the Alpine resorts of Montana-Vermala, Crans, Champérey, and Verbier that were noted in the previous section, many more resorts are located in the eastern end. One of the most charming and internationally popular of these ski resorts is Saas-Fee. In summer, this village, surrounded by high Alps, is for visitors who want a sense of isolation and are not interested in going to some city every day. It is located 16 miles (26 km) south of Visp, on the Rhône.

Nearby, 22 miles (36 km) southwest of Visp, is Zermatt, the region's most famous ski and summer resort, known not only for skiing but also for good restaurants, hiking, sunny terraces, and as the base for assaults on the nearby Matterhorn.

Cars are not allowed in either Saas-Fee or Zermatt, but may be parked at the station where service by rail or minibus is available. It is only 86 miles (140 km) from Visp to Lausanne, and another 43 miles (70 km) to Geneva.

The South-Central Tip
(Italian-Speaking Canton—Ticino)

For visitors who come into the canton of Ticino from the north, through the Saint Gotthard tunnel, over the Saint Gotthard pass (Paso del Santo Gottardo), or over the San Bernardino pass, the change in everything from the language to the food, architecture, music, and life-style is surprising. It is like crossing an international boundary rather than a provincial one, yet Italian-flavored Ticino has been Swiss since the sixteenth century. The unusual atmosphere derives from mixing Italian notions of the good life with the Swiss passion for order, efficiency, and law.

On the sunny south side of the Alps, the mountains here are high enough for plenty of snow, but this is principally an area where the climate is mild enough for magnolia and mimosa, palm trees, flowers, and citrus. An international region, Ticino's predominant language is Italian, but about 10 percent of the populace speaks Swiss-German, and another 30 percent are foreign residents who speak anything from Danish to Portuguese. The common language is English. Lakes Maggiore and Lugano, both shared with Italy, are the focus for visitors to the region. By juxtaposing Mediterranean influences and Alpine grandeur, these lakes make the area a very attractive home base.

Many of the rentals are in, or near, the towns of Locarno and Lugano. Locarno, the smaller of the two, is a wonderful town on the shore of Lake Maggiore. Lugano, on the shore of the Lake Lugano, is the grand dame of the lake country resort towns and, like Locarno, would be a good home base. With a manageable population of 30,000, it has smart shops, good restaurants, and an atmosphere of elegance. If you prefer not to stay in town, make this clear to the agencies you contact; however, do try to stay on or near the lakes.

Bellinzona, the capital of Ticino, is north of the lakes and makes a good base for anyone wanting to avoid the press of summer tourists in better-known Lugano and Locarno. Besides the historical and artistic attractions in these principal towns, lake steamer excursions are a must, and drives through the mountain valleys are a delight.

BEST TIMES OF YEAR TO VISIT. A drawback to this area is one that afflicts all of Europe's most attractive places: summer crowds. Because of the mild climate and the low elevation of the lakes and lake towns (Locarno is under 700 feet), spring and fall are also lovely times to visit. Garden and meadow flowers begin their display in February, heighten in March, and give way to wisteria, azalea, and cherry blossoms in April. If you are free to go when you wish, choose March, April, May, September, or October, and avoid the high-season months of June, July, and August.

LOCATION AND TRANSPORTATION. From Lugano it is about 43 miles (65 km) south to the city of Milan, and 145 miles (235 km) north to Zurich. All of Switzerland is open to exploration from a home base in this south-central region. Also, a trip to Venice (and the Italian cities of Verona and Padua along the way) can be accomplished from the Swiss lake region. It is, for example, only 205 miles (330 km) from Lugano to Venice, a journey of four hours by train or highway. The mainline railroad runs between Zurich and Milan, via Bellinzona and Lugano, with a major spur between Bellinzona and Locarno. With rail, buses, and lake vessels available a car is not essential for a stay in the region, but it is a great convenience.

ADVANCE BOOKING TIME. For June, July, and August—six months. For February through May—two months. For September and October— two months. For November through January—up to two weeks.

The Southeastern Region
(Romansh/Multilingual)

The area where even the Swiss go to get away from it all, the Grisons (Graubünden in German), is the largest and least populated canton in Switzerland. Three languages are spoken: ancient Romansh along the central east-west axis, German to the north and south, and Italian in the southern tips that border Italy.

It is a few hours' drive from Interlaken eastward to Chur (pronounced "Koor"), the principal city of the Grisons. Because the highway, which is not an expressway, climbs through passes that exceed 7,000 feet, the approach from the west makes the area feel somewhat isolated from the rest of the country. This feeling is compounded by seeing signs bearing town names and words in the unfamiliar Romansh language. No more German mountain *horn* names, or Italian *monte*, but *piz*, meaning "peak" in Romansh. Lakes are now called *lei* instead of the Italian *lago*, French *lac*, and German *See*.

After dropping out of the high and often desolate country and arriving at Chur, it astonished us to realize that we were less than an hour from Zurich by autobahn, and even closer to the cities and towns on the shore of Lake Constance.

THE ENGADINE VALLEY: For mountain lovers who must visit Switzerland during the high summer season, but want to avoid the crowds that descend on the better-known and more popular areas to the west, a one-week stay in the Engadine Valley (the valley of the Inn [En] River) southeast of Chur is ideal. The villages of the Lower Engadine retain their character from earlier days, and most of the valley remains unspoiled. St. Moritz, the principal community of the Upper Engadine, is one of the world's best-known resorts. It is a fashionable, dynamic, and expensive international play spot. In winter St. Moritz hits its stride, but in the other months it is also a place to go for hiking, swimming, tennis, and riding, as well as shopping in exclusive, high-priced stores. St. Moritz has the highest concentration of rentals in the Engadine, mostly deluxe in standards and high in price, available through seven of the agencies listed at the beginning of this chapter. For more modest, moderately priced properties in the valley, Interhome, Inc. USA has the largest selection.

EAST OF CHUR: Elsewhere in the Grisons, the two most popular village resorts are Davos and Klosters, both in the Alpine country about 43 miles (70 km) east of Chur. Davos is a large, busy ski and summer resort where almost everything can be rented for slightly less than in St. Moritz and the more fashionable Klosters, a few miles north. Charles, the Prince of Wales, fancies Klosters, both for the skiing and the relatively restrained and elegant atmosphere. Six of the agencies listed at the beginning of this chapter offer rentals in Davos, while the best bet for Klosters is Villas International.

WEST OF CHUR: Off the highway leading to the Saint Gotthard tunnel and Interlaken are the smaller, quieter villages of Laax and Flims. This area of wooded hills and small lakes lends itself to a relaxed stay, yet offers easy access to Chur. To the west, the Bernese Oberland is within easy striking distance. Rentals in this area are available through Hometours International.

LOCATION AND TRANSPORTATION. From Chur, Laax, Davos, and Klosters, the main highway south passes through the Saint Bernardino tunnel and into Ticino, the Italian-influenced canton. It is 93 miles (150 km) of outstanding scenery from Chur to Lugano. Northward, the highway splits, the left branch going to Zurich and the right to Saint Gallen and Lake Constance, following the Rhine River valley and traveling along the border of Liechtenstein. A circular journey through Liechtenstein, into Austria's Montafon and Arlberg regions, and back down to the Engadine Valley is a varied and scenic trip.

The mainline railroad from Zurich ends at Chur, but there is regular service from Landquart, just north of Chur, to Davos and Klosters. St. Moritz is served by rail from Chur, and a cog railway runs from Chur to Laax and Flims.

Although transportation systems through this eastern region are adequate, the area is best traveled by car, especially if you want to get away from the main tourist paths.

ADVANCE BOOKING TIME. For June, July, and August—6 months. For December, February, and March (ski resorts)—six months. For January (ski resorts)—three months. For the rest of the year—up to one month.

13

United Kingdom

◆

◆ THE AGENCIES

Each agency is followed by the general locations of the properties it represents: England, Scotland, or Wales. If there is no specific concentration of properties in any area, such as Cornwall, Devon, or Sussex, they are noted to be "throughout." Recognizable area names such as Cotswolds and Thames Valley may be used as well as county names.

In this guide, London is dealt with as a separate entity, and the districts—such as Mayfair, Kensington, and Bloomsbury—where agencies have rentals are shown after the word *London*. If there is no district notation, the agency offers properties throughout all the central parts of the city.

For more specific information on the agencies and their properties, refer to Chapter 3.

AARP Travel Service (London—Westminster, Mayfair)

Abacus Agency (London—Chelsea/Belgravia, South Kensington, Mayfair)

At Home Abroad (England—Sussex, West Country, Heart of England; London)

Beds Abroad, Ltd. (London—Belgravia, Knightsbridge)

Blake's Vacations (throughout England, Scotland, and Wales; concentration in East Anglia)

British Travel Association (throughout England, Scotland, and Wales; London)

Castles, Cottages & Flats of Ireland and the U.K. Ltd. (throughout England, Scotland, and Wales; Bath, London)

Coast to Coast Resorts (throughout England; some in Scotland and Wales)

Condo Vacations (throughout England; some in Scotland and Wales)

De Loof Limited (London—Belgravia, Chelsea, South Kensington, Mayfair)

Eastone Overseas Accommodations (throughout England and Scotland; some in Wales; Edinburgh, London—Chelsea, Kensington, Mayfair)

Europa-Let (throughout England and Scotland; some in Wales; London—Bloomsbury, Kensington, Mayfair, and environs)

Families Abroad, Inc. (England—Southwest and Southeast; Scotland—Edinburgh; London)

Four Seasons Villas (throughout England; London—Knightsbridge, South Kensington, Pimlico, Westminster)

Four Star Living, Inc. (throughout England, Scotland, and Wales; London—Belgravia, Kensington, Pimlico)

Grand Circle Travel, Inc. (London—Pimlico)

Grant-Reid Communication (throughout England, Scotland, and Wales; London—Bayswater, Kensington, Knightsbridge, Mayfair, Pimlico)

Hastingwood Assoc., Ltd. (London—Belgravia, Knightsbridge; Avon—Bath)

Heart of England Cottages (Heart of England, Shakespeare Country, Thames & Chilterns)

Hearthstone Holidays (throughout England, Scotland, and Wales; Edinburgh, London)

Heritage of England (throughout England, Scotland, and Wales)

Hideaways International (London—Kensington, Westminster)

Hometours International (London—Kensington, Mayfair)

Idyll, Ltd. (few selected locations in Scotland and Wales; London—Belgravia, Bloomsbury, City of London and its environs)

In the English Manner (London—Chelsea, Kensington, Knightsbridge, Mayfair; hosted rooms in manor houses throughout Britain)

Livingstone Holidays (throughout England, Scotland, and Wales; Bath, London—Belgravia, Bloomsbury, Chelsea, Kensington, Mayfair)

London Apartments (USA) Ltd. (London—Bayswater, Bloomsbury, Kensington, Knightsbridge, Mayfair, Victoria)

NW Bed & Breakfast—Travel Unlimited (London—Chelsea, Knightsbridge, Pimlico; canal boats)

Orsava, Inc. (throughout England; some in Scotland and Wales)

Overseas Connection (London)

Pilgrim's Way (throughout England, Scotland, and Wales; London—Belgravia, Bloomsbury, Chelsea, Kensington, Mayfair, Pimlico, Westminster)

Rent A Home International (throughout England; some in Scotland and Wales; London—various locations)

Rent A Vacation Everywhere (RAVE) (London—various locations)

Tour-Host International (throughout England; some in Scotland and Wales; London—various locations)

Vacation Home Rentals (VHR) Worldwide (throughout England; London—central and environs)

Villas International (throughout England, Scotland, and Wales; London—central districts and environs)

Wayside Travel (Heart of England, Shakespeare Country, Thames & Chilterns)

Williams & Co. (throughout England; some in Scotland)

Wilson & Lake International (throughout England, Scotland and Wales)

To work things out independently, contact one of the British companies shown in Appendix B. There may be some savings in the rental prices, but there will be no service or assistance from a U.S. or Canadian agency. Although dealing with deposits and payments is cumbersome with some of the companies, Britain is one country where direct contact is the least risky.

♦ INTRODUCTION TO GREAT BRITAIN

The United Kingdom comprises England, Scotland, Wales, and Northern Ireland. In this guide "Great Britain" or "Britain" refers to England, Scotland, and Wales collectively. We have not included Northern Ireland, despite its beautiful countryside, the breathtaking north coast of Antrim and Londonderry counties, and interesting cities such as Londonderry and Armagh. Few vacation rentals are available there. Instead, it can be visited from locations covered in Chapter 8 "Republic of Ireland." If you wish to stay in Northern Ireland, accommodations can be found by contacting the British Travel Authority in the United States or Canada.

It would be virtually impossible to cover every part of Great Britain. The thirty-nine agencies listed above are only those that represent British rental companies in the United States and Canada, and although a few represent only one British company, others represent up to six. Many British companies do not have North American representatives, although there is increasing interest in the market. In fact, the problem of finding a good cottage or apartment to rent is being replaced with the problem of selecting from among them. Furthermore, hundreds of individual properties—from castles to cottages—are not represented by any agency, and depend solely on advertisements and listings with the British Tourist Authority, the British Automobile Association, or the Royal Automobile Club for their bookings. By conservative estimates, the number of vacation rentals in England, Scotland, and Wales ranges from 25,000 to 30,000, of which the North American agencies above, and the selected British companies in Appendix B, represent perhaps 20,000. If you wish to add to the choices, contact the British Tourist Authority for its booklet; the addresses of its offices are in Appendix C.

We have visited Great Britain several times; for half of 1984 we lived in Kent, 50 miles southeast of London. During these times we saw a great deal of the country, but we also developed a mental list of the many places we wanted to visit at some future time. So our itinerary for this book included things we have seen—and things we hoped to see. We set up our contacts with the companies accordingly, from the tip of Cornwall to the north of Scotland, from the waterlands of East Anglia to the coast of Wales, and, of course, London.

We chose twenty areas and cities because of their variety, their proven interest to American visitors, and their interest to us. They were also visited with an eye toward available rentals and how they would serve as home bases from which to explore and enjoy the surroundings. The areas are covered in geographical order.

In England: Norfolk, Lincolnshire, North Yorkshire, the Lake District, the Cotswolds, the Chilterns and the Thames Valley (west of London), Dorset, Devon, Cornwall, Hampshire, West Sussex, Kent, and the cities of London and Bath.

In Scotland: Borders region, the Grampian Highlands, Dumfries and Galloway, and the cities of Edinburgh and Aberdeen.

In Wales: Gwynedd (north coastal) and Dyfed (south coastal).

Although our list does not exhaust the interesting places in which to stay in Britain, it does encompass the great majority of all the available rentals. These are good starting points, especially if you're planning a first visit or have not yet decided just where to settle.

If you are seeking a special "theme" vacation—golfing in Scotland, walking the moors, or attending the theater in London or Stratford—tell the agents (or check with British Airways, which has an excellent variety of programs in and around the London area). If you are an avid walker for whom Scotland's sparsely populated Grampian Highlands are still too crowded, rentals are scattered across the remotest areas of the coast and hinterlands of Scotland's Northwest Highlands. For island lovers, rentals are available on the Scottish islands, the Isle of Man, Wales' Isle of Anglesey, the Scilly Islands, and the Channel Islands off the coast of France.

♦ THE COUNTRY

Perhaps no other country in Europe, or in the world, has been written about as extensively as has Great Britain. The British document themselves and their country prodigiously, from guides to their stately homes and detailed histories of their royal families, to ordinance survey maps that show every bend in the road and everything there is to see along the way. Guidebooks to Britain alone, covering every imaginable topic, occupy several feet of shelf space in any bookstore of even modest size. This chapter will not, therefore, concern itself with Great Britain, but with an overview of how to spend a few weeks there.

A good first step is to contact the nearest office of the British Tourist Authority. The offices are very busy, especially from January to June, so try to establish what information you need before calling. Also, we have found British Airways to be a helpful resource, especially for advance booking for tickets to London theaters, musical performances, tours, and other city events, as well as for out-of-town activities such as Shakespeare plays at Stratford-upon-Avon. By flying on the carrier of your destination country, the vacation starts earlier: British food and service (or French, or Italian, depending on the destination country) begins when you board. Also, the national carrier usually knows more about its home country and, we have found, usually offers better advice and information.

Most Americans who have never been to Britain become aware after a few days there that their ideas about England's resembling the United States are not correct. And the farther one gets off well-traveled tourist trails, both physically and psychologically, the more evident the differences are. These are not a matter of good or bad, better or worse, but merely of the reality that there are more stylistic differences that affect day-to-day life than are imagined by most Americans. To begin to describe them would not only take a separate chapter, it would spoil your pleasure in discovering just how foreign Great Britain is to most Americans and, to a lesser extent, to Canadians. The longer one stays, the more foreign it all seems, especially if you're living in a rental and consequently participating in the community's daily life (going to the grocers, the "launderette," and so on), rather than staying in hotels and eating in restaurants as the majority of tourists do. A few of the differences are evident in the British approach to renting what they call "self-catering" properties, and they need to be taken into account in order to help make your visit easy. Living temporarily in a vacation rental in Britain is not like renting a condominium, beach cottage, or mountain cabin in the United States.

GENERAL NOTES ON RENTALS AND RENTING IN THE UNITED KINGDOM. Unfortunately, and with good reason, some British rental companies believe that Americans complain about accommodations unjustifiably. We were often asked to explain to Americans that many British rentals are older and of a different character and style from those in North America. Complaints also were caused by the fact that British daily life and social customs are so unlike those of middle Americans and Canadians.

When Americans and Canadians (or the British, for that matter) visit Greece, Italy, Spain, Morocco, or other non–English-speaking countries, differences in standards and life-style are more or less expected. However, because we think the British are more like ourselves, we measure British style and customs against our own. A broader outlook and a little forewarning will ease matters greatly. This also applies to those aspects of the British rental business to which North Americans are not accustomed.

DEFINITIONS, TERMINOLOGY, AND DETAILS. The following definitions are important as you deal with agents and study catalogs.

Self-catering is the term used in the United Kingdom (and some other European countries) for vacation rentals, and *holiday* is the word for "vacation."

The word *cottage* has a somewhat different meaning in British rental parlance than it would in the United States. It can be used to describe what *we* think of as a cottage (single-family dwelling, usually not very large, often cozy or quaint), in which case it is a "detached" cottage. Or it can be one unit or apartment among several in a larger house—usually rural or in a village—or a unit in a row of units (town-house style). It can also mean half of a duplex ("semi-detached"). It is essential, therefore, that the agent understand exactly what you want to rent. If you want a cottage as we use the term, specify that you want an individual, single-occupancy, detached house. Or, if making a selection from a catalog, read the description thoroughly and confirm it with the agent. If it does not matter to you, or if you prefer a "cottage" in a larger house, a duplex, or a town house, make this clear.

The term *unit* generally means a nonindividual or, in British English, "non–self-contained," accommodation in which the laundry room, terrace, and perhaps garden and hallways are shared with others in similar units.

The first floor in Britain (and all of Europe) is what we call the second floor; that is, our ground floor and first floor are the same, but in Europe the count begins with the floor above the ground floor. *Lower ground* floor or *garden level* means a floor halfway below the surface level. This description is especially important when selecting an apartment in a city.

A *bathroom* must contain a bathtub or shower in addition to the other facilities. What Americans call a half-bath is described as having a handbasin and WC.

Apartment usually means the same as in American and Canadian English, but the term *masionette* also refers to what we think of as an apartment, or one side of a duplex. A *flat* is an apartment occupying a single floor, usually the whole floor.

RENTAL PERIODS: Saturday to Saturday is the normal rental period, except in the low season (roughly late September to early June in most areas) when "mid-week" bookings of three or four days' duration can often be made. In London, Edinburgh, and other major cities, three- or four-day minimums usually apply except in the peak summer months, and changeover days are far more flexible than in rural cottages. For rural rentals during high season, consider arriving in Britain a day or two early and taking a hotel or B&B in the vicinity of your rental before the occupancy date.

ELECTRICITY: The cost of electricity is often *not included* in the rent (except in city apartments). Many rural and village properties are set up with a coin-operated meter, most of which accept only 50-pence pieces. Be sure to determine from the catalog or the agent if electricity is included. If not, *be sure to arrive with some 50-pence coins* in case it is a coin-metered setup. In some properties the renter is asked to read the meter upon arrival and departure, then settle with the owner on the spot, or with the agent later. Voltage, as it is throughout Europe, is 220 AC, but British plugs are immense, different from the others.

TOWELS AND LINENS: In rural and village properties, these are seldom provided for British renters, but are available to renters from overseas. *Be sure to confirm with the agent or British company that you need towels and linens.* There may be a small extra charge.

WELCOME NOTE AND INFORMATION: If you are not met on arrival by the owner or agent, look inside the rental for a folder or booklet containing information about how to operate things and giving the location of the laundry, grocers, and other services, and contact telephone numbers.

SWITCHES: The British seem to be mad about electrical switches; perhaps it is a safety precaution. There are always switches on the wall or the baseboard sockets, so if a lamp or appliance does not operate by its own switch, look at the socket it is plugged into. This includes the TV, the range (called a "cooker"), the cooking surface (called a "hod"), and even the oven, refrigerator, and electric hot-water heater. *Check all wall and baseboard sockets for the switch position* (and, if appropriate, make sure your metered time has not run out) before calling the owner or agent.

APPLIANCES AND UTENSILS: Long a tea-drinking society, the British shift toward coffee (but not away from tea) has principally emphasized the instant kind. As a result, many rural and village rentals are not supplied with a coffee maker. Teapots, yes, and an electric kettle for boiling water, but if you want brewed coffee, spend a pound or so at the grocers on a small Melitta-type cone and filters. Good ground coffee is available. Dishwashers are uncommon in average rentals, so if this is important, tell the agent; you will, however, be limiting your choice of properties. Many utensils are recognizable; however, in most kitchens there is a rectangular stainless steel dish with a rack attached—this device is where the British place their hot, buttered breakfast toast to cool.

SHOWERS: In older buildings, very few bathrooms have fixed showers, and it seems that the British, a bathing society, are not inclined to install showers even in more modern bathrooms. A few tubs have hose attachments for a hand shower, and some have a single, mixed-water spout, but many have just hot- and cold-water spouts. "Use a saucepan to rinse with," one landlady told us. If you have a disability that requires a shower, make this clear to the agent or British rental company. Unless a shower is vital, consider overlooking it, since this will limit your choices somewhat.

GROCERIES: Grocery stores run the gamut from large, modern Safeways and other supermarkets to the small grocers who handle staples and "tinned" goods but no vegetables, fruits, or meats. Or they handle vegetables and fruits, but no tins or meats, and so forth. In towns and villages there is always a grocery store, but in the cities they can be somewhat difficult to find. Usually, there are neighborhood groceries and strategically placed Safeways. In the city centers look for Marks & Spencer, a national department store chain with large grocery sections. These stores offer a vast selection of foods, especially wrapped and

prepackaged, from fresh vegetables to pork pies and Welsh pasties—
somewhat expensive, but very handy for vacationers.

BEST TIMES OF YEAR TO VISIT. Britain's length and its proximity to
the Gulf Stream help define its seasons. Due to the warm western ocean
currents, the United Kingdom has a very mild climate for its latitude; all
of it is well north of the continental United States, and the north of
Scotland is roughly on a line with the north of Labrador and Juneau,
Alaska. In Cornwall and the other southwest counties, it rarely gets cold,
but there can be weeks of leaden skies and rain. To the north, winters can
be cold, wet, snowy, and disagreeable. Consequently, hundreds of thousands of sun-starved Britons flee their island for vacations in balmier
climes.

Spring comes early in the south country, normally as early as mid-
March, and by early April the weather is usually very pleasant. But spring
arrives later in Scotland, especially in the Highlands, so if consistently
good weather is important, wait until May.

The warmest, sunniest months are June through September, which
is when tourists flock to Great Britain. However, school lets out late there,
often in mid-June, and most Britons with children stay home until exams
are over. Thus, May and early June are better times to go than the very
busy period from mid-June to mid-September. Considering crowds and
weather, the optimum times to visit are roughly as follows:

Southern England, western Wales: April 1 to mid-June, September to
late October.

Central England and Wales: mid-April to mid-June, September to
mid-October.

Northern England, Scotland, and Wales: late-April to mid-June and
September.

PRICES. Rural cottages and village apartments are modestly priced,
less than most properties of comparable standards in France, Italy,
Germany, and even Spain. However, many price schedules are exceed-
ingly complex, having as many as eight or ten changes throughout the
year. These reflect not only the peak, high, mid, and low tourist seasons
but also domestic holidays that foreigners know little about: bank holidays, national holidays, and school holidays. When the domestic demand for cottages increases, so do the prices. Often it is just by a few
pounds, which makes us wonder why they bother, but that is the way it is.
Still, competition among the rental companies is very keen, and our
inquiries show that most are fair.

Prices for apartments in London tend to be high or very high, but about 10 to 30 percent cheaper than hotel rooms of equal standards. More information follows in the London section.

Most agencies' catalogs are produced in Britain and are quite well done and accurately descriptive. Price schedules should be enclosed, although they usually have been printed for the U.S. market and will include the agents' fees or commissions.

WHERE TO STAY. No point in Britain is more than 80 miles from the sea, a statistic that makes the country seem rather small. Nevertheless, its configuration means distances between extremes are too great to make day trips possible. From London to Inverness, Scotland, is about 560 miles (miles, not kilometers, are used in Britain) by highway, and it's another 175 miles north from Inverness to John O'Groats at the tip of Scotland. Even east to west is deceivingly distant: more than 400 miles separate Norwich, near the east coast, and Penzance, on the tip of Cornwall. If you want to see the most of Britain in a limited time, or if you cannot choose one area you want to visit, two home bases need to be selected. Given the large number of rentals throughout Britain, decisions need not be hampered by a lack of accommodations.

◆ THE REGIONS

This section is divided into three parts: England, Scotland, and Wales. England, in turn, is divided into three tiers—North, Central, and South— and the city of London. Each tier has been subdivided longitudinally into east and west portions, resulting in six geographic subregions.

Unless you know Britain well, the first step is to get a good general guide and a map of the entire country. If you are considering a stay in London, as all visitors should, you'll also need a London map that shows the districts by name (Chelsea, Bloomsbury, Mayfair, and so forth) so that you can note where these are in relationship to the things you especially want to see and do. A good source of maps and information is the British Tourist Authority (see Appendix C for addresses). Once you narrow down your areas of interest, find the agencies in the list at the beginning of this chapter that offer properties in these areas. Then turn to Chapter 3 to find more specific information on the agencies and select those you want to contact.

England

The forty-six counties of England are generally divided into nine regions, but in this guide we divided the country into six. The regions, beginning at the south, are Southeast, Southwest, East-Central, West-Central, the Rose Counties, and the Lake District. Identifiable areas in each region are noted in either the section heading or the descriptive text. This ties in county or geographical names to their locations in the country, and matches them with the areas where there are rental properties. The profiles below provide a sense of each of the six areas. London is dealt with separately, after the other sections on England. Wales and Scotland follow London.

PRICES. Cottages, ranging from small and simple to large and elegant, can be rented for anything from £75 to £475 per week. For the higher figure ($760 [U.S.] at an exchange rate of $1.6 per British pound) you can expect a fairly large country home with a tennis court, gardens, and perhaps a pool. For half that price you will find very comfortable, nicely furnished, one- and two-bedroom independent houses in choice locations. At the lower end, in the £100-($160)-per-week range, the "cottages" are typically either small, simply furnished, converted farmhouses or out buildings, or studio or one-bedroom apartments in small (three-to-six-unit) buildings, often clustered as part of a former farm.

There is also a scattering of manor houses for rent throughout England. Normally these are large, exclusive, and beautifully furnished. Staff is often available, and gardening and maintenance are, of course, included in the rent, which typically runs from £1,700 to £2,250 per week ($2,700 to $3,600). The manor house specialists are In the English Manner, Williams & Co., Livingstone Holidays, and Wilson & Lake International, although other agencies handle a few.

Standard double hotel rooms in larger destination towns such as York, Norwich, Bath, and Lincoln range in price from £45 to £75 ($72 to $120) per night, which equals to $504 to $840 per week. This means that a two or three-bedroom, well-appointed, individual house in a choice location on attractive grounds can be rented for the price of a room in a three-star hotel. Standard for standard, a one-bedroom apartment in town costs approximately 65 to 70 percent of a hotel room. Rural cottages cannot be compared to city hotels, but we found that pleasant one-bedroom cottages generally cost less than typical B&Bs.

Despite their idiosyncrasies, rentals in Britain are generally better for the money than those in other parts of Europe.

THE SOUTHERN TIER

THE SOUTHEAST: This compact area spans Kent's rolling hills, woods and farmlands in the east, and Hampshire in the west, plus the English channel coast from the Thames estuary westward to Portsmouth and the Isle of Wight. The northern portion of the area is surrounded and influenced by London. This area offers tranquil rural beauty; attractive, historically interesting towns; castles and stately homes; proximity to the sea; and proximity to London. The eastern towns of this region—Canterbury, Rye, Lewes, Rochester, Tunbridge Wells, and Maidstone—are particularly worth visiting. In the western half, Winchester and Lymington are the towns of special interest and beauty. The prettiest countryside is in the Kent Downs, the High Weald, Sussex Downs, New Forest, or, closer to London, the Surrey Hills. (If any agent is unsure about where these areas are, check with another one.) We settled in Tunbridge Wells, Kent, because we especially liked the countryside of the High Weald, an area of several hundred square miles that stretches from the coast near Hastings west into West Sussex. The other scenic areas mentioned above are also good, especially if easy visits to London are appealing.

To avoid the drawbacks of city and commuter traffic, we recommend that you not locate within the London ring road, the M25 motorway that surrounds the city about fifteen miles from the center. Rail service is very good, so visits to the city from anywhere in the region can easily be accomplished (see the section on transportation, below).

Few North Americans will want to stay in the larger English Channel coast cities and resorts. This is not to say that coastal villages such as Bognor Regis, and near-coastal villages like Chichester and Arundel, are not inviting; they are. But the less heavily populated towns are easier and more interesting to stay in, or around, than the larger resort towns of Brighton, Hastings, and Eastbourne, and the cities of Portsmouth and Southampton.

Rentals are available throughout this area, and because it is easily accessible from London, it is a popular countryside for city dwellers to visit for weekends and holidays. Rentals in the more desirable areas are booked well in advance for the summer season, mid-June to mid-September.

Numerous agencies offer rentals in this area, so contact any with the counties of Kent, Surrey, East and West Sussex, Hampshire, and Berkshire after their names—or any that list properties throughout Britain. To make a direct contact, or if you plan to be in the United Kingdom during the off-season months (roughly mid-September through May) and want to arrange a rental on the spot, try one of the British companies shown in Appendix B. Among these is Freedom Holiday Homes, a small, personalized, Kent-based company that has a good selection of rentals, and a good reputation, in Kent and East Sussex (U.S. tel: 800-462-4486).

There are no disadvantages to renting in this area if you avoid the large coastal cities and resort towns, and stay well outside the ring road. A drive along the coastal area from Dover to Southampton can be done in half a day; two weeks can be spent exploring the region and taking day trips to London (by rail, preferably), still leaving much to see and do.

Highways and railroads serve this area well, partly because much of it is within commuter distance to London, and partly because the ferryports at Dover, Sheerness, Folkestone, and Portsmouth serve as conduits for traffic between Britain and Continental Europe. No place in the region is more than two hours apart by train. A car enables you to get off the main thoroughfares to smaller communities, castles, and stately homes, but this can also be done by public transportation. Check the local tourist offices for tours and bus information.

For a visit to France, ships sail daily from Dover to Calais and Boulogne (and return), and from Southampton to Cherbourg and Le Havre (and the Channel Islands and return). Other routes are Sheerness to the Netherlands, and Felixstowe to Zeebrugge (Belgium). Contact any travel agent for confirmation, information, and tickets.

Advance booking time (dates are approximate) needed in peak season (June 25 to September 10)—six months. In high season (mid-May to June 25 and September 10 to October 1)—three to six months. In mid-season (April 1 to mid-May and October)—one to two months. And for low season (November, December, January, and most of March)—none.

Odd periods, which most foreigners know nothing about (school midterm breaks, national holidays, bank holiday weekends, and so on), affect both prices and advance booking times. These dates may vary from year to year, so be sure to obtain the latest price listings from the agents.

THE SOUTHWEST: Except for Wiltshire, all the counties of this region are coastal. Dorset is on the English Channel; Somerset and Avon lie to its north along the coast of the Bristol Channel and the industrialized Severn River estuary. Devon and Cornwall share the southwest peninsula, washed by the English Channel at the south and the Atlantic Ocean at the north.

The Southwest comprises four somewhat distinct areas: the English Channel coast; the rolling hill country of Wiltshire and Dorset; the forests, moors, and orchard land of Somerset and Devon; and the rugged Atlantic coast of Devon and Cornwall, which boasts sheer cliffs, sandy beaches, and sea.

The English Channel coast, from Southampton west to Penzance and Land's End at the tip of Cornwall, is a chain of resort towns broken by the industrial ports of Bournemouth, Weymouth, and Plymouth. These larger cities are rich in British history, particularly its centuries as the world's principal sea power. They are certainly worth a visit, but there is no need to rent in or near any of them. Although many of the smaller coastal towns are attractive and pleasant, especially when the sun shines, they have few of the abbeys, cathedrals, museums, and historic centers and streets that most North Americans visit Great Britain to see. Fowey and Falmouth in Cornwall, and Lyme Regis in Somerset all merit a visit. But if you want to rent a place directly on the coast, advise the agent to avoid the larger resort towns.

Back from the coastal zone, along the east-west line from London to Land's End, is an orderly rural land dotted with beautiful small towns, any of which would be an ideal setting for a week or two. Some of England's most interesting and important historic towns are in this region. Just visiting Bath, Exeter, Wells, Taunton, Glastonbury, and Salisbury will occupy many days.

Whether because they occupy the western reaches of the southwest peninsula, or because they are the land of Camelot, Cornwall and Devon seem apart from the rest of England. The farther west, the more tranquil and remote the countryside appears, but it is still only four hours by motorway or rail between Plymouth and London. Nevertheless, Cornwall is an area for leisure seekers who enjoy poking around small towns, walking the moors, and exploring rugged coasts. Devon is much the same, but slightly more populated, especially on the Channel coast and around the city of Exeter. From a cottage in Devon, day trips to Cornwall are an easy matter, and vice versa. Perhaps the deciding factor between staying in Cornwall or Devon is that Cornwall *seems* more rural and remote.

The eastern reaches of the Severn River estuary toward Bristol are more industrialized and less attractive, and although Weston-super-Mare near Bristol is a resort popular with the British, we find little to recommend it.

In Devon, we spent time around the tiny village of Thorverton, just north of Exeter, where Mary Spivey—the very knowledgeable proprietor of The Independent Traveller—taught us as much about the British rental business as we could have learned in several more months of traveling. This small company excels at working with clients personally and ferreting out good rentals, not only in Devon but elsewhere in the southwest and in London and its western environs (Thames Valley) as well. In the United States, contact Castles, Cottages & Flats, Ltd.; for direct contact see Appendix B for the address of The Independent Traveller in Devon.

Other good companies are Wilson & Lake International, U.S. representative for Taylings, and Europa-Let.

The headquarters of the Cornish Traditional Cottage Company are near the small village of Lostwithiel. The very large, beautifully restored, old stone main house of this small estate serves not only as the elegant home of the Powells, the company's owners, but also as their office, plus half a dozen small but attractive apartments. It is one of about 300 well-chosen properties in Cornwall handled by this firm. From this rural setting, as with any others in the vicinity, all of Cornwall is easy to explore. Warmed by the Gulf Stream, this area is particularly popular with vacationers from eastern England. Perhaps 500 to 600 vacation rental cottages are available in this county. Cornish Traditional Cottage Company makes direct-contact booking easy, and during low season a rental can be arranged on the spot or by a phone call (see Appendix B for the address). The company's agents in the United States are British Travel Associates; Castles, Cottages & Flats, Ltd.; and Heritage of England. In Canada, the agent is Hearthstone Holidays.

Although they, too, are primarily rural, Wiltshire and Avon seem a little less rural and a little more ordered than the western counties. The beautiful valley of the Avon River (different from the more northern Avon upon which Stratford lies) flows through both counties, through the cities of Bristol on the north coast, and Bath, Warminster, Salisbury, and Bournemouth on the Channel. A cottage in the valley near any of the three inland towns would be ideal for anyone eager to be closer to London and willing to forgo the more isolated coasts of Cornwall and Devon.

For those who prefer an urban location, the small city of Bath (Avon) is an excellent choice. Numerous apartments are available, both central and in the environs. For elegant central apartments, contact Castles, Cottages & Flats, Ltd. or Hastingwood regarding Fountain House. For more modest apartments, also contact the former or, directly, Bath Holiday Homes (address in Appendix B), or Europa-Let. Bath is a very popular city, rich with the living history of the Roman Empire, so book well in advance (six to nine months for summer; two to three months for mid-March to mid-June and September through October). The spring and autumn months are ideal.

A sampling of the cottages in this region suggests that the owners, and the companies that represent them, are very serious about the rental business, maintaining high standards of neatness and cleanliness. Few of the rural properties, however, could be called elegant. They tend to be modest, comfortable cottages rather than manor houses or large homes that have been converted.

There is rail service between London and the tip of Cornwall, along most of the Channel coast, with spurs to the Atlantic coast towns of Barnstaple, Newquay, and St. Ives. The area is, nevertheless, best explored by car, especially Devon and Cornwall, where many of the interesting smaller communities are not served by rail. An alternative is the public bus system.

For a visit to France, large ferries sail between Plymouth and Roscoff, in Brittany. There are also sailings between Weymouth and Cherbourg, and Weymouth and the Channel Islands (Jersey and Guernsey). And for something entirely different, a long-route port-to-port ship runs on a regular schedule between Plymouth and Santander (Spain). It is a twenty-four-hour voyage, so be sure to book a cabin. Check with any travel agency, or with Brittany Ferries in Plymouth.

Advance booking time (dates are approximate) needed for peak season (June 25 to September 10)—six months. For high season (mid-May to June 25 and September 10 to October 1)—three to six months. For mid-season (April 1 to mid-May and October)—one to two months. And for low season (November through January)—none.

THE CENTRAL TIER (north of London, from the east coast to Wales). The broadest part of Great Britain includes the "bulge" at the east, and ends at the west with the promontories of Wales, which reach into the Irish Sea. The central tier area of England encompasses the regions shown on most maps as East Anglia, the Shires, the Thames & Chilterns just northwest of London, and the Heart of England bordering Wales at its west. More minutely divided, there are twenty counties in this central third of the country.

EAST-CENTRAL ENGLAND: East Anglia is the low country of England, the waterland, and the area least touched by industrial change. It comprises Cambridgeshire, Essex, Norfolk, and Suffolk counties, noted not for dramatic scenery but for the remarkable changelessness of their cities, towns, and villages. The past seems to be the present, and is evident in Norman castles, medieval churches, thatched cottages, timbered Tudor houses, and eighteenth-century manor houses. Much of the prosperity and cultural development that marked the fourteenth through sixteenth centuries is manifested in the great university towns of Cambridge and, to the west, Oxford, as well as in the area's principal cities, Norwich, Ipswich, and Colchester. For those who enjoy beautiful reminders of England's past, this area abounds in cathedrals, abbeys, castles, and museums. Each little market town has its own character, an unusual melding of ancient and new.

Blake's Holidays and Hoseasons (represented by Blake's Vacations and by Coast to Coast Resorts and Orsava, Inc., respectively, in the United States) established themselves many years ago as rental companies for sailboats, houseboats, and cruisers on the vast inland waterways known as the Norfolk Broads. They expanded into rental cottages throughout Britain, although concentrating on properties in East Anglia. Many of their rentals in this area are associated with lakes and waterways and the boats that sail on them. Across fifteen feet of terrace and lawn, on two sides of the town-house apartment in Wroxham where we stayed, a dozen or more boats were tied. These are available for rent by the week, with or without renting an apartment, and smaller day boats (without berths) can be rented by those who prefer to spend their nights on land. This attractive town-house complex in Wroxham is less than a mile from Blake's main offices, 10 miles north of Norwich by highway (or 50 meandering miles by water). A nice approach to staying there is to arrive a day or two before the Saturday changeover and stay in the nearby Norfolk Mead Hotel, a handsome Georgian country house. Four cottages are on the grounds are also available. The Mead can also be booked through Blake's Vacations.)

Also located in East Anglia—in Fakenham, Norfolk—is the headquarters of English Country Cottages, one of Britain's largest and most respected rental companies. Many of its rentals are in East Anglia, but it handles hundreds more throughout Britain. The principal U.S. agent is Heritage of England, but others such as British Travel Associates and Villas International can also make reservations.

Adjoining East Anglia to the northwest are the counties known as the Shires. In a continuation of the East Anglia coast, miles of beaches are spotted with towns where many Britons go for their holidays. However, to North Americans, who don't have to cross the Atlantic to get to the beach, the main interest here is the juxtaposition of quaint market towns, historic cities, and the green countryside. Less flat than East Anglia, the Shires is scenically more interesting, ranging from the undulating Lincolnshire Wolds to the Peak District National Park in the northwest county of Derbyshire. The highland moors rise to 2,000 feet at the park's northern end. Between the park and the Wolds lie Nottinghamshire and Sherwood Forest, smaller but still much the way they must have been in the days of Robin Hood.

More populous than East Anglia, the Shires are rich with towns and cities of historic significance—Nottingham, Chesterfield, Lincoln, Louth, and Stamford. This area is also popular with walkers and bikers who enjoy the Wolds and, especially, the Peak District. An apartment or cottage in one of the smaller towns, or a cottage in the countryside, makes an ideal base for exploring all of central England as well as the Shires.

Surprisingly, there are relatively few rental properties in the Shires, but they can be found, principally through Castles, Cottages & Flats and Heritage of England. Also, Coast to Coast Resorts and Orsava, Inc., representing Hoseasons, offer rentals in "holiday parks," which are functional, modern, purpose-built resorts that seem strangely out of place to North Americans. All of Britain, however, is not made up of narrow lanes and quaint houses; these rentals are inexpensive (in the £80 to £120 [$140 to $200 per week] range) and adequate for those who plan to spend most of their time out exploring the countryside.

WEST-CENTRAL ENGLAND: Located between East Anglia and the Shires on the east and Wales on the west, this may be England's most orderly scenic area. Even the meadows appear to be well tended, and each turn in the road opens a new picturebook scene. Thames & Chilterns County lies to the northwest of Greater London, and the Heart of England is farther west.

Rolling hills rise into Peaks National Park at the north of this region, and also along the Welsh border. The low hill ranges of the Cotswolds and the Chilterns separate and form watersheds for the area's beautiful rivers: the Avon, Severn, and Wye, and for the Windrush, Evenlode, Cherwell, and Thame. The last four join and feed the Thames. The gentle hills shelter dozens of villages, some of them just a few houses, and in the broad river valley the region's yellow limestone brings a warmth to urban buildings, castles, abbeys, and country homes.

The Thames that runs through Wiltshire, Oxfordshire, and most of Buckinghamshire appears quite different from the Thames that flows through London; it is astonishing that such a broad brown river could, in such a short distance, become a tranquil stream cutting through meadows, willow borders, and pretty towns. North of the Thames Valley, the area's second most famous river, the Avon, flows through Warwickshire and, of course, through Stratford-upon-Avon, in Shakespeare Country.

Day trips throughout the region from any point in it can be made to some of England's best-known, most interesting towns and cities: Cheltenham, Cirencester, Broadway, Gloucester, Stratford, Shrewsbury, Warwick, and Worcester in the Heart of England; and High Wycombe, Marlow, Newbury, Oxford, Saint Albans, Windsor, and Woodstock in Thames & Chilterns. For castle and palace lovers there are Warwick Castle, Sudley Castle, Berkeley Castle, Windsor, and, at Woodstock, Blenheim Palace.

Toward the west is Birmingham, the second largest city in Britain. An important industrial center, it has excellent shopping and numerous museums and historical sites. The main city to the east is London, easily accessible from anywhere in the area (it is 95 miles from Stratford-upon-Avon, for example).

A British company, The Cottage Register, has a very nice selection. Although not especially expensive, these properties are invariably attractive, well maintained, and well located. The area of most rentals is from the southern Cotswolds north into Shakespeare Country. (The principal U.S. agents for this company are Heart of England Cottages; Castles, Cottages and Flats, Ltd.; and Livingstone Holidays [California]. Others to contact are Wayside Travel [Midwest] and Villas International. In Canada, contact Hearthstone Holidays or Condo Vacations.)

Closer to London, the Thames & Chilterns area is not unlike the adjacent Heart of England. At least to the foreigner, the gentle hills of the Oxfordshire Cotswolds are hard to distinguish from those of Gloucestershire, and the towns of the wooded Chiltern Hills are as appealing as those farther to the west. Of course, the nearer to London, the greater the impact of the city. Except for convenience to London, there is no reason to stay too close. If you like proximity to a city, a cottage in the countryside around Oxford is a good choice, but any village in the area will make an ideal home base. The local organization specializing in rentals in this part of west-central England can be contacted directly: Thames & Chilterns Tourist Board, 8 Market Place, Abingdon, Oxon OX14 3UD, England. It may be awkward to work out payment details, but it can be done; the rentals are all fairly priced and, of course, selected and inspected by the Tourist Board (U.S. tel: 800-462-4486). In addition to the agencies shown in the previous paragraph, British Travel Association, Europa-Let, Pilgrim's Way, Heritage of England, and Wilson & Lake International also represent good properties in Thames & Chilterns, as well as in the Heart of England.

For those seeking larger, more distinctive, and especially elegant homes, this area boasts a good selection of manor houses and country homes with grounds and in private settings. Some of these more distinctive properties can be rented with or without staff; others offer rooms for a few guests in a hosted situation. Contact Williams & Co., Livingstone Holidays, and In the English Manner.

The fact that virtually all the large British companies offer self-catering properties throughout this region attests to its desirability. If there is any place that fits the image and promotional photos of England, this is it. Consequently, it is quite crowded from mid-June to mid-September, slightly less so in the few weeks before and after this period.

A good railroad network radiates from London into the central tier of England. Many of the smaller towns, however, are not on a line, especially in East Anglia but also in the Cotswolds and Chiltern Hills. In this region, no cities on a mainline are more than two and a half hours from London.

Although most of the major towns are served by rail, a rental car gives you freedom and the ability to get away from the more populous places. If you rent a car in London and are headed for East Anglia, try to avoid the Dartford Tunnel, where the M25 ring road goes under the Thames east of the city. It is curious that a country capable of drilling a tunnel under the English Channel cannot eliminate the monstrous traffic queues for the inadequate Dartford Tunnel.

From the east of this region (East Anglia and the Shires), easy day trips lead into Kent and its special places such as Canterbury and Rye. Harwich, on the coast of East Anglia, is the most active port in England for long-run ocean ferryliners. If you want a change of country and an ocean adventure, there are sailings almost daily to Hamburg (West Germany), Esbjerg (Denmark), Göteborg (Sweden), Hoek van Holland (Netherlands), and, in summer, Kristiansand (Norway). Voyages are from nineteen to twenty-four hours in duration, so a cabin is recommended, although deck passage and reclining seats are available on most trips. The price is modest, the food on board is good, and both one-way and round-trip tickets can be purchased. Contact any tourist office or travel agency in Britain for information.

From the west of the Heart of England and Thames & Chilterns, trips into the southern counties such as Dorset, Somerset, and Devon, and even into Cornwall and west into Wales, can be undertaken easily.

Advance booking times (dates are approximate) needed for peak season (mid-June to mid-September)—six months. For high season (mid-May to mid-June and mid-September to October 1)—three to six months. For mid-season (April 1 to mid-May and October)—one to two months. For low season (November through March)—up to two weeks.

NORTHERN ENGLAND

THE ROSE COUNTIES: The southernmost part of this region, the Rose Counties are north of, and bordering, the Shires, the Heart of England, and on the west, Wales. These counties occupy the country from coast to coast, about 135 miles at the widest point. The principal features of the countryside are the renowned Yorkshire Moors and Yorkshire Dales, large national parks. The moors suggest an ominous and brooding area, but their wildness can be tamed by exploring them from a cottage base in the vicinity of Helmsley, Thirsk, Pickering, or another stone village in the area. Or, for that matter, from an apartment in the city of York.

The Yorkshire Dales occupy much of the region's northwest, a countryside easily identified by anyone who has seen the television series "All Creatures Great and Small." Southwest of the dales, the pretty area of Lancashire's Forest of Bowland borders the more industrialized Cheshire County and the cities of Liverpool and Manchester. In the southern reaches, Peaks National Park is shared with the central tier counties. The entire region is dotted with towns of considerable historical interest, from the walled city of Chester in the extreme southwest, to Ripon in North Yorkshire and the old seaside town of Scarborough.

The architecture changes from the daub-and-wattle, timbered buildings and thatched roofs of many of the southern counties to gray stone, not only in the cities but in the villages and farms. Virtually every rental property in the region, and there are many, is a stone cottage, or a "cottage" in a larger stone house. The severity of the architecture is softened by the countryside, and most of the rentals seem neat, tending toward the plain but comfortable, perhaps reflecting the independent nature of the people of this region.

One way to select a specific locale to visit for a week or more is to think in terms of the moors or the dales, and choose the one you prefer. The former tend to be more wild and isolated, the latter more tame; read about them before you decide. From any spot in the region all others can be visited easily. If you are inclined to stay near a city, a specific area called the Vale of York is especially appealing.

The agencies offering the widest selection of rentals in the area of the moors, the dales, the Yorkshire coast, and the Vale of York are Blake's Vacations, British Travel Association, Heritage of England, and Villas International. Holiday Cottages Yorkshire Limited (Water Street, Skipton, North Yorkshire BD23 1PB) is a small local company with about 150 rentals in the area but no agent in North America.

Travel throughout the area is best done by car, but intercity buses and mainline rail service connect York with London to the south and with Newcastle and Edinburgh to the north. There is also rail service into Leeds, and across the country to Carlisle, with a somewhat roundabout connection at Windemere into the Lake District. Southeast of York is the port city of Hull (properly Kingston-upon-Hull), the area's largest city. For a complete change of country scene, there are daily sailings between Hull and Zeebrugge (Belgium) and between Hull and Europort (Rotterdam, Netherlands). The voyages take about fifteen hours, so a cabin is a good idea for the overnight schedule. The ships are large, new, and attractive; the food is fair; and the price is modest. On the other end, Zeebrugge, and the exquisite nearby town of Bruges (Brugge), make for the most rewarding of the two journeys. Contact any tourist information office or travel agent.

Advance booking time needed for peak season (mid-June to early September—six months. For high season (May 15 to June 15 and September 10 to October 1—four to six months. For mid-season (April 1 to May 15 and October)—one to two months. And during the rest of the year—up to one month.

THE LAKE DISTRICT: Occupying the northwest corner of England, Cumbria County and the Lake District are among the country's most popular areas, especially with British vacationers and weekenders, but also with foreign visitors. The countryside blends hills, mountains (England's tallest at more than 3,000 feet), and lakes (including Windemere, England's largest). During the summer months, and on long spring and fall week-ends when the weather is sunny and warm, many of the narrow roads that wind through the hills are lined with the cars of picnickers, walkers, and climbers. On the sunny October day that we joined them, it seemed that there were as many people on the hillsides as there were sheep, and that's saying a lot. Those who were not climbing hills or hiking the lakeshore paths were in the shops, restaurants, and sidewalks of the pretty towns of Ambleside, Grasmere, Bowness, Keswick, and Winde-mere. Then there were those who shunned the hills to sail on Lakes Windemere or Ullswater, to cruise aboard lake steamers, or to take shoreline trips on the steam train.

The crowds did little to dampen our good feeling toward the area. In fact, since most of the outsiders were British, not foreign tourists, the crowded conditions we experienced were not bad when compared to those of the summer months, when Continental Europeans and Ameri-cans join the hordes. The lesson, therefore is obvious: To enjoy this beautiful area and its charming towns, go in the late spring (May to mid-June) or early fall (September). Much earlier or later than this increases the chance of inclement weather (it rains considerably there), and in between is the time of peak tourist activity. If the bustle of the towns and lakes in peak season is of no concern, be sure to book well in advance.

Not all of Cumbria is occupied by the Lake District (the largest national park in England). The area surrounding the district is rich with fascinating places to visit, including castles, stately homes, and, to the north, the ancient, gray stone city of Carlisle. Distances in this narrow section of Britain are not great, and day trips to York, for example, or to the Yorkshire Moors or Dales, can be taken easily (Windemere is less than 100 miles from York).

Any agency offering properties throughout England can arrange bookings in this popular area—Castles, Cottages & Flats; Hearthstone Holidays (Canada); Blake's Vacations; British Travel Association; Europa-Let; Heritage of England; Vacation Home Rentals (VHR) Worldwide; and Wilson & Lake International principal among them. We were pleased by the rentals shown to us by Heart of the Lakes, a modest-size regional company with a good selection, both in the towns and nearby (see Appendix B for the address for a direct contact). Lakelovers is also small, but has a nice selection; it has no formal agent in the United States, but can be booked through Pilgrim's Way or contacted directly at the address in Appendix B. A third British company is Grey Abbey Properties Ltd., unusual in that it owns, rather than represents owners of, some eighty-five cottages and apartments, mostly in the northern part of the district. (See Appendix B for this address also.)

The nature of the Lake District is such that a car is very useful, although there is bus service between the lake towns. Also, Windemere is served by a spur rail line off the mainline that runs between London, Lancaster, Carlisle, and Glasgow. East-west rail routes connect Carlisle and Lancaster with Newcastle-upon-Tyne and York.

Advance booking time needed for peak season (mid-June to early September)—six months. High season (May 15 to June 15 and September 10 to October 1)—four to six months. For mid-season (April 1 to May 15 and October)—one to two months. And during the rest of the year—up to one month.

BORDERLANDS: This region, comprising the counties of Cleveland, Durham, Northumberland, and Tyne & Wear, is among those least visited by North Americans. Of course, there is no shortage of travelers who come here specifically to see the ancient battlegrounds and the castle fortresses built to protect this almost indefensible no-man's-land. Bamburgh, Alnwick, and Dunstanburgh castles are especially impressive, and Barnard Castle is softened somewhat by the attractive town surrounding it. This is also a country of old abbeys, priories, pele towers (fortified houses), and a scattering of stately homes.

There are relatively few vacation rentals in this area, yet it is most appealing to those interested in getting off the beaten track and learning the history of the wars and struggles over disputed lands. We did not spend time here, only passed through en route to the Borders region of Scotland. Still, we found the town of Durham particularly interesting, and Northumberland National Park is most beautiful.

For rentals in this region, contact Heritage of England and Blake's Vacations.

The only north-south rail service is by the mainline between London and Edinburgh, serving Newcastle-upon-Tyne, and along the Northumberland coast through Berwick-upon-Tweed, England's most northern town. The single east-west line runs between Newcastle and Carlisle, just north of the Lake District. From this region, day trips into Scotland as far as Edinburgh, Glasgow, and Pitlochry, are possible.

In the summer months port-to-port ships sail between Newcastle and Bergen (Norway), Esbjerg (Denmark), and Göteborg (Sweden), all fairly long voyages. Excellent sea-land itineraries can be worked out by anyone who has the time. One route could be Newcastle to Bergen, Bergen to Scotland's Shetland Islands, the Shetlands to Aberdeen, and from Aberdeen return to anywhere in Britain. Contact any large travel agency in Britain for details.

Advance booking time needed for July and August—three to four months. For May, June, September, and October—one to two months. And during the rest of the year—up to one month.

LONDON. To go to Great Britain for the first time and not visit London would be a sad omission. However, because it is the air gateway to Britain, especially from the United States and Canada, it is a city almost impossible to miss, so the question is how long should one stay. The answer depends on your interests and budget.

London guidebooks describe so many things to enjoy and be enriched by that it can be frustrating to apportion limited time. Visiting museums, galleries, churches, monuments, and shops is not so difficult but, for first-time tourists especially, the problem is to make the most of every day.

BEST TIMES TO VISIT: Although the lower winter rates in most London apartments are in effect from around November 1 through March 31, a few increase rents for a short period before Christmas to capture shoppers' dollars. The difference between high and low seasons can be relatively significant, often in the range of 25 percent, which means that an apartment that rents for £500 ($800) per week in high season will rent for £375 ($600) in the winter months. Unfortunately, the winter season as interpreted by London rental agents is relatively brief, and the five months are indeed wintry: days are short at this latitude, and chilly, rainy weather punctuated by rare sunshine is the norm. The advantage is that the tourist population is small. Tourist crowds peak in July and August, are large from early June through September, and ebb after that until they begin to grow again from mid-April. Thus, it is hard to go at a season of lowered prices unless you are willing to take a chance on the weather. Otherwise, April, May, and late September through October combine the virtues of thinner crowds and usually good weather.

PLANNING YOUR VISIT: Before deciding where to stay, it is useful in dealing with a city of this size and complexity to have a basic plan of how to spend your time. For example, although it is actually not difficult, the prospect of buying tickets to London theaters, the National Opera, Covent Garden, the Promenade Concerts, Shakespeare at Stratford, and other events can be daunting, and the mechanics can be time-consuming. One answer is to let someone who knows London help out, either with advice or direct assistance. We have found the British Travel Au-

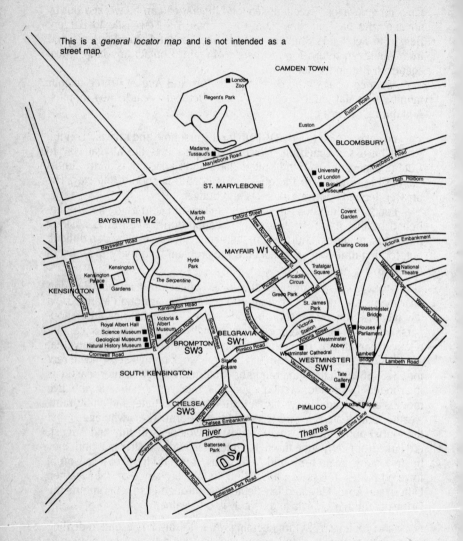

This is a *general locator map* and is not intended as a street map.

CAMDEN TOWN

London Zoo

Regent's Park

Euston

BLOOMSBURY

Euston Road

Theobald's Road

High Holborn

Madame Tussaud's

Marylebone Road

ST. MARYLEBONE

University of London

British Museum

Covent Garden

Marble Arch

Oxford Street

New Bond St.

Old Bond St.

Regent Street

Charing Cross

Victoria Embankment

BAYSWATER W2

MAYFAIR W1

Picadilly

Piccadilly Circus

Trafalgar Square

Whitehall

National Theatre

Waterloo Bridge

Waterloo Road

Bayswater Road

Hyde Park

Green Park

St. James Park

The Mall

Kensington Church St.

Kensington

Kensington Palace

Gardens

The Serpentine

KENSINGTON

Kensington Road

Royal Albert Hall

Science Museum

Geological Museum

Natural History Museum

Victoria & Albert Museum

Brompton Road

Sloane Street

BELGRAVIA SW1

Grosvenor Place

Victoria Station

Victoria Street

Westminster Abbey

Westminster Bridge

Houses of Parliament

Millbank

Lambeth Bridge

Cromwell Road

BROMPTON SW3

Pimlico Road

Westminster Cathedral

WESTMINSTER SW1

Lambeth Road

SOUTH KENSINGTON

Sloane Square

Vauxhall Bridge Road

Tate Gallery

CHELSEA SW3

Royal Hospital Road

PIMLICO

Vauxhall Bridge

Chelsea Embankment

Cheyne Walk

Battersea Bridge Road

River

Thames

Nine Elms Lane

Battersea Park

Battersea Park Road

thority very good on the first count, and British Airways is excellent on the second. British Airways has a variety of programs that enable clients to arrange in advance for tickets to everything from theater and dinner cruises on the Thames to music festivals (Edinburgh, Bath, Wexford) and day trips out of the city. British Airways and travel agents have brochures with the details. Unlike the simplicity of a country village, the complexity and population of London makes everything time-consuming, so the more details that are worked out in advance, the easier your stay will be after arrival.

WHERE TO STAY: Assuming that you have found good reason to stay for a week, or even for three or four days (some apartments can be booked for less than a week), the next steps are to find the right location and the right price.

According to the British Travel Authority, North American visitors complain about short-term London rentals at a rate four times greater than they do about other vacation rental properties in Britain. We tried to learn the reasons, and found them to be complex and interrelated. The first is the cost; the second is value (what you get for what you pay); the third is outside surroundings; the fourth is age and amenities; and fifth is the reality versus the expectations. For first-time visitors, or for those who have not been to London for several years, some predeparture perspective will help. To the average urban apartment dweller in the United States or Canada, a London apartment will seem more spacious and comfortable than it will to those who live in three- and four-bedroom homes with nearly as many bathrooms, and whose experience in limited quarters comes from hotel rooms, which are expected to be relatively small.

Central London is a very large area carved into a number of districts. A guidebook will describe these districts, and our brief profiles of the neighborhoods containing the preponderance of short-term rental apartments will help you decide where to look.

Used below, the term *relatively* means relative to general rental prices in other areas of the city, all else being equal. In certain areas, prices are higher simply because these areas are more fashionable or exclusive than others. There is a premium, for example, on locations near Harrods, Old Bond Street, or Sloane Square. An apartment will cost less in Pimlico than one of equal size and standards in adjacent Chelsea. Also, the farther from the city center, the lower the prices, all the way out into the countryside (see the section on Thames & Chilterns, earlier in this chapter in the Central Tier section).

> *Bloomsbury:* Rental prices are relatively modest. This is the academic and museum district, home of the British Museum, the University of London, the University College Hospital, and the

Royal Academy of Dramatic Arts. Otherwise, this is a quiet residential area with streets of food stores, small shops, restaurants, pubs, and specialty cafés. There is good transportation: Euston, Saint Pancras, and Kings Cross railroad stations; underground and bus stops. The modest, comfortable apartment we stayed in toward the north of Bloomsbury was quiet and convenient. A large Safeway is nearby, and it is within walking distance of the British Museum. (Apartment Services, Ltd.—addresses in list at the end of this chapter and in Appendix B.)

Mayfair: Rental prices are relatively high. Bounded by Oxford Street on the north, Bond Street on the east, Green Park on the south, and Hyde Park on the west, this is a desirable area. The U.S. Embassy and many of the larger and better hotels are here. Shopping is on Oxford Street and Old Bond Street. There is good intracity transportation, but no railroad station.

Bayswater: Rental prices are relatively moderate. Located along the north of Hyde Park and Kensington Gardens, this is a quiet area of apartment houses and large period residences, many of which have been converted to apartments. There are offices, smaller hotels, and a few restaurants. The area is convenient to Oxford Street shopping (Bayswater Road becomes Oxford Street). There is good underground and bus access and, for railroad service, Paddington Station is convenient.

Kensington and Earl's Court: Rental prices are relatively moderate. Adjacent areas to the west and southwest of Kensington Gardens are a little distant from the core of the city, so rent prices are lower there than in the areas closer to the city center. We once stayed at the 51 Kensington Court apartments and found the location excellent. (Information and booking through London Apartments (USA), Ltd.; Grant-Reid; Hometours, International). In nearby Kensington High Street, a good transportation artery, has many restaurants with fare ranging from fast food to fine food. Kensington Gardens, Albert Hall, the Victoria and Albert Museum, the Science Museum, the Natural History Museum, and a Safeway are all within easy walking distance. Other agencies for Kensington include Eastone, Europa-Let, Four Star Living, and Villas International.

South Kensington and Knightsbridge: Rental prices are relatively high. This area is south of Kensington Gardens and Hyde Park; toward the west is the Victoria and Albert Museum. The east (Knightsbridge) is close to Harrods, American Express, and the stores of Brompton Road. Many good restaurants are in the area. Kensington Road, Brompton Road, and Sloane Street are all good transportation arteries, and underground stations are convenient.

Chelsea: Rental prices are relatively high; higher toward Belgravia, lower toward the southwest. Bordered by South Kensington and the Thames, Chelsea merges with Belgravia to the east. This is an area of fashionable residences and better apartments, and of streets with elegant boutiques, good small restaurants, and antiques stores. If you find a modestly priced apartment with a Chelsea (SW3) address, it is probably fairly distant from the city center. Good bus transportation runs along the Chelsea Embankment, King's Road, and Fulham Road, but there are only two underground stations.

Belgravia: Rents are relatively high in this fashionable area, which blends into Chelsea on the west and Westminster on the east. Between Sloane Square and Hyde Park to the north, at least a dozen countries have their embassies. There are good restaurants, shops, pleasant residential streets, and easy access to popular spots such as Harrods, Buckingham Palace, and Victoria Station. Sloane Square illustrates the paradox of London. Addresses on Sloane Street, Sloane Gardens, Holbein Place, and other streets in the vicinity of the square are quite in vogue; indeed, most of the homes are elegant, but they are best viewed from the inside. Due in part to some lack of concern for appearances, the bustling square and the streets leading into it show the grime and general overuse of inner cities, belying the interior elegance of these residences and apartments. Perhaps this contributes to some of the North Americans' complaints. This is, nonetheless, a desirable location.

Pimlico: Rents are relatively modest. This mostly residential area is surrounded by Chelsea, Belgravia, Westminster, and the Thames (actually a district of the City of Westminster). The location is excellent for persons preferring to be nearer the Tate Gallery, Westminster Abbey, and Houses of Parliament than to the shopping streets of Mayfair and Knightsbridge. Victoria Station and the British Airways in-town terminal are in this area. References in agency material to the Victoria area mean Pimlico, near Victoria Station. One of the largest apartment complexes in London, Dolphin Square, is in Pimlico. Not quaint, elegant, or imaginative, it compensates by being secure, comfortable, and self-contained (swimming pool, shops, grocers). It can be booked through virtually every agent in the list at the beginning of this chapter. It is being remodeled one floor per year from the top down, so if you make reservations here, insist on one of the top (remodeled) floors; the others are drab.

Westminster: Rents are relatively moderate. Comprising the Victoria Embankment, Parliament, Big Ben, Westminster Abbey, the Tate, and No. 10 Downing Street (off Whitehall), the Thames-side area of Westminster is the most recognizable to foreigners. This eastern area is not residential, but to the west it joins Pimlico and Belgravia. It is a good location for access to museums, the National Theaters across the river, and other city sights, but is not known for its shopping.

The City & Barbican: Rents are relatively modest. The financial hub of London is here, with few residences and apartments except toward the Barbican Center. The area merges with Holborn and Bloomsbury to the north, and is convenient to Covent Garden, the theater district, and Saint Paul's. Bus and underground transportation throughout London radiates from here.

Rental prices vary widely within any of the ten areas, but overall, the most fashionable and expensive are Mayfair, South Kensington, Knightsbridge, Belgravia, and Chelsea. For generally more moderate rentals, try Bayswater, Kensington (a bit higher in the Earls' Court end), and Westminster. At the generally lower end of the rental price range are apartments in Pimlico, the City, and Bloomsbury.

London is expensive, but not outrageous, as cities go; to visitors from New York, Chicago or San Francisco it would not seem unreasonable. Hotel rates provide a base from which to evaluate apartment prices. The following figures are approximate. Prices will generally increase a little each year in terms of pounds sterling, but will vary in U.S. and Canadian dollars as exchange rates fluctuate. The £ figure is the constant, the U.S. dollar conversions are at $1.60 per pound; these rates are per standard room (not per person), and prices include the 15 percent value-added tax (VAT).

Class		Per night		Per week	
*****	Hyatt Carlton Tower	£210	$335	£1,470	$2,352
****	Holiday Inn Mayfair	160	255	1,120	1,792
****	Royal Garden	150	240	1,050	1,680
****	Royal Court	125	200	875	1,400
***	Cadogan	135	216	945	1,512
***	Vanderbilt	85	136	595	1,952
**	Regent Palace	42	67	294	430
No-star hotels & B&Bs		30–50	48–80	210–350	336–560

The British government will soon begin the process of establishing rating standards for short-term rental apartments and cottages, such as the star system for hotels. In the meantime, many of the owners and rental companies classify apartments according to an A, B, C ranking (or Superior, Comfortable, and Economy). We used High, Moderate, and Modest for rental classes. Comparisons indicate that the prices of central-area London apartments run from about 70 percent to 90 percent of prices at hotels of equivalent standards.

Unlike country cottages, London's serviced apartments include in their prices all utilities (except telephone charges), change of linens once or twice per week, and change of towels from daily to once per week. Higher-category apartments generally provide maid service daily, mid-category usually three to five times per week, and economy once or twice per week. The approximate prices in the table below are average for each category, and are per apartment (not per person) per week. On the average, deduct 15 percent from these rates for winter occupancy.

Category	Studio		One-bedroom	
High+ (Luxury) (A+)	£1,100	$1,760	£1,400	$2,240
High (Superior) (A)	600	960	800	1,280
Moderate (Comfortable) (B)	425	680	500	800
Modest (Economy) (C)	250	400	325	520

The best value comparison between apartments and hotels should be drawn between the prices of a studio and a hotel room. Generally, the lower the rating of the hotels and equivalent apartments, the closer they are in price. In other words, the higher the price, the greater the savings, the greatest bargains are for families, or for friends who share an apartment. Many one-bedroom apartments have a studio couch in the living room and can accommodate four people.

A description for a typical apartment in the moderate (two-to-three-star standard) range might read as follows: "Pleasant double-bedded one-bedroom flat on fourth floor of converted Edwardian mansion; lift (elevator); sitting/dining room with sofabed; bathroom with bath, WC, and basin. Well-equipped kitchen. Services: weekly cleaning, telephone, washer, entry phone. Includes electricity, heat, linen, and towels. Convenient to Russell Square, British Museum. One-week minimum; shorter terms possible in off-season. (£320 low, £420 high.)"

A description for a typical apartment in the superior (three-to-four-star equivalent) category, one notch up, should read something as follows: "Studio located in the Mayfair residential area, convenient to West End shopping, entertainment, and the diplomatic and commercial districts. Nearest shopping area: Oxford Street, Old Bond Street. Nearest underground: Green Park. Period Georgian house recently converted into apartments. Amenities: daily maid service, porterage, all utilities, security entry system, telephone; towels changed daily, linens every second day. Three-day minimum except one-week minimum July and August (£520 low, £630 high.)"

For an apartment in the luxury (five-star) category, you should expect elegant appointments and atmosphere, and rooms larger than those in a five-star hotel. Add something like: "Studio furnished with selected antiques and original paintings; period fireplaces; fresh flowers daily, welcome provisions awaiting in modern kitchen. Concierge service; secretarial services available for corporate accounts. One-to-three-day minimum except in peak months. (£1,000 low, £1,200 high.)"

In the economy category, the furniture will be simple and the rooms are seldom much larger than hotel rooms. There is once per week maid service and weekly change of linens and towels. Many of these economy apartments are being rented while the owners are on vacation, so until you arrive and check with the agent, you won't know exactly where the property is located (although it will be in the area you specified). It may be any of a half dozen or so (out of hundreds) being vacated while the owners are on vacation. Because of high turnover, the agency performs a continual juggling act. The savings over a hotel of equal standards may not be great, except for families or groups of four or more. In the lower price range the principal advantages are more space, a kitchen, and the possibility of preparing at least a few meals in. Rooms in typical unrated and one-star hotels tend to be especially confining.

Persons on limited budgets who want the best possible accommodations for the money should locate in outlying areas. The farther the property is from the central area, the lower the rent. For example, within a forty-five-minute commute, a comfortable two-bedroom house in the Thames Valley west of London will rent in the range of £160 ($256) in winter to £260 ($416) in summer. For information on outlying properties, contact Castles, Cottages & Flats, Ltd. or British Travel Association (or contact The Independent Traveller directly—see address at the end of this chapter or in Appendix B), or Europa-Let.

In summary, it takes some effort to assure that you are getting fair value. Budget hotels and apartments can be very poor indeed; so can moderately priced ones if you are not careful. This is especially disturbing when "moderate" prices are actually quite high in North American terms. However, with basic information about London's neighborhoods, the difference in rent prices among them, hotel prices, and what to expect in apartments and rents, you can locate the right apartment.

HOW TO FIND THE RIGHT APARTMENT: The key to the right apartment is to find the right agent. Almost every one of the thirty or so agents listed in this chapter represent properties in London. Many overlap each other, often charging different commissions and fees for the same apartment.

With a few exceptions, the smaller agencies—which have a personal acquaintance with the companies and properties they represent—are preferable, often because the principals themselves know London well. Some specialize in London apartments, rather than properties all over Europe, and can therefore offer reliable advice and pay personal attention to each client's needs and budgets. A few represent only one or two apartment blocks, or a single complex. Another option for travelers planning to divide their time between London and a cottage elsewhere in Britain is to contact agents that have reliable properties in both locations (refer to the agency list at the beginning of the chapter).

Given these considerations, the following list is just a place to start; refer to Chapter 3 for more information on the agencies. Agents marked with an asterisk (*) are smaller ones specializing in Britain or in London proper; the others are international, and London apartments represent only a part of their inventories. The companies with an *x* following the asterisk are directly affiliated with an English company and therefore add little or no commission to the London prices.

Abacus Agency (*x): moderate to superior
Beds Abroad, Ltd.: moderate to superior
British Travel Association (*): moderate to superior
Castles, Cottages & Flats of Ireland and the U.K. Ltd. (*): modest to moderate
Eastone Overseas Accommodations: modest to moderate
Europa-Let: modest to moderate
Four Seasons Villas: modest to superior
Grant-Reid Communication (*): modest to superior
Hastingwood Assoc., Ltd. (*x): superior to luxury
Hearthstone Holidays (Canada) (*): modest to moderate
Hideaways International: moderate to luxury
Hometours International: moderate to superior
In the English Manner (*): superior to luxury
Livingstone Holidays (*): modest to superior
London Apartments (USA) Ltd. (*x): modest to luxury
Pilgrim's Way (*): modest to superior
Villas International: superior to luxury
Williams & Co. (*): superior to luxury
Wilson & Lake International: modest to moderate

The British Travel Authority (BTA) publishes a small booklet called "Apartments in London," which lists dozens of apartment buildings, blocks, and rental organizations. Some of these are represented in the United States or Canada, some are not. Rental companies also advertise in the booklet; the BTA does not screen or endorse any of the companies it lists. These companies can be contacted directly whether or not they have an agent here. The plus side is that you may save the agent commission or fee. The minus side is that all correspondence and telephone contacts will be international and, second, there will be no domestic company to answer questions, offer advice, or deal with any prerental or postrental problems. Some of the companies send catalogs, but others find the cost of international airmail prohibitive, so all you can do is ask for one. If you plan to book directly, be sure to start the process early (six to eight months ahead for summer bookings, two months for other times). International telephone rates are not terribly high, so do not hesitate to phone. Some companies accept major credit cards, others require bank drafts in pounds sterling (available from U.S. and Canadian banks for a fee). Of course, if you are in London without accommodations, just telephone and rent an apartment on the spot. In this situation nearly all of the companies accept major credit cards.

In aggregate, the following British companies offer apartments in the entire range of standards and prices. Their prices seem fair relative to the size, quality, location, and services.

ABACUS AGENCY
20 Park Hill, Ealing
London W5 2NJ
Tel: 011-44-01-491-6498

Moderate to superior; Belgravia, Chelsea, South Kensington. U.S. agent is a no-fee company branch; brochure.

APARTMENT SERVICES LTD.
2 Sandwich Street
London WC1H 9PL
Tel: 011-44-01-388-3558

Modest to moderate; personalized service; mostly Bloomsbury, also Barbican City, Westminster. Has U.S. agents; catalog.

DOLPHIN SQUARE
Grosvenor Road
London SW11
Tel: 011-44-01-834-9134

Moderate; large self-contained complex in Pimlico. Almost any agency can book; brochure.

DRAYCOTT HOUSE
10 Draycott Avenue
London SW3 2SA
Tel: 011-44-01-584-4659

Luxury; Chelsea.

HASTINGWOOD ASSOCIATES
3 Sloane Gardens
London SW1
Tel: 011-44-01-730-4403

Luxury; Belgravia, Knightsbridge. U.S. agent is no-fee company representative; brochure.

THE INDEPENDENT TRAVELLER
Dinneford Spring
Thorverton
Exeter EX5 5NU
Tel: 011-44-39-286-0807

Modest to moderate; some luxury; personalized; environs and central; also in other parts of southern England. Has U.S. agents; catalog.

LONDON APARTMENTS, LTD.
51 Kensington Court
London W8 5DB
Tel: 011-44-01-937-4248

Modest to superior; Bayswater, Bloomsbury, Kensington, Knightsbridge, Mayfair, Pimlico. U.S. agent is no-fee company branch.

This handful represents a total of a thousand or more apartments from modest to luxury. There are dozens more, but these are companies we can recommend from personal experience. The North American agencies listed at the beginning of the chapter represent many more.

We can see no particular reason to have a rental vehicle in London. A London newspaper recently reported that the average traffic speed (cars, buses, taxis) in central London during rush hours is much slower than the rate of carriages in Victorian times. The point is well made. Taxis are plentiful and cost relatively little; the Underground is fast and efficient; and the double-deck buses are fun.

Advance booking time (dates are approximate) needed for May 1 to September 31—four to six months. For April and October—two to four months. For November 1 to April 1—up to one month.

OTHER USEFUL CONTACTS

BRITISH AIRWAYS
Tel: 800-247-9297
(airline tickets; theater, show, and tour advance bookings)

BRITISH ARTS FESTIVAL TICKETS
Tel: 800-223-6108
   212-944-0290 (NYC)

BRITISH RAIL & FERRY INFORMATION
Tel: New York: 212-599-5400
   Los Angeles: 213-624-8787
   Dallas: 214-748-0860

BRITISH SPORTS EVENTS
(including Lawn Tennis Championships at Wimbledon)
Tel: 800-223-4446
   212-302-7077 (NYC)

LONDON SHOWS
Tel: 800-962-9246
   212-944-0290
   or British Airways (800-247-9297)
(when booking air transportation)

WALK-IN INFORMATION IN LONDON ONLY; DO NOT MAIL INQUIRIES

BRITISH TRAVEL CENTER
12 Regent Street
London W1
Tel: 01-730-3400

SCOTTISH TOURIST BOARD
19 Cockspur Street
London W1
Tel: 01-930-8661

WALES TOURIST BOARD
34 Picadilly
London W1
Tel: 01-409-0969

Scotland

In broad terms, Scotland is divided into the Lowlands, and the Highlands and islands. The first are roughly the southern half, and the Highlands rise north of an imaginary line drawn between the Firth of Forth on the east and the Firth of Clyde on the west.

Traveling north from England, a sense of isolation sets in once you cross the Scottish border. This happens twice, actually; once upon crossing the Cheviot Hills and dropping into the counties of Borders and Dumfries and Galloway, and again, more profoundly, upon leaving the narrow populated zone anchored by Edinburgh and Glasgow and moving northward into the Grampian Highlands. Less than 2 percent of the population lives in this northern region, occupying nearly a quarter of the area of the island of Great Britain. This statistic conveys the nature of the Highlands, an area where visitors go for peace, solitude, hiking and walking, fishing, and enjoying the beautiful and rugged countryside, free from the pressures of cities and tourist throngs.

THE LOWLANDS. Rental cottages are available throughout Scotland, and apartments can be rented in Edinburgh, Glasgow, Aberdeen, and other cities and towns, so where to stay is a matter of individual choice. Although the name "Lowlands" suggests flat, low countryside, in actuality this area is higher and more rugged than much of England; it is low only in contrast to the more mountainous region to the north. The Southern Uplands rise from the Teviot River Valley just north of the border, then give way to the Central Lowlands. Except for the journey to Arran Island off the west coast, the area can be explored by day trips from any home location.

Rolling farmland, soft mountainous areas, ancient and interesting towns, castles and the shells of abbeys, and the cities of Glasgow and Edinburgh all exist in the Lowlands. Its variety makes it an excellent region to settle in for a week or more, perhaps in a village cottage for part of the time and an Edinburgh apartment for the other part. Only 45 miles separate Edinburgh and Glasgow, so there is no need to uproot yourself to visit another area or city. Even from the southern reaches of Borders it is not a difficult journey into the northern region to visit towns such as Perth and Pitlochry.

In the center of Borders, in the vicinity of the tiny (one-pub) village of Lilliesleaf, where we stayed, the area is rich in historical places. Nearby are Melrose, Jedburgh, Galashiels, and Kelso. Although it is less than a two-hour drive from Lilliesleaf, we moved into a small gem of an apartment in the center of Edinburgh to explore the city (and found it much to our liking). It is a great but manageable capital of about half a million people. Glasgow, at nearly double the size, is a bit more complicated, but despite its rather industrial appearance from the motorways, it does have value for visitors. North of Glasgow, after an unimpressive intervening suburban area, Loch Lomond lifts the spirits and introduces visitors to the beauties of Scotland's spectacular large lakes. In the county of Fife—directly across the country from Loch Lomond and an easy trip from Edinburgh—the town of Saint Andrews is to golf what Wimbledon is to tennis.

Holiday Cottages (Scotland), Ltd., the modest (250+ properties) local company with which we were particularly impressed, concentrates on cottage rentals throughout Scotland, especially in Borders, other parts of the Lowlands, and Edinburgh. It was interesting to step into Holiday's headquarters, a small, ancient house in a tiny hamlet, and find a computerized operation combining personalized service and technical efficiency. A pioneer of the cottage rental business in Britain, Jill Bristow knows all the properties personally and maintains a close watch on their quality and upkeep. The address is: Holiday Cottages (Scotland), Ltd., Lilliesleaf, Melrose, Roxburghshire TD6 9JD, Scotland; tel: 011-44-835-7481. North American agents are Castles, Cottages, & Flats, Ltd. in the United States and Hearthstone Holidays in Canada.

THE HIGHLANDS AND THE ISLANDS. Except for the cities of Aberdeen, Perth, Dundee, and Inverness, and smaller but notable towns such as Pitlochry, Oban, and Elgin, the Grampian and Northwest Highlands can best be described as extensive and open. Beyond the cities, little evidence of twentieth-century pressure intrudes. In winter, the Cairngorm Mountains rising from Spey River valley become the skiing and winter sports center of Britain, with peaks reaching well above 4,000 feet. In summer they are an area for walks and hikes, especially into the Cairngorm Nature Reserve.

Northward beyond Inverness, and westward beyond the long valley occupied by Loch Linnhe and Loch Ness, the countryside becomes even more grudging of modern incursions. Although rental cottages are available on the mainland; on Skye, Mull, Colonsay and Tiree Islands; and a few on the Inner and Outer Hebrides, they are widely scattered. Privacy and peace can be guaranteed here, with delightful fishing villages and summer resorts to break the isolation. If you are planning a summer visit, wait until at least mid-May to improve your chances of good weather.

Closer to the population centers, but still quite isolated and peaceful, the valley of the Spey River is the site of the main highway between Edinburgh and Inverness, intersected by an occasional highway leading to the west coast. We found this area appealing both because of its physical beauty and because it is central to the entire Highlands region. Day trips or easy overnighters can be made to the western coast, to the western offshore islands (longer to the Outer Hebrides), to the north tip, east to the city of Aberdeen, or back south to Perth and Edinburgh.

We spent time in this location in a rental similar to many properties in Scotland. Long self-sufficient in terms of raising produce, cattle, timber, even husbanding herds of deer and providing for stag hunts, some of the great estates, comprising many thousands of acres, no longer need large staffs of workers. Modern machinery, more efficiency, and a changing focus have replaced many of the men and their families over the years, and the estate houses where they used to live have been renovated, modernized, and listed with companies for rent. Such is the case with the Ardverikie Estate on Loch Laggan, about 50 miles south of Inverness. The large old stone houses, the stream, the meadows, the hills, the long slender lake, the castlelike estate mansion, and the hospitality of the property manager typify all that is good about a visit to this part of Scotland. (Ardverikie Estate rentals are also among those offered by Holiday Cottages [Scotland] Ltd. and by Castles, Cottages & Flats, Ltd. in the United States and Hearthstone Holidays in Canada.)

Prices run the gamut, as do the rentals, from simple isolated cottages to apartments in larger estate homes, and large homes themselves. Size and quality varies. There is also considerable difference between low-season and high-season prices. Typically, the simplest one-bedroom cottage will run about £75 ($120) per week in low season, £105 ($170) in mid-season, and £120 ($192) in high season. Rural or village rentals in the middle to upper price ranges are usually very comfortable and fairly large, two-to-four-bedrooms, with a typical rent of £125 ($200) per week in low season, £165 ($265) in mid, and £200 ($320) in high. Apartments in Edinburgh and Glasgow run more, although not nearly as high as those in London. The one-bedroom apartment we stayed in, nicely located on Edinburgh's Royal Mile, is typical at about £250 ($400) per week in low season and £300 ($480) in high. *To all the above prices, add 15 percent value-added tax.*

In addition to the agencies noted in the previous paragraph, there are several others with rentals in Scotland, among which Blake's Vacations, Europa-Let, Heritage of England, and Livingstone Holidays offer a good selection.

If you want to rent an apartment in Edinburgh directly from an owner or manager, and do not mind booking sight unseen with no description, write the City of Edinburgh Advance Reservations Department, Waverley Market, 3 Princess Street, Edinburgh, EH 2 2QP, Scotland, and ask for the list of self-catering accommodations and order form. It will take a little effort and some risk, but no commissions will be charged. When dealing directly with a Scottish company or individual, payment will usually have to be made by bank draft in pounds sterling (such drafts are available at most U.S. and Canadian banks).

If your visit to Scotland is planned for any time between mid-October and mid-May (except Christmas week and school midterm breaks), you can usually count on renting on the spot without reservations. Just telephone or go to the offices of the Scotland-based companies shown here and in Appendix B.

Mainline railroads connect all the major cities of Scotland (and tie Scotland to the cities of England), going as far north as Aberdeen on the east coast and Inverness to the west. Less frequent service is available all the way north to Scrabster, and west to Kyle of Lochalsh (ferry from here to the Isle of Skye), to Mallaig, and to Oban. There is ferry service between Oban and the Isle of Mull and the Hebrides. The Orkney Islands off the north coast are served by ferry from Scrabster, and for something entirely different, an ocean ferry journey from Aberdeen to the Shetland Islands is an interesting possibility. Ships sail three times per week on the fourteen-hour voyage to Lerwick, Shetland (with connections in summer to Bergen in Norway, the Faeroe Islands of Denmark, and Iceland). Contact the BTA or any travel agent in Britain for information.

Despite good rail and bus systems, most of the rental properties are off the main lines and tourist trails, and a car is essential in almost all cases.

Advance booking time (dates are approximate) needed for high season, (late June to September 1—six months. For mid-season (late May through June and September)—two to three months. For low season (October to late May [except Christmas and Easter])—up to one month.

Wales

Geographically, Wales is the western end of Britain's central tier; its western border is the Irish Sea, its eastern border the counties of the Heart of England. To cross the border from England, however, is to enter into a different country, which Wales once was. In terms of history, culture, and language, these distinctions live side by side. Signs that read "CROESO I GYMRU" ("Welcome to Wales") and the names of the counties—Clwyd, Dyfed, Glamorgan, Gwent, Gwynedd, and Powys—are clues that Welsh is quite different, but of course English is spoken universally.

Wales is not large, so the whole of it can be explored by day trips from a cottage rented anywhere within its borders. The only two cities of any size, Cardiff and Swansea (pop. 280,000 and 180,000, respectively), are on the south coast, and from there northward the populace is thinly spread throughout farms, villages, and towns of fewer than 20,000 people.

Any visitor should plan to enjoy at least four aspects of Wales. First is the inland, with the national parks of Snowdonia in the north and Brecon Beacons toward the south. Both are noted for their scenic woods, mountains, and streams. Second is the coast, from Cardiff all the way to Prestatyn, including the long, thin, Pembrokeshire National Park along the southwest coast and the many villages that lie on the promontories, along the estuaries, and, in the north, around the Isle of Anglesey. A third aspect is historical Wales, manifested in its cathedrals and abbeys, but more impressively in its many castles, from the forbidding walls and mass of the ruined Caerphilly to the classic grace of Caernarvon. The fourth aspect is revealed in the process of enjoying the other three: the towns and villages, hospitable people, good food, old and wonderful pubs, and unhurried life-style.

The north of Wales, including the Isle of Anglesey, seems especially remote from London and the Heart of England, although it is fewer than four hours by train from London's Euston Station to Bangor. Some Welsh people feel that the needs of northern Wales are not a high priority with the British government, and it is true that to the outsider this land shows little sign of late twentieth-century British development. Therein lies its charm and beauty. However, the torturous northern coastal highway of Clwyd is being replaced by a four-lane freeway that will surely gratify weekenders from Liverpool and Manchester who used to line the highway for miles trying to get home. Such is progress.

Strangely, of the half dozen Welsh rental companies, none has agents in North America. The owner of one company Snowdonia Tourist Services (address: Ynys Tywyn, High Street, Porthmadog Gwynedd LL49 9PG, Wales; tel: 011-44-766-513-829), was worried about some of the simpler cottages meeting American standards, but this should not deter anyone. If this is of concern, the answer is to reserve a cottage of average standards or above. In any case, a wide variety of rentals is available, from cozy cottages and beautiful larger homes to apartments in village buildings and even in castles. Rentals (as well as castles and towns) are concentrated in the northwest and the southwest, and both are good locations for a home base. There is also a scattering of properties in central Wales and in the very pretty Brecon Beacons area.

In the northwest corner of Wales, six miles east of Caernarvon, is Bryn Bras Castle, where we took an apartment to experience castle living. The comfortable apartments run from average standards to above average, and can accommodate from two to six persons. In castles it is usually best to book one of the higher standard rooms rather than the former staff quarters in order to enjoy the surroundings. Rates run from about £75 ($125) to £140 ($225) per week in low season to double that in July and August. The kitchens at Bryn Bras have recently been completely modernized. There is no agent in North America for this castle, but rentals can be arranged through Castles, Cottages & Flats, Ltd., or direct bookings can be made by writing or telephoning Bryn Bras Castle, Llanrug, Gwynedd LL55 4RE, Wales; tel: 011-44-286-870-210. Two other castles with apartments are in the southwest: Saint Bride's Castle in Haverfordwest, Dyfed, and the elegant Roch Castle in Pembrokeshire National Park near Saint David's at the tip of the peninsula. (Both are available through Blake's Vacations.)

Sixteen North American agencies represent English rental companies that in turn, represent owners of Welsh properties. Of these firms, a number are large, representing rentals throughout the world; a few specialize in Britain, including Wales. These smaller ones are:

Blake's Vacations
British Travel Association
Castles, Cottages & Flats, Ltd.
Europa-Let
Grant-Reid Communication
Hearthstone Holidays (Canada)
Livingstone Holidays
Pilgrim's Way
Wilson & Lake International

In the off-season, roughly October through April, it is usually possible to rent an apartment or a cottage on the spot. So if you are in Britain without a reservation, or want to work directly with a Welsh rental company, in northern Wales try Bryn Bras Castle or Snowdonia Tourist Services in Porthmadog at the addresses shown above. A small, very nice group of cottages on the Isle of Anglesey at Beaumaris (the east end, just across from Bangor), is the Henllys Farm House Apartments on the grounds of Henllys Hall, now a hotel; the address is Beaumaris, Anglesey LL58 8HU; tel: 011-44-248-811-303. For central Wales, contact Wales Holidays (The Bank, Newton, Powys SY16 2AA; tel: 0686-25267), and for southwest Wales, Coastal Cottages of Pembrokeshire (Abercastle near Haverfordwest, Dyfed SA62 5HJ; tel: 03483-7742) is a good choice. Stays of only three or four days instead of the usual Saturday to Saturday can almost always be arranged in the low-season months.

From the south of Wales, day trips to London are possible; the travel time by motorway or train is a matter of two to three hours. Beyond that, the trip becomes too long. There is a highway along the coast, and several others crisscross Wales, but there is no rail line along the southern part of the west coast. The north-south rail line runs between Swansea and London with connections at Shrewsbury west to the coast at Tywyn. The northern part of the west coast railway runs from Aberystwyth through Porthmadog and connects with the London-Crewe-Holyhead mainline. It is possible, therefore, to get around the area fairly well by train, except for the southern west coast and, of course, through much of Snowdonia or Brecon Beacons National Parks. This takes a car and, we found, so do most of the rental properties. Wales is very rural, and even though there is fair bus service, without a car you will need to be prepared for long walks.

For an interesting change of scene, there are daily sailings out of the port towns of Fishguard and Holyhead to Ireland, the former to Rosslare Harbour and the latter to Dublin. These are crossings of about four hours' duration; the ferries can take cars. Of the two, the trip to Dublin is the most appealing, because Rosslare is not near any special destination city.

The ferryport near Holyhead is on the tip of Holy Island, across a narrow channel from the west end of the large island of Anglesey, which, in turn, is across a narrow channel from the northern Wales town of Bangor. Anglesey itself is an important area to visit, rich in ancient ruins and castles. Beaumaris Castle, one of Britain's most beautiful, is just a short trip by bus or car from Bangor.

From a cottage or apartment in northern Wales, it is an easy and worthwhile trip by car or train to the city of Chester, just across the border in the English county of Cheshire. Liverpool is just to the north for anyone who wants to visit.

Wales is not a very popular place to visit in the low-season months from mid-October to April (except at Christmas, national holidays, and school midterm breaks), so the price of rentals drops dramatically after the summer season. But even during the summer months it is not difficult to find a comfortable, internally modernized cottage in the range of £100 ($160) to £120 ($190) per week. At the other end of the spectrum, the main part of Roch Castle, mentioned above, can be rented for £485 ($775) per week in April; the rent goes up to £785 ($1,255) per week in the peak months of July and August. This is for five bedrooms, two baths (with showers), four toilets, and six acres of grounds that are shared with the renters of the slightly smaller, three-bedroom, west wing (which rents from $400 to $700). There are rental properties in every price between the two extremes, and the values are very good.

Advance booking time (dates are approximate) needed for high season (mid-June to September)—six months. For mid-season, (mid-May to mid-June and September and October)—two to three months. And during the rest of the year—up to one month.

Appendix A

North American–Based Rental Agencies

◆

AARP TRAVEL SERVICE
5855 Green Valley Circle
Culver City, California 90230
Tel: 800-227-7737
      212-417-2277

ABACUS AGENCY
P.O. Box 15295
Ann Arbor, Michigan 48106
Tel: 313-572-0700

AT HOME ABROAD
405 East 56th Street
New York, New York 10022
Tel: 212-421-9165

B. & D. DE VOGÜE TRAVEL SERVICES
1830 S. Mooney Boulevard
Suite 113
Visalia, California 93277
Tel: 800-727-4748
      209-733-7119

BEDS ABROAD, LTD.
188 Highwood Avenue
Tenafly, New Jersey 07670
Tel: 201-569-5245

BLAKE'S VACATIONS
4939 Dempster Street
Skokie, Illinois 60077
Tel: 800-628-8118
    312-982-0561

BRITISH TRAVEL ASSOCIATION
P.O. Box 299
Elkton, Virginia 22827
Tel: 800-327-6097
    703-289-6512

CASTLES, COTTAGES & FLATS OF IRELAND
& THE U.K., LTD.
P.O. Box 261
Westwood, Massachusetts 02090
Tel: 617-329-4680

CHEZ VOUS
220 Redwood Highway
Suite 129E
Mill Valley, California 94941
Tel: 415-331-2535

COAST TO COAST RESORTS
860 Solar Building
1000 16th Street N.W.
Washington, D.C. 20036
Tel: 800-368-5721

CONDO VACATIONS
717 West Pender Street, 3rd Floor
Vancouver, British Columbia V6C 1G9
Canada
Tel: 800-663-0368
    604-688-2504

CUENDET—POSARELLI VACATIONS
180 Kinderkamack Road
Park Ridge, New Jersey 07656
Tel: 201-573-9558

DE LOOF LIMITED
111 South Fourth Avenue
Ann Arbor, Michigan 48104
Tel: 800-553-2582
313-995-4400

DER TOURS
1290 Bay Street
Toronto, Ontario M5R 2C3
Canada
Tel: 416-964-3290

EASTONE OVERSEAS ACCOMMODATIONS
6682 141st Lane North
Palm Beach Gardens, Florida 33418
Tel: 407-622-0777

EUROPA-LET, INC.
P.O. Box 3537
Ashland, Oregon 97520
Tel: 800-462-4486
503-482-5806

FAMILIES ABROAD, INC.
194 Riverside Drive
New York, New York 10025
Tel: 212-787-2434
718-766-6185

FOUR SEASONS VILLAS
P.O. Box 848
Marblehead, Maine 01945
Tel: 800-338-0474
617-639-1055

FOUR STAR LIVING, INC.
964 Third Avenue, 39th Floor
New York, New York 10022
Tel: 212-758-2236

FRANCE GRANDES VACANCES
P.O. Box 2517
Venice, California 90924
Tel: 213-450-1304

THE FRENCH EXPERIENCE
171 Madison Avenue
New York, New York 10016
Tel: 212-938-3800

FRENCH HOME RENTALS
5515 Milwaukie Avenue
Portland, Oregon 97502
Tel: 503-233-1224

GRAND CIRCLE TRAVEL, INC.
347 Congress Street
Boston, Massachusetts 02210
Tel: 800-831-8880
      617-350-7500

GRANT-REID COMMUNICATION
P.O. Box 810216
Dallas, Texas 75381
Tel: 800-327-1849
      214-243-6748

HASTINGWOOD ASSOC., LTD.
104 East Main Street
Stockbridge, Michigan 49285
Tel: 800-992-2925
      517-851-8000

HEART OF ENGLAND COTTAGES
P.O. Box 888
Eufaula, Alabama 36027
Tel: 205-687-9800

HEARTHSTONE HOLIDAYS
P.O. Box 8625, Station L
Edmonton, Alberta TC6 4J4
Canada
Tel: 403-465-2874

HERITAGE OF ENGLAND
P.O. Box 297
Falls Village, Connecticut 06031
Tel: 800-533-5405
    203-824-5155

HIDEAWAYS INTERNATIONAL
P.O. Box 1464
Littleton, Massachusetts 01460
Tel: 800-843-4433
    617-486-8955

HOMETOURS INTERNATIONAL
1170 Broadway
New York, New York 10001
Tel: 800-367-4668
    212-691-2361

IDYLL, LTD.
P.O. Box 405
Media, Pennsylvania 19063
Tel: 212-565-5242

IN THE ENGLISH MANNER
P.O. Box 936
Alamo, California 94507
Tel: 415-935-7065

INTERHOME, INC. USA
36 Carlos Drive
Fairfield, New Jersey 07006
Tel: 201-882-6864

INTERNATIONAL LODGING CORP.
89-27 182nd Street
Hollis, New York 11423
Tel: 718-291-1342

INTERNATIONAL SERVICES
Piazza di Spagna 35
00187 Rome
Italy
Tel: (011-39-6) 784-0288
U.S. Contacts
110 East End Avenue   or P.O. Box 3537
New York, New York 10028   Ashland, Oregon 97520
Tel: 212-794-1534   Tel: 800-462-4486
                                               503-482-5806

ITALIAN VILLA RENTALS
P.O. Box 1145
Bellevue, Washington 98009
Tel: 206-827-3694

LaCURE VILLAS
11661 San Vicente Boulevard
Suite 1010
Los Angeles, California 90049
Tel: 800-387-2726
        800-387-2715
        800-387-2720
and
275 Spadina Road
Toronto, Ontario M5R 2V3
Canada
Tel: 800-387-1201 (Ontario and Quebec)
        416-968-2374

LISMORE TRAVEL
106 East 31st Street
New York, New York 10016
Tel: 800-547-6673
        212-685-0100

LIVINGSTONE HOLIDAYS
1720 East Garry Avenue
Suite 204
Santa Ana, California 92705
Tel: 714-476-2823

LONDON APARTMENTS (USA) LTD.
5 Hidden Valley Road
Lafayette, California 94549
Tel: 800-366-8748
    415-283-4280

LYNOTT TOURS
350 Fifth Avenue
Suite 2619
New York, New York 10018
Tel: 800-221-2474
    212-760-0101

NW BED & BREAKFAST TRAVEL UNLIMITED
610 S.W. Broadway
Portland, Oregon 97205
Tel: 503-243-7616

ORSAVA, INC.
P.O. Box 6275
Marietta, Georgia 30065
Tel: 404-578-9091

OVERSEAS CONNECTION
70 West 71st Street
Suite C
New York, New York 10023
Tel: 800-542-4007
    212-769-1170

PILGRIM'S WAY
P.O. Box 1307
Havertown, Pennsylvania 19083
Tel: 215-649-1868

RENT A HOME INTERNATIONAL
3429 Freemont Place No. 318
Seattle, Washington 98103
Tel: 206-545-4963

RENT A VACATION EVERYWHERE (RAVE)
328 Main Street East
Suite 526
Rochester, New York 14604
Tel: 716-454-6440

RENT IN ITALY
3801 Ingomar Street N.W.
Washington, D.C. 20015
Tel: 202-244-5345

RIVIERA HOLIDAYS
31 Georgian Lane
Great Neck, New York 11024
Tel: 516-487-8094

SUSAN T. PIDDUCK, CUENDET AGENT
1742 Calle Corvo
Camarillo, California 92010
Tel: 805-987-5278

SWISS TOURING, USA
5537 N. Hollywood Avenue
Milwaukee, Wisconsin 53217
Tel: 414-963-2020

TOUR-HOST INTERNATIONAL
141 East 44th Street
Suite 506
New York, New York 10017
Tel: 800-445-2690
     212-953-7910

UTELL INTERNATIONAL
10606 Burt Circle
Omaha, Nebraska 68114
Tel: 800-448-8355
    402-498-4300

VACANCES EN CAMPAGNE
P.O. Box 297
Falls Village, Connecticut 06031
Tel: 800-533-5405
    203-824-5009
    212-838-4045

VACANZA BELLA
2443 Filmore Street
Suite 228
San Francisco, California 94115
Tel: 415-821-9345

VACANZE IN ITALIA
P.O. Box 297
Falls Village, Connecticut 06031
Tel: 800-533-5405
    203-824-5009

VACATION HOME RENTALS (VHR) WORLDWIDE
235 Kensington Avenue
Norwood, New Jersey 07648
Tel: 800-NEED A VILLA
    800-633-3284
    201-767-9393

VILLA LEISURE
P.O. Box 209
Westport, Connecticut 06881
Tel: 203-222-9611

VILLAS & APARTMENTS IN PORTUGAL
Janino Bastos Advisory Service
500 East 83rd Street
New York, New York 10028
Tel: 212-535-3262

VILLAS INTERNATIONAL
71 West 23rd Street
New York, New York 10010
Tel: 800-221-2260
    212-685-7585

WAYSIDE TRAVEL
10101 Fifth Kolin Avenue
Oak Lawn, Illinois 60453
Tel: 312-423-2113

WILLIAMS & CO.
2841 29th Street N.W.
Washington, D.C. 20008
Tel: 202-328-1353

WILSON & LAKE INTERNATIONAL
330 York Street
Ashland, Oregon 97520
Tel: 800-545-5228
    503-488-3350

WORLD-WIDE HOME RENTAL GUIDE
142 Lincoln Avenue
Suite 652
Santa Fe, New Mexico 87501
Tel: 505-988-5188

Canada

The British rental companies (in parentheses) represented by the following agencies in Canada are known and recommended by the authors, and properties have been selectively sampled. London apartments and Continental properties, if any, have not been sampled, but all the agencies shown enjoy a good reputation in Canada. Most are relatively large. Other Canadian agencies are described in Chapter 3, and are included in the appropriate country chapters, and in the main body of Appendix A.

CAMELOT TOURS
777 Warden Avenue
Suite 5a
Scarborough, Ontario M1L 4C3
Tel: 416-750-4448
(Blakes; see Blake's Vacations in Chapter 3)

EUROPEAN VILLAS
27 Gordon Rowe Crescent
Richmond Hill
Toronto, Ontario L4C 8R9
Tel: 416-737-6132
(Country Holidays)

EXECUTIVE TRAVEL APARTMENTS
1101 Bay Street
Suite 1805
Toronto, Ontario M5R 2W8
Tel: 800-387-1432
     416-923-3000
(Apartments in London & Paris)

Appendix B

Addresses of Selected European Rental Companies

The following companies represent just a few of the many European rental companies. Those selected for inclusion fall into at least one of three categories: (1) the authors had personal contact with the company principals, sampled the properties, and visited the operation offices; (2) the company was recommended by a known and trusted person or organization; (3) the company is considered reputable by others in the business (praise from competitors). As with any travel outside well-worn tourist paths, or accommodations in other than four- to five-star, North American-style hotels, there can be no guarantees—but your best bet is to deal with agencies and companies of good reputation.

This listing is principally for the convenience of travelers who arrive in Europe without rental accommodations and wish to rent on the spot. This can usually be accomplished in low season, and often in mid-season with a more limited selection but is not recommended during high and peak seasons. Because the tourist and price seasons differ throughout Europe, refer to the appropriate country chapters for scheduling information.

For direct bookings from overseas, some European companies require payment in bank drafts in the currency of their home country; these foreign currency drafts are available at most U.S. and Canadian banks for a modest fee. Other companies accept major credit cards. There are English speakers at all company offices listed.

Some U.S. rental agencies assisted the authors on the condition that their European clients remain anonymous. Despite the implications of this arrangement, we have honored it. However, many of these European companies are publicized in the United States and Canada through their respective government tourist offices. Thus, companies appearing in other materials available to the public may appear in the listing despite the requests of their North American agents.

The terms *modest, moderate,* and *luxury* suggest the prices and standards of each company's properties.

The numbers following the name of the country enable you to dial overseas calls directly. The first number (011) the international telephone access code, is always the same; the second number, the country code, differs from country to country, but is constant within a country. The telephone numbers following company addresses are the city routing and company numbers. For example, the country code for Austria is 43; the city code for Bludenz is 5552, and the phone number for PEGO is 65-666. Therefore, the full number to dial direct from North America is 011-43-5552-65-666.

Austria (011-43-)

PEGO
Sägeweg 1
A-6700 Bludenz
Tel: 5552-65-666

Throughout Austria.

France (011-33-)

INTERNATIONAL CAP D'ANTIBES
"Le Royal" 125
Boulevard du Cap
06600 Cap d'Antibes
Tel: 93-61-22-17

Moderate to luxury villas in Antibes and vicinity.

NPH ANTIBES
240 Avenue Jules Grec
06600 Antibes
Tel: 93-65-95-00

Luxury city apartments in Antibes.

LES CITADINES
3 et 5 Boulevard Grosso
06000 Nice
Tel: 93-44-39-00

Moderate city apartments.

PIERRE ET VACANCES—LE TANIT
14 Avenue de la Rostagne
06160 Juan-les-Pins
Tel: 93-61-91-91

Moderate city apartments.

VICKY COLE; BOWHILLS
A. Courance
47150 La Capelle Biron
Tel: 53-71-60-51

Moderate rural villas in western France.

PARIS APARTMENTS

EMBASSY
8 Avenue de Messine
75008 Paris
Tel: 42-62-6214

Agency; modest to moderate.

LE CLARIDGE
74 Champs Elysées
75008 Paris
Tel: 43-59-6797

Building; moderate to luxury.

ORION PARIS LES HALLES
4 rue des Innocents
75001 Paris
Tel: 45-08-0033

Building; modest.

RESIDENCE DU ROY
8 rue François
75008 Paris
Tel: 42-89-5959

Building; moderate.

Federal Republic of Germany (West Germany)

Contact the nearest German National Tourist Office in the United States or Canada and request the DZT "Self-Catering" catalog; this publication lists many vetted properties throughout West Germany. Direct booking is with the Accommodation Reservation Service in Frankfurt. All necessary information is included in the catalog.

Republic of Ireland (011-353-)

DONEGAL THATCHED COTTAGES
Attn: Conor Ward
Rosses Point
County Sligo
Tel: 71-719-97

Moderate rural individual cottages.

KILLARNEY LAKELAND COTTAGES
Muckross, Killarney
County Kerry
Tel: 64-315-38

Moderate rural individual cottages.

The Irish Tourist Board (P.O. Box 1083, Dublin 8), sells a catalog of self-catering properties for £2 Irish plus mailing charge, but it is time-consuming and somewhat complicated to obtain. The Irish Tourist Board in New York *may* have a few copies at any given time. When in Ireland, the best approach to booking is to contact the Tourist Information Office (14 O'Connell Street, Dublin 1; tel: 01-735-043. This office can reserve any of hundreds of properties throughout Ireland. Bookings can also be made through any other Tourist Information Office in Ireland.

Italy (011-39-)

CUENDET & CIE., SPA
53030 Strove/Siena
Tel: 577-301-112

Wide choice: Tuscany, Umbria; U.S. agents Susan Pidduck and Cuendet-Posarelli; small fee.

HABITALCASA
2 Viale Roma
San Gimignano
Tel: 577-941-733

Modest to moderate; Florence, Siena, western Tuscany.

INTERNATIONAL SERVICES
Piazza di Spagna 35
00187 Rome
Tel: 6-784-0288
    U.S.: 212-794-1534
         800-462-4486

Moderate to luxury; throughout Italy, includes islands; American owner.

SOLEMAR
Via Cavour 80
50129 Florence
Tel: 55-218-112

Wide choice: Tuscany, Umbria.

TOSCANAMARE
Piazza 24 Maggio 25-26
55044 Marina de Pietrasanta
Tel: 584-23-844

Villa clusters on the Tuscan coast.

Portugal (011-351-)

THE ALGARVE

APARTHOTEL SOLFÉRIAS
Sitio do Mato Serrão
8400 Lagoa, Algarve
Tel: 82-57-401

Moderate apartments.

CLUBE PRAIA DA OURA
Praia da Oura, Apartado 27
Albufeira, Algarve
Tel: 89-531-35-8

Moderate town house resort.

QUINTA DA BALAI
Albufeira, Algarve
Tel: 89-525-75

Moderate to luxury villa resort.

QUINTA DOS CARRIÇOS
Praia de Salema
8650 Vila do Bispo, Algarve
Tel: 82-65-202

Small, modest apartments, camping.

LISBON AREA

ULTRAMAR PROPRIEDADES, LDA
Rua do Regimento Dezanove de Infantaria, No. 67 ric
2750 Cascais
Tel: 1-284-4526

Agency, good selection, modest to moderate.

Spain (011-34-)

AGENCIA PICAMAL
Calle Norte, 6
Gerona
Tel: 72-20-05-53

Modest to moderate; various locations.

APARTAMENTOS CENTRO NORTE
Mauricio Legendre, 16
28046 Madrid
Tel: 91-733-34-00

Building; moderate apartments.

Switzerland (011-41-)

INTERHOME
Buckhauserstrasse 26
8048 Zurich
Tel: 1-497-24-97

Largest rental company in Europe; wide selection, modest to moderate.

UTORING AG
Beethovenstrasse 24
8022 Zurich
Tel: 1-497-2727

Modest to luxury; throughout Switzerland.

United Kingdom
(011-44-)

If calling from within Britain, delete the 011-44 and dial 0 before the numbers below.

ENGLAND

BATH HOLIDAY HOMES
3 Frankey Buildings
Bath BA1 6EG
Tel: 225-332-221

Modest to moderate; city and environs.

CORNISH TRADITIONAL COTTAGES
Lostwithiel, Cornwall PL22 OHT
Tel: 208-872-559

Good selection, modest to moderate; Cornwall specialists.

ENGLISH COUNTRY COTTAGES LTD.
Claypit Lane
Fakenham, Norfolk NR21 8AS
Tel: 328-4041

Large selection throughout Britain; modest to moderate and some larger homes.

FREEDOM HOLIDAY HOMES
Weaver's Den Cottage
Frittenden, near Cranbrook,
Kent TN17 2EP
Tel: 58-080-251

Modest to moderate; specialists in Kent and Sussex countryside.

GREY ABBEY PROPERTIES
P.O. Box 23, Coach Road
Whitehaven, Cumbria CA28 9DF
Tel: 946-3346

Small company, owns most of its properties in northern Lake District; modest to moderate.

HEART OF ENGLAND COTTAGES
Iveson House
Ampney St. Peter
Cirencester, Gloucester GL7 5SH
Tel: 285-87-217

Good selection in Cotswolds into Shakespeare Country; moderate to luxury and manor houses.

HEART OF THE LAKES
Rydal Holme, Rydal
Ambleside, Cumbria LA22 9LR
Tel: 539-432-321

Small company, good selection in central Lake District.

THE INDEPENDENT TRAVELLER (MARY SPIVEY)
Dinneford Spring, Thorverton
Exeter, Devon EX5 5NU
Tel: 392-860-807

Small company with broad knowledge and resources; modest to moderate, in Devon, southwest England, London, Thames Valley.

For other luxury homes and manor houses, contact the Blandings agent in the United States, Williams & Co. (see Chapter 3 and Appendix A).

LONDON

ABACUS AGENCY
20 Park Hill, Ealing
London W5 2JN
Tel: 1-997-6497

Good selection in central and west London; moderate to luxury (no-fee U.S. agent: see Abacus in Appendix A).

APARTMENT SERVICES LTD.
2 Sandwich Street
London WC1H 9PL
Tel: 1-388-3558

Small, personalized company; well selected, modest to moderate; mainly Bloomsbury, Westminster.

DOLPHIN SQUARE
Pimlico
London SW1V 3LX
Tel: 1-834-9134

Large, self-contained complex; moderate.

DRAYCOTT HOUSE
10 Draycott Avenue
London SW3 2SA
Tel: 1-584-4659

Upper-moderate to luxury in Chelsea.

THE INDEPENDENT TRAVELLER
Dinneford Spring
Thorverton,
Exeter, Devon EX5 5NU
Tel: 392-860-807

Modest to moderate, central and area into near Thames Valley.
Good choices.

KENSBRIDGE APARTMENTS
Kensgate House
38 Emperor's Gate
London SW7 4HJ
Tel: 1-589-2923

Modest to moderate; Chelsea and Kensington.

LONDON APARTMENTS, LTD.
51 Kensington Court
London W8 5DB
Tel: 1-937-4248

Good Selection in own and represented properties; west and central; modest to luxury. (See Appendix A for no-fee agents in U.S.: London Apartments (USA) Ltd. and Grant-Reid.)

SCOTLAND

HOLIDAY COTTAGES (SCOTLAND) LTD.
Lilliesleaf, Melrose
Borders TD6 9JG
Tel: 8357-481

Small, personalized company; good selection; modest to luxury throughout Scotland.

FINLAYSON HUGHES
Bank House, 82 Atholl Road
Pitlochry, Pertshire PH16 5BL
Tel: 796-1512

Good selection throughout Scotland; modest to luxury.

WALES

POWELLS COUNTRY COTTAGES
197 High Street
Saundersfoot, Dyfed SA69 9EJ
Tel: 834-813-232

Modest to moderate in south and central Wales.

SNOWDONIA TOURIST SERVICES
Ynys Tywyn, High Street
Porthmadog, Gwynedd LL49 9PG
Tel: 766-513-829

Modest to moderate in north and central Wales; Snowdonia National Park.

Appendix C

Foreign National Tourist Offices in the United States and Canada

♦

This is a listing of the tourist offices of the governments of the countries covered in this guidebook.

United States

AUSTRIAN NATIONAL TOURIST OFFICE
500 Fifth Avenue
New York, New York 10110
Tel: 212-944-6880

500 N. Michigan Avenue
Suite 544
Chicago, Illinois 60611
Tel: 312-644-5556

4800 San Felipe
Houston, Texas 77056
Tel: 713-850-9999

11601 Wilshire Boulevard
Suite 2480
Los Angeles, California 90025-1760
Tel: 213-477-3332

BRITISH TOURIST AUTHORITY
40 West 57th Street
New York, New York 10019
Tel: 212-581-4700

John Hancock Center
Suite 3320
875 N. Michigan Avenue
Chicago, Illinois 60611
Tel: 312-787-0490

Cedar Maple Plaza
2305 Cedar Springs
Dallas, Texas 75201-1814
Tel: 214-720-4040

350 S. Figueroa Street
Los Angeles, California 90071
Tel: 213-628-3525

FRENCH GOVERNMENT TOURIST OFFICE
610 Fifth Avenue
New York, New York 10020
Tel: 212-757-1125

645 N. Michigan Avenue
Chicago, Illinois 60611
Tel: 312-337-6301

2305 Cedar Springs Road
Suite 205
Dallas, Texas 75201
Tel: 214-720-4010

9454 Wilshire Boulevard
Suite 303
Beverly Hills, California 90212
Tel: 213-271-6665

1 Hallidie Plaza
Suite 250
San Francisco, California 94102
Tel: 415-986-4174

GERMAN NATIONAL TOURIST OFFICE
747 Third Avenue
New York, New York 10017
Tel: 212-308-3300

444 S. Flower Street
Suite 2230
Los Angeles, California 90071
Tel: 213-688-7332

IRISH TOURIST BOARD
757 Third Avenue
New York, New York 10017
Tel: 212-418-0800

ITALIAN GOVERNMENT TRAVEL OFFICE
630 Fifth Avenue
New York, New York 10111
Tel: 212-245-4822

500 N. Michigan Avenue
Chicago, Illinois 60611
Tel: 312-644-0990

360 Post Street
Suite 801
San Francisco, California 94108
Tel: 415-392-5266

PORTUGUESE NATIONAL TOURIST OFFICE
590 Fifth Avenue
New York, New York 10036
Tel: 212-354-4403

NATIONAL TOURIST OFFICE OF SPAIN
665 Fifth Avenue
New York, New York 10022
Tel: 212-759-8822

845 N. Michigan Avenue
Chicago, Illinois 60611
Tel: 312-642-1992

San Vincente Plaza Building
8383 Wilshire Boulevard
Suite 960
Beverly Hills, California 90211
Tel: 213-658-7188

SWISS NATIONAL TOURIST OFFICE
608 Fifth Avenue
New York, New York 10020
Tel: 212-757-5944

150 S. Michigan Avenue
Suite 2930
Chicago, Illinois 60601
Tel: 312-630-5840

260 Stockton Street
San Francisco, California 94108
Tel: 415-362-2260

Canada

AUSTRIAN NATIONAL TOURIST OFFICE
(Office national autrichien du tourisme)
Suite 3330
2 Bloor Street East
Toronto, Ontario M4W 1A8
Tel: 416-967-3381

736 Granville Street
Suite 1220
Vancouver, British Columbia V6Z 1J2
Tel: 604-683-5808

1010 ouest rue Sherbrooke
Suite 1410
Montreal, Quebec H3A 2R7
Tel: 514-849-3709

BRITISH TOURIST AUTHORITY
(Ministère du tourisme de la Grande Bretagne)
94 Cumberland Street
Suite 600
Toronto, Ontario M5R 3N3
Tel: 416-925-6326

FRENCH GOVERNMENT TOURIST OFFICE
(Maison de la France representation francaise du tourisme au Canada)
1 Dundas Street West
Suite 2405, Box 8
Toronto, Ontario M5G 1Z3
Tel: 416-593-4723

1981 rue McGill College
Suite 490
Montreal, Quebec H3A 2W9
Tel: 514-288-4264

GERMAN NATIONAL TOURIST OFFICE
(Office national allemand du tourisme)
2 Fundy, Place Bonaventure
C.P. 417
Montreal, Quebec H5A 1B8
Tel: 514-878-9885

IRISH TOURIST BOARD
(Office national du tourimse irlandais)
3rd Floor, 10 King Street East
Toronto, Ontario M5C 1C3
Tel: 416-364-1301

ITALIAN GOVERNMENT TRAVEL OFFICE
(Office national italien du tourisme)
1 Place Ville Marie
Suite 2414
Montreal, Quebec H3B 3M9
Tel: 514-866-7667

PORTUGUESE NATIONAL TOURIST OFFICE
(Office national du tourisme du Portugal)
Concourse Level
2180 Yonge Street
Toronto, Ontario M4S 2B9
Tel: 416-487-3300

500 ouest rue Sherbrooke
Suite 930
Montreal, Quebec H3A 3C6
Tel: 514-843-4623

SPANISH NATIONAL TOURIST OFFICE
(Office national espangnol du tourisme)
Suite 1400, 102 Bloor Street West
Toronto, Ontario M5S 1M8
Tel: 416-961-3131

SWISS NATIONAL TOURIST OFFICE
(Office national suisse du tourisme)
Suite 2015, P.O. Box 215
Commerce Court West
Toronto, Ontario M5L 1E8
Tel: 416-868-0584